A Message to Coaches From USA Track & Field

On behalf of USA Track & Field, we hope you find this *USA Track & Field Coaching Manual* a useful tool. This book features contributions from USATF's Development, Coaching Education, and Sports Science Committees and highlights techniques and drills that should prove helpful to beginning and veteran coaches alike.

The mission of USATF is to provide vision and leadership in athletics in the United States, and to promote the pursuit of excellence from youth to masters, from the grass roots to the Olympic Games. The *USA Track & Field Coaching Manual* embodies that vision and leadership, and we are grateful to the many coaches who have contributed their expertise to this project. Your ongoing contributions—whether you coach a youth club or at a major university—are very much appreciated.

We hope this publication becomes a valuable resource for you, and we wish you continued success in your coaching careers.

Patricia F. Rico
President

Craig A. Masback
Chief Executive Officer

CONTENTS

PREFACE

As the national governing body for the sport, USA Track & Field has promoted, incurred, and witnessed its share of changes during the decade plus since publishing a previous version of this book. The name of the organization has changed from The Athletics Congress. A new director has been selected. Women's participation and performances have risen to new heights. Continued refinements in conditioning programs have produced more powerful and finely-honed physical specimens than ever in the sport's history.

This *USA Track & Field Coaching Manual* (2000) reflects the innovations, emphases, and improvements in our sport since *The Athletics Congress's Track and Field Coaching Manual* was published in 1989. The book features an outstanding cast of contributors — 33 of the sport's most successful coaches — presenting the latest and best information on testing, teaching, training, and competing in every event for both men and women.

This book is divided into five parts, allowing you to turn straight to an event of interest for comprehensive coverage. Part I, Coaching Essentials, presents many of the most important facets of managing a successful program with useful insights on planning, promoting, and recruiting. A special chapter on predictive testing of athletes will help you more objectively and accurately determine the potential of developing athletes and project their performances in various track and field events.

Part II, Running Events, contains seven chapters loaded with material on proper mechanics, training regimens, and competitive strategies for the sprints, hurdles, distance races, and relays.

The next four chapters form Part III — Jumping Events. In this section you'll find extensive information on technique and training for the long jump, triple jump, high jump, and pole vault.

Throwing Events, Part IV, consists of chapters on the shot put, discus, javelin, and hammer. Two keys to success for athletes in these events are efficient mechanical form and generating maximum power.

Part V covers racewalking and the multi-events of heptathlon and decathlon. These chapters are especially helpful when you have athletes who may not shine in a single running, jumping, or throwing event, but who have a great work ethic, are highly conditioned, and have a will to win.

This book is the most authoritative and comprehensive guide to coaching the sport. Read and refer to it often as you work to develop and improve your program. You'll benefit from the expertise and experience of the many excellent coaches who contributed to this work. Your athletes will benefit from your better instruction and training. Both you and your athletes will see the results when you compete in forthcoming seasons.

CREDITS

Figures and Text

Figures 3.3, 3.4, 5.4, 6.1, 6.7, 6.8, 7.1, 9.1, 9.2, and 14.11 reprinted, by permission, from G.A. Carr, 1999, *Fundamentals of Track and Field,* 2d ed. (Champaign, IL: Human Kinetics), 4, 158, 56, 67, 54, 56, 75, 28, 29, and 201.

Table 3.1 reprinted, by permission, from USA Track & Field, Inc., "USA Track & Field Level II Coaching Education Program."

Chapter 11 portions of text reprinted, by permission, from D. Hayes, 1981, *Practical Coaching Techniques – The Triple Jump,* (Ames, IA: Championship Books & Video Productions).

Figure 11.2 reprinted, by permission, from J. Hay, University of Iowa, Exercise Science Department, Iowa City, IA.

Chapter 16 portions of text reprinted, by permission, from B. Webb and B. Sing, 1989, The Javelin. In *The Athletics Congress's Track and Field Coaching Manual,* 2d ed., edited by V. Gambetta (Champaign, IL: Leisure Press), 189-199.

Figure 16.2 reprinted, by permission, from T. Naclerio, 1988, *The Teaching Progressions in the Shot Put, Discus, and Javelin,* (Rockaway, NJ: Tony Naclerio), 279.

Figures 18.1, 18.2, 18.3, 18.4, 18.5, 18.6, 18.7, and 18.8 reprinted, by permission, from J. Salvage and G. Westerfield, 1996, *Walk Like an Athlete,* (Marlton, NJ: Walking Promotions).

Photos

Pages 249 and 299: © Active Images.

Page 1: © 1996 Rich Cruse.

Pages 11, 19, 33, 51, and 109: © Brian Meyer/Photo Run.

Page 113: © Anthony Neste.

Pages 75, 173, and 256: By Tom Roberts.

Pages 141, 281, 296, and 302: © Joe Rogate.

Pages 63, 136, and 217: © Victah Sailer/Photo Run.

Page 235: © SportsChrome.

Pages iii, 3, 35, 61, 93, 98, 106, 123, 139, 159, 199, 219, 248, 265, 279, 286, 287: Courtesy of USA Track & Field.

PART I

COACHING ESSENTIALS

1 Organizing a Successful Program

Joseph L. Rogers

To organize a successful track and field program, a coach should begin, not by placing the sole emphasis on winning, but by first laying the necessary foundation for success. Coaches at all levels should foster a positive environment by developing a coaching philosophy that takes the athletes' best interests to heart. Of equal importance is the hiring and training of coaches to make it the most knowledgeable staff possible. A successful program—one that stands the test of time—depends on effectively organizing practices and putting together well-run meets. In other words, planning is critical. To keep the program at the same level of success year after year, coaches must also learn the best ways to promote their programs and recruit the most talented athletes. Take the time to lay the groundwork, and winning will be the natural by-product of your efforts.

Philosophy

Coaches' philosophies are dictated by their objectives. A coach should answer the questions, "Why do I want to be a coach, and what are my objectives?" Many factors may motivate one to become and continue as a coach. Often, coaches have been athletes who want to continue to be involved with the sport that they love. There is also much satisfaction in watching younger athletes develop and achieve, and in contributing to the growth and development of young lives. Coaches may live vicariously through the athletes they help. Or coaches may believe that they are the main reason their athletes succeed and want to take most of the credit for that success. Some of the reasons for being a coach are very self-serving and do not have the best interests of the athlete in mind. The guiding principle for developing a coaching philosophy should be concern for the athletes' best interests. A coach has the potential to become a very positive force in the physical and psychological development of the athlete. It is often said that athletics develop character. However, we have all seen successful athletes who demonstrate poor character. Athletics do provide an environment for positive character development when the leadership—that is, the coaches—provides the right attitudes and expectations for its charges. If the leadership demonstrates unethical behavior, a willingness to bend the rules, or a general dishonesty in order to pursue success, the athlete will believe that winning at all costs is the correct philosophy of life.

All coaching decisions should be guided by considering the effects the decisions will have on the athletes as well as their performance. Those decisions about training, competition, and athlete behavior must place the well-being of the athlete ahead of winning or success. This does not mean that achieving success should not be a priority. What it means is that the well-being of the athlete must not be sacrificed for the glory of winning.

Coaching Knowledge and Background

Successful coaching requires a basic understanding of several different disciplines. While few coaches can be a master in all of the areas, the more that you can absorb, the greater will be your ability to teach the needed skills and to train and motivate the athlete to be successful.

Physiology

The study of the various systems of the body is important in understanding how training affects the systems to improve performances. The following are key systems to learn about.

- Musculoskeletal system—Strength/power development
- Nervous system—Speed, coordination, skill development
- Cardiopulmonary system—Endurance
- Vascular system—Endurance
- Nutrition—Fuel for energy production

Motor Learning

Motor learning is the study of how humans learn skills. It includes an understanding of the relationship of the brain to the nervous proprioception, and of how kinesthetic feeling is developed through practice. The body can learn by visual cues (sight), verbal description (hearing), and feeling (kinesthetic awareness). An individual may learn best by one cue rather than another and at a different rate than another individual. The maturation of learners plays a major role in their ability to learn, since the brain and nervous system may or may not be adequately developed to master a complicated skill.

Psychology

The study of human behavior is critical in developing a coach-athlete relationship that allows athletes to have confidence in you, the coach. Motivation is a vital aspect of getting athletes to push through the pain barrier that brings them to a higher level of capacity and achievement. The coach must be able to identify the needs and desires of youth of different ages. When athletes desire to use athletics to achieve their needs, your job of getting the athletes to dedicate themselves to the task is much easier.

Biomechanics

Biomechanics is the study of physical mechanics relative to motion and skill performance. It involves understanding balance, leverage, angular motion, linear motion, velocity, and acceleration.

First Aid

A certified trainer is not always on site at practices or competitions. So coaches should have a basic understanding of first aid in order to provide immediate protection for the athletes in their charge. It is important to treat an injury with appropriate action until medical help is available. The coach should use treatment modalities that protect athletes while they recover, and allow for maximum recovery before the athletes return to practice and competition.

Communication

The coach needs to understand how to get across the necessary information for learning to take place. Coaches also need to understand how to listen to the athletes to learn of their needs. This critical ability gives vital feedback to the coach in the learning process. It also shows a respect for the athletes, which helps develop good coach-athlete communication. The coach also needs to be able to communicate with community groups who help support the program. Communication with parents is also a very critical skill.

Public speaking is an important skill, since coaches are commonly asked to speak at various community service organizations and athletic banquets. Writing skills are also important. You may be asked to write a story for the local paper about how your team succeeded, which will ensure a positive story and help bring recognition to your team.

Organizing Practices

The ability to effectively coach your athletes and team will be determined by several factors. Some factors, like the quality of facilities and equipment, the size of the coaching staff, and the amount of invested time may lie somewhat outside of your control. There will always be financial constraints dictated by your institution. However, the key is learning how to make effective use of what time and staff you *do* have.

Using Time Efficiently

A key element in effective coaching is assigning coaching duties to your assistants in a manner that allows them to spend their time with all their responsible areas most effectively. You want to give an adequate amount of time and effort to each event. A common problem for coaches is to shy away from those events where they don't feel knowledgeable or competent. Often, that leaves athletes to fend for themselves, which results in injury, poor development, or loss of interest. As a coach, it is very important to learn as much as possible about those events in which you are weak in background knowledge. At least learn enough to teach good fundamentals and safe procedures. Even if one of your assistants does the coaching for an unfamiliar event, as head coach you should have an understanding of the fundamentals. After all, you may have to groom another assistant in the near future.

Learning the proper fundamentals now will save you time in the long run. If you don't strive to gain as much background knowledge as possible, you could be teaching your athletes improper technique, and it takes much longer to correct bad technique once it becomes a habit. Take the time to learn the fundamentals up front.

How do you gain information? There are many resources. The library is a good place to start. Books on track and field as well as individual events are available. If your local library is lacking in such books, see if interlibrary loans are possible. A university library is an excellent resource, if there is one near you. Numerous publications containing technical information about the events are also available. Talk to other coaches you know who have been successful. They probably have access to many good resources. Join your state coaches association. Associations put on many clinics annually where a lot of information can be gained. Many university coaches in your area also offer clinics and camps. Contact them. Check with your local USATF association for additional available clinics and coaching education programs.

Organizing Your Staff

Whether you're the sole coach for your athletes or the head of a team of coaches, the following are effective ways to organize all events. A team of six knowledge-able coaches would be great, but often economically unfeasible. Keep in mind that even if you have little help, you are not doomed. Where there's a will, there's a way!

One-Person Coaching Staff

In some small schools, the lack of financial resources may force you to work with no help at all. This is not as common as it used to be, but it can still happen. If you find yourself in this situation, try to recruit some volunteer help from coworkers, friends, or parents of some of your athletes. If you lack volunteer help, you may be able to recruit some good managers from the student body. Trying to coach 15 or 16 events by yourself will certainly challenge your effectiveness, but you can still have a program that produces athletes who learn, have fun, and experience the thrill of competition. You will need to decide how to divide your time with all events and try to have personal contact with each event at least twice a week. Table 1.1 shows how that might be done within a five-day period.

The schedule shown in table 1.1 does require that athletes who are not coached on a certain day will have to practice on their own. This requires that you give them activities that you can rely on them to carry out safely and effectively. Keep them occupied with things that don't require a large amount of difficult effort, and don't place them in dangerous situations. Older and more experienced athletes who act as team leaders can help motivate teammates to work independently. Good team managers can also act as extra eyes and ears while you work with other events. The most important point here is to be organized. Have planned training scheduled so that all athletes keep active. Unsupervised periods with the freedom to practice as the athletes wish often leads to horseplay and/or no productive time.

Two-Person Coaching Staff

With a two-person coaching staff, you can virtually double the amount of time spent per event. How you divide up responsibility for events should depend upon each coach's knowledge and interest.

Example

    Coach A: All running events

    Coach B: All field events

While this division requires emphasizing different events on different days, it works very well for the running events. However, because of the technical complexity of the different field events, the field event coach may be on the track for several hours longer than the running coach in order to cover all aspects of field event training. So the running coach may want to direct a field event. Since the

TABLE 1.1   DIVISION OF TIME FOR A ONE-PERSON COACHING STAFF

	Monday	Tuesday	Wednesday	Thursday	Friday
First hour	Distance runners	Sprinters	Hurdlers	Distance runners	Hurdlers and sprinters
Second hour	Vertical jumpers	Throwers	Horizontal jumpers	Throwers	All jumpers
Third hour	Weight training and conditioning by events				
	Distance runners and throwers	Sprinters and jumpers	Distance runners and throwers	Sprinters and jumpers	Throwers

sprinters and hurdlers often participate in a jumping event, the coach who works with the sprinters or hurdlers could cover one of those events.

Three-Person Coaching Staff

For a three-person coaching staff, the options for dividing responsibilities expand to a much more effective approach:

Example 1

Coach A: Distance events, and one jumping event

Coach B: Sprints, hurdles, and two jumping events

Coach C: Throws, weight training for all events

Example 2

Coach A: Distance events, hurdles

Coach B: Sprints, relays, and jumping events

Coach C: Throws, pole vault

Example 3

Coach A: Distance, pole vault

Coach B: Sprints, hurdles, long jump

Coach C: Throws, high jump

There are many other possible combinations. The number of jumping events or throwing events varies from state to state. Some states include the javelin or hammer, while others may include only the shot put and discus. In other states, the traditional long jump, high jump, and pole vault events are joined by the triple jump.

The pole vault is a very complex and difficult event to master, requiring more coaching time to ensure proper instruction and safety. The same point can be made about the javelin, discus, and hammer. While the shot put requires concern about safety, it is less complex than the other throws, and the learning time may be less. All of these factors should be taken into consideration while assigning coaching responsibilities.

Four-Person Coaching Staff

For a four-person coaching staff, the options for dividing responsibilities expand even further.

Example 1

Coach A: Distance, middle distance

Coach B: Jumps

Coach C: Throws

Coach D: Sprints, hurdles, relays

This has become one of the most common approaches, allowing the coaching staff time to work with all groups daily. But other variations are possible, such as the following:

Example 2

Coach A: Distance, middle distance

Coach B: Hurdles, pole vault

Coach C: Sprints, relays

Coach D: Throws, all groups' weight training

Example 3

Coach A: Distance, middle distance, high jump

Coach B: Sprints, relays, long jump

Coach C: Hurdles, pole vault

Coach D: Throws

Five-Person Coaching Staff

With a five-person coaching staff, you might use one of the following divisions:

Example 1

Coach A: Distance, middle distance

Coach B: Sprints and relays

Coach C: Hurdles

Coach D: Throws

Coach E: Jumps

Example 2

Coach A: Distance, middle distance

Coach B: 400 meters, 4 × 400-meter relay, and longer-distance hurdles

Coach C: Sprints, 4 × 100-meter relay, and shorter-distance hurdles

Coach D: Throws

Coach E: Jumps

Six-Person Coaching Staff

For a six-person coaching staff, you could adopt one of the following divisions.

Example 1

Coach A: Distance, middle distance

Coach B: Sprints, long jump, triple jump

Coach C: Hurdles, relays

Coach D: Throws

Coach E: High jump

Coach F: Pole vault

Example 2

Coach A: Distance, high jumpers

Coach B: Sprints, relays

Coach C: Hurdles, long jump, triple jump

Coach D: Pole vault

Coach E: Throws

Coach F: Middle distance, longer-distance hurdles

Promoting Your Program

One of the ways to develop a successful program is to have large numbers from which to develop your athletes into a competitive team. To get students to come out for your team, it is important to sell your program. For an individual to get interested in being on a team, there must be something to draw him or her. The status of being on the team will draw some people. If your team has been successful, you have a built-in advantage, because lots of prospective athletes want to be a part of a winning team. There are many other aspects of sport that draw the interest of young people: having fun, being with their friends, social interaction, belonging to a group, individual achievement, awards, letter jackets, and others. The most important motivating factor for almost everyone is individual recognition. The more ways that you can draw individual attention to your team members, the more likely you will stimulate interest in being a part of your program.

Ways to create recognition:
- Announce the athletes' achievements on the school PA system.
- Get meet results and top performances into the local papers.
- Put up a bulletin board to highlight team and individual achievements.
- Create an athlete of the week award.
- Hold a postseason banquet to honor the team.
- Post school records in a prominent location in the school or gym.
- Develop all-time performance lists that give athletes goals to target.
- Draw attention to the outstanding academic achievements of team members.
- Create trophy case displays in school to show off trophies and awards.
- Take individual pictures of your athletes, and post the pictures of those who made that week's best efforts.
- Write your own newsletter to pass out in school expounding on the achievements of individual athletes or the team.
- Put together a brochure of your team that highlights individuals, your schedule, and record holders.
- Create a videotape of your team's competitions, successes, and of the team having fun. This will be an excellent recruiting tool.
- Promote intramural track meets to involve the whole school and create more interest in the sport.
- Create summer clinics and organize all-comer meets for community youth.

Whenever your athletes can hear or see information about themselves that gives them a sense of accomplishment among their peers, they will become more motivated.

A good way to increase attendance at home track meets is to hold the meet on a Friday evening or a weekend evening. Get another school organization to host a dance following the meet at the school. To help increase attendance at the collegiate level, consider inviting fraternities and sororities, or make the meet part of an alumni celebration. Especially in the spring, there are not many competing school social activities. Many students will come out to see the team in action prior

Individual recognition is a key factor in keeping athletes motivated. Here Mark Crear is recognized by the entire world for his performance in the 1996 Olympic Games.

to the dance. Many athletic events at all levels are tied to a social event. Doing this helps to appeal to a wide audience.

By promoting your program, you will attract many athletes; motivation is what will keep them there. Motivation is a key requirement for successful coaching. Challenging your athletes is one form of motivation. Give them challenging goals, show them how to pursue those goals, and help them get there. As mentioned earlier, good communication skills are a necessity for a coach. You must show your athletes that you care about them as well as want them to succeed athletically. You must recognize that they are each important. You do that when you acknowledge them and show them they are important to you whether they are the top performers or the lowest on the team. You must learn to listen carefully to each athlete. You need to be able to "read" your athletes— recognize their ability to work hard and to pursue goals, and when they are mentally down and should not be criticized. Often, we take for granted that an athlete is motivated and needs no encouragement; but everyone needs encouragement. Your ability to read your athletes will ensure that you push them in the right direction. You do not have to be some sort of Pollyanna, but a positive, encouraging personality does go a long way to boost the athletes' motivation. Be honest in your evaluations and criticisms. Let them know that when you criticize them it is honest and done to help them improve. Be sure they understand your criticism is for the performance and not the person. Motivation is almost a promotional technique in itself. Seeing a happy group of athletes will encourage others to join.

Recruiting

Where do you look for talent? Obviously, look to athletes who compete in other sports in other seasons. Football, soccer, basketball, swimming, diving, gymnastics, and wrestling all have strength, endurance, and skill requirements that are similar to those for track and field. Also, you may find some track and field talent in athletes who are cut from other teams.

Speak to the physical education teachers in your school system and see if they offer a unit of track and field in their curriculum. If they do not, offer to help develop one with them. Also, find out if they do fitness testing for strength, power, endurance, and agility. Evaluating those tests can reveal talent. (See chapter 2 on predictive testing.) If you are a high school coach, contact physical education teachers in the junior high or middle schools that feed into your high school. Ask if you might come to their schools and give a presentation to their classes about your team and the opportunities that are available to them in the future. This provides an excellent opportunity to present the videotape that you produced showing your team at practice, at meets, successful events, and your athletes having fun. Seek out opportunities to also speak to parent and community groups such as the Parent-Teacher Organization (PTO). The more you can get the word out that your program provides challenges, recognition, and fun, the more you increase the chance for greater participation.

Organizing Home Meets

One way of developing spectator interest in your team is to put on well-run meets where your athletes can display their talents. It is critical that your meet displays competition that is exciting and understandable. One thing that can cause spectators to lose interest during track meets is a lack of information, such as not knowing the height of the crossbar or who is leading in an event. Having enough good officials is key to hosting effective meets. There are three vital officials whose tasks are critical to a well-run meet. First and foremost, have a knowledgeable announcer who keeps the spectators informed. Use display boards at each field event site to list the performer, the performance, or the height of the crossbar. Keep the meet moving on a tight time schedule. Meets that last longer than two hours may not hold spectator interest. The second key official, who maintains the meet schedule, is the clerk of course. The third and equally important official is the head timer/head finish judge.

1. **Announcer:** One of the key ways to interest spectators is to have a good announcer who can keep everyone informed of the whole competition. The announcer should have all the information available about all competitors in all events. To provide current information, an official with a walkie-talkie moves around to the various field events, informing the announcer of the height of the crossbars, the best jumps or throws, and how many competitors are still left in the competition. The announcer should have a complete list of lane assignments of every athlete competing in each running event. An assistant announcer who can help keep all of this information current will help produce a very interesting meet. Personalizing the performers to the fans creates additional interest.

2. **Clerk of Course:** This is an official to whom all runners report prior to the race. The clerk checks to see if all competitors are wearing the appropriate numbers. He or she takes the competitors to the assigned starting positions and gives final instructions about running in lanes, breakpoints, and exchange zones before turning the runners over to the starter. The clerk is the person who keeps the meet on schedule and prevents delays by athletes who procrastinate. It is very important to have communications between the clerk and the announcer by walkie-talkie.

3. **Head Finish Judge:** In smaller meets, the head timer and head finish judge may be the same official. However, in meets where there will be eight or more finish places, it is better to divide the tasks between two people. The head finish judge assigns the place pickers to each race's finish, then records the order of finish from those decisions. The head timer assigns each timer a place to time, then

records their results and determines all official times. The head finish judge then gets the data from the head timer to be placed on the event result form and sends the form to the scorekeeper and announcer.

The efficient completion of the duties of the above three officials determines if a meet stays on schedule. If you do not have anyone to officiate these duties, you should train several people upon whom you can rely to work your home meets. Many other officials are critical to the running of a meet. The following is a checklist of the officials needed for large invitationals or championship meets.

List of Officials for Championship Meets

___ Meet director

___ Starter(s)

___ Referee

___ Head field judge

___ Clerk(s) of course (two for single-gender meet, three or four for both-gender meets)

___ Head finish judge

___ Head timer

___ Runner for head judge and head timer

___ Lap counter

___ Timers (three on first place, and enough to time all scoring places) (Wherever possible, use two or three timers per place timed.)

___ Judges (same as with timers)

___ Inspectors (umpires) (6 to 10 are needed)

___ Wind gauge operator(s) (one for running events and one for horizontal jumps)

___ Weights and measures judge

___ Phototimer operator (one runner is helpful)

___ Film reader (person who evaluates results from phototimer)

___ Scorer

___ Starting block clerk (moves the blocks to the right starting line)

___ Typist(s)

___ Scorer's assistant to post results

___ Announcer(s)

___ Announcer's assistant

___ Hurdle crew (one per flight of hurdles)

___ Awards clerk

___ Head official for each field event

___ One performance indicator board official for each field event

___ Two measurers to assist head official at each throwing event

___ One implement retriever for each throwing event

___ Two measurers to assist head official at horizontal jumps

___ One pit raker at each horizontal jump

___ One crossbar replacer at each vertical jump

___ Marshal(s) (officials who keep all competition areas clear of noncompetitors, coaches, and spectators)

___ Physician and/or athletic trainers

In order for performances to be recognized as records, certified officials are a must. For high school championships, the state athletic association provides for the testing and certification of officials. Other certification is done by the national governing body, USA Track & Field. Each field event should be run by at least one certified official. That official can be assisted by noncertified personnel. For dual meets, it is not always possible to get as many certified officials as you need. For those situations, you should have officiating clinics for those people who will be helping you. You must ensure that the officials that you put in place know the rules of competition, and the procedures for measuring, timing, or calling the order of competitors.

To put on a good show, you need a lot of help. You should line it up well in advance, in order to be confident that everything will work smoothly. Other key people that are needed are scorekeepers, typists, and marshals. As the head coach, you will often find yourself in the role of meet director. It is vital to have the meet operations organized ahead of time and well planned. Once all the officials and operational help are in place, the meet can almost run itself. If you are not well organized, you will find yourself running around throughout the meet, solving problems and carrying out duties that someone else should be doing. This will leave little time for you to coach or observe your team.

Prior to the start of the season, you should write to all persons who potentially can work as officials at your meets. Send them a schedule of the home meets with dates and start and finish times. Ask them to return a form on which they check off the meets that they can work and the officiating duties that they prefer to do. Also, make sure they give you updated address and phone information.

Groups from which to secure officiating help:

- State high school association (ask for a list of certified officials)
- USA Track & Field Association (ask for their list of officials)
- Off-season coaches from your school
- Other interested teachers and school staff members
- Parents of your athletes (use in roles that do not involve decision making or rules interpretation)
- Booster Club members
- Former athletes and alumni
- Physical education majors at local universities or community colleges

Putting together a list of tasks to do before, during, and after the meet will help you keep track of what needs to be done to pull off a well-run meet. Use the following checklists or tailor them to fit your needs.

Meet Checklists

Several days prior to meet:

___ Contact by phone or in person all needed officials.

___ Assign pre- and postmeet duties to team members.

- Noncompeting athletes.
- Premeet duties for those competing late in meet.
- Postmeet duties for those competing early in meet.
- All team members can assist with postmeet cleanup.

___ Fill out your own team entries.

___ Post a meet time schedule for your team.

___ Check track facility and equipment for any needed repair.

___ Prepare meet operational forms on clipboards for the following:

- Head finish judge
- Head timer
- Clerk of course
- Announcer's time schedule
- Wind gauge operator's report form
- Individual field event score sheets
- Meet score sheets for official scorer

___ Place brief synopsis of rules for event on back of clipboards.

___ Check photoelectric timing device for battery charge and readiness.

___ Check film for photoelectric timing device.

Day before meet:

___ Line all sectors for throwing field events.

___ Rope off all landing areas well outside the sector lines for the throwing events. Use pennants or other colorful materials.

___ Turn and level sand in jumping pits.

___ Place trash barrels in key locations.

___ Roll grass landing for the throws using heavy lawn rolling device and tractor.

___ Stack hurdles neatly near each location and set the crossbar at the proper height for the first hurdle race. Set the adjustable hurdle weights (where applicable) at the proper location prior to the first race.

___ Post the order of events and meet entries at key locations around the track.

___ Check pole vault and high jump standards to see if they are functioning properly.

___ Lubricate any equipment whose moving parts may be frozen or sticking.

If your track is not all-weather, with permanent markings for all start, finish, or exchange zone lines:

___ Drag and roll cinders track.

___ Line all lanes.

___ Mark the following:
  • Finish lines
  • Start lines
  • Staggered start lines for races in lanes
  • Exchange zones and fly zone marks
  • Curved start line for races over 800 meters
  • Hurdle position marks

___ Set up check-in area for athletes to report to the clerks.

___ Set up awards area.

___ Set up a secure area where competing athletes can leave their warm-up clothing during their events.

___ Set up the stand for finish judges in proper area.

The day of the meet:

___ Set out crossbars, standards, starting block cart, rakes, shovels, and brooms.

___ Set up performance indicator boards.

___ Set up all electronic equipment and needed extension cords.
  • Photoelectric timer
  • Wind gauges
  • Field event timing devices

___ Place film for phototimer.

___ Set out and check stopwatches.

___ Place lap counter and indicator near finish line.

___ Set up and check PA system.

___ Set up tape player for national anthem.

___ Check out walkie-talkies and make sure they function.

___ Check distance-indicating markers for throwing events.

___ Set out whistles for starter and head finish judge.

___ Set out batons.

___ Set out scorecard for official scorer.

___ Set out typewriter, paper, stapler, adhesive tape for producing official results.

___ Set out copy machine.

___ Set up for distribution of awards and recording of distribution.

___ Set up an officials' check-in area where you will distribute the following:
   • Field event clipboards
   • Tape measures
   • Pencils for recording data
   • Baskets in which clipboards, tape measures, and pencils can be placed. One for each event.
   • All other forms for officials mentioned earlier
   • Red and white flags for inspectors (umpires)
   • Rule books

___ Set up implement weigh-in area with measuring and weighing devices.

After the meet:

___ Distribute meet results to all visiting coaches.

___ Distribute meet results to all media present.

___ Supervise site cleanup.

___ Call in or fax results to local paper if reporters are not present.

___ Call in or fax results to local radio station.

___ Post meet results, individual scoring totals, competition splits, field event performance series, meet or school records, personal bests.

___ Write a brief critique of your team's performance.

Summary

Implementing the steps outlined in this chapter may seem like a daunting task. However, taking the time in the beginning to plan, promote, organize, and recruit will make your job during each season much easier. It will also create a solid foundation on which to build a winning team.

2 Predictive Testing of Athletes

Phil Henson
Paul Turner

The United States has never had an organized system of identifying and selecting potential Olympic athletes at a young age. Due to the vast size and diversity of the United States and the lack of direct control over young athletes, this type of program has been viewed by the United States Olympic Committee (USOC) as unfeasible. Also, as long as the United States was winning the bulk of Olympic medals simply by "showing up," most people considered talent selection unnecessary.

Times, however, have changed. No longer is it possible to dominate Olympic and World Championship competitions by simply "showing up" and bringing those who have filtered to the top of an event on their own. Other nations have improved their selection and training programs to the point that they are much more competitive.

The United States is no longer the dominant power that it once was. Canada, Great Britain, and several Caribbean and West African nations now provide real challenges in the sprints, once a U.S. monopoly. Germany, the republics of the former Soviet Union, and several emerging nations remain strong in the field events. The most dramatic power shift, of course, is in the distance events, where Kenya, Ethiopia, and Morocco have nearly eliminated the United States from contention in major international meetings.

In the 1970s and 1980s, it was obvious that the Soviet Union and East Germany became very efficient in utilizing their countries' talent, particularly in the explosive events. During these two decades, the two countries dominated the throwing and jumping events, especially in the women's competition. Did they have better talent than the United States, or did they simply do a better job of identifying the athletes with talent and involving them in sport at younger ages? It is obvious that the talent pool of the United States was greater than that of East Germany, and that the talent levels in the United States probably were higher due to its higher standard of living, when compared with that in the Soviet Union or the German Democratic Republic. Therefore, we can assume that one key area where the United States faltered was in identifying talented athletes and directing them.

One of the great historical strengths of U.S. track and field has been its close connections with the education system. Most youngsters become involved during their junior high school or senior high school days and then continue on through college or university and on to the national teams.

Although the U.S. education system has served the sport of track and field well during this century by providing competitive opportunities, facilities, professional coaching, and even college scholarships, these contributions also can be a source of weakness for the sport, for the following reasons:

- High school or even junior high school may be too late in some sports or events to initiate involvement. Where would gymnastics or swimming be if athletes' first competitive opportunity came at the high school level?

- The school calendar usually ends in May or early June, which often results in short competitive seasons. What happens during the remainder of the year?

- What happens when athletes finish their education or complete their eligibility? Unless they have achieved a world-class level of performance already, they probably face an early end to their competitive careers.

- Most importantly, what happens to those young people who do not migrate naturally toward track and field? How many young people become involved in drugs, gangs, or even menial part-time jobs in place of athletics?

The 15-year-old boy who is 6 feet, 8 inches (about 203 cm) tall will probably be directed into basketball in most schools. Likewise, the young man who is 6 feet, 2 inches (about 188 cm) tall and weighs 240 pounds (about 109 kg) will probably be encouraged to play football by coaches and peers. However, what about the average-sized boys and girls walking the halls of U.S. elementary and secondary schools? Without daily physical education, most youngsters with exceptional physical talent simply go unnoticed in the school systems. There is an alarming trend to abolish physical education at this level. Unless young people or their parents initiate involvement in the school's track and field team, most coaches have no way of identifying the talent at their disposal. The problem in the United

States has been magnified in recent years by an increasing reliance upon part-time coaches. Junior high and senior high school coaches who do not teach in the same building or even in the same system as their coaching assignment are at a distinct disadvantage when it comes to recognizing and recruiting young student athletes. This situation is further complicated by the fact that the United States, unlike many European countries, does not have a strong system of sports clubs to augment the role of the education system in providing track and field opportunities.

Talent Evaluation Program

What the United States needs is an organized, broad-based system of identifying young people with exceptional talent at an early age. Obviously, some areas such as endurance and static strength can be developed through training and hard work. However, other areas such as speed and explosive power are largely innate and may be closely related to muscle fiber type cannot be readily changed through training. Muscle fiber type may be a determining factor in events requiring speed and explosive ability. Performance potential can be identified through 11 fairly simple measurements and field tests. (See page 22.)

The United States has several widespread testing programs that encourage physical fitness. The American Association of Health, Physical Education, Recreation and Dance (AAHPERD) test and the President's Test for Physical Fitness are the most common. These tests, however, are not designed to detect explosive strength, the main ingredient in most track and field events and the one most closely associated with muscle fiber type.

The proposed talent evaluation program would be administered much like a physical fitness test and would use existing sports clubs, parks and recreation programs, sports camps, and school physical education classes as testing venues. The test results would be compiled and standards established for gender and age in each test category. Young boys and girls who scored well on the field test would be encouraged to become involved in track and field. The test results also would be used to recommend the event area in which an individual should concentrate. These tests have been shown to predict actual performance levels, once youngsters have learned basic technique. This phase has been particularly useful in motivating young athletes to strive to achieve their theoretical potential.

Recent studies conducted at Indiana University with the help of a USA Track & Field grant revealed that it is possible to accurately predict performance in selected track and field events using relatively simple field tests. The results are most accurate when the athlete already has some experience in the competition event that he or she is expected to perform. Further studies using the same field tests should help identify what additional events would be best for the athlete.

Performance Tests

The tests used in the following talent evaluation procedures were selected both for their ability to effectively help predict future track and field performance(s) and for their ease of application. These tests generally are well known and can be readily executed using a minimum of equipment and evaluators. This enhances the use of this test battery in the field.

Eleven criteria are evaluated during the testing.

1. Height
2. Weight
3. Body composition
4. Standing long jump
5. Vertical jump
6. Five bounds for distance
7. Sixty-meter dash from a standing start
8. Thirty-meter dash from a standing start
9. Thirty-meter dash from a moving start
10. Stride frequency during 30-meter dash from a moving start
11. Stride length during 30-meter dash from a moving start

Equipment

To perform the track and field prediction tests, the following equipment is needed:

- Clipboards
- Pencils
- Data recording forms
- Measuring tapes for imperial and metric systems
- Four stopwatches
- Skinfold calipers
- Vertical jump board
- Scales

Testing Procedures

Performance tests are given in the same order for all athletes to eliminate any possible order effect. Except for the anthropometric measures (height, weight, % body fat), all tests are given twice and the best trial is used in the calculation. The following outlines the proper procedures for performing each test.

Height

Measure height in inches with the athlete standing flush against a vertical surface.

Weight

Measure each athlete's weight in pounds. Their shoes should be taken off prior to the test.

Body Composition

Each athlete's body fat percentage will be determined by skinfold measurements using calipers. For female athletes, measurements are made at the iliac crest and at the tricep. For males, the measurements are on the quadricep and subscapular. The following are the specific procedures for this test:

1. Place the thumb and forefinger of the left hand far enough apart that a fold of skin can be pinched up firmly and clearly from the underlying tissue.

2. Firmly hold the fold between the fingers while the measurement is being made with the calipers.

3. Apply the calipers to the fold below the fingers so that the pressure at the point is exerted by the caliper faces, not the fingers. Readings to the nearest half-millimeter are adequate.

Body fat can be determined by the following formula:

Body Density (male) =
$$1.1043 - (.001327 \times \text{quadricep}) - (.00131 \times \text{scapula})$$

Body Density (female) =
$$1.0764 - (.00081 \times \text{iliac crest}) - (.00088 \times \text{tricep})$$

% Fat (male) = [(4.57/Body Density) – 4.142] × 100

% Fat (female) = [(4.201/Body Density) – 3.813] × 100

Total Body Fat = % Body Fat × Body Weight

Lean Body Weight = Body Weight – Total Body Fat

Since these calculations are rather long, a table of body fat percentages has been derived from the above equations. (See pages 29–32.)

Standing Long Jump

The subject begins from a stationary position with both feet square against a predetermined starting line. Measurement (in inches) is made from the starting point to the landing point closest to the starting point (e.g., where the heel of the foot landed). Two trials are performed, and the best performance is used in the calculations. Equipment needed is a long jump pit and a tape measure.

Vertical Jump

Using a jump board, the athlete's standing reach is ascertained. Then, from a stationary position, the athlete jumps and touches as high as possible on the jump board. Two trials are given, and the athlete's vertical jump is determined by subtracting the standing height from the highest jumping height. All measurements should be recorded in inches. Equipment needed is a wall at least 11 feet high and a tape measure. Commercial adjustable vertical jump stands are helpful, but not necessary.

Five Bounds for Distance

From a stationary position with both feet square against a predetermined starting line, the subject executes five bounds (actually four bounds and a jump) ending in a long jump pit. Therefore, the pattern would be R-L-R-L-jump, or vice versa. Two trials are given, and the best distance is used. Measurement is made from starting point to landing point closest to the starting point. Record this number in inches. This is also an excellent predictor of triple jump ability, and the distance will be similar. Equipment needed is a long jump pit and a tape measure.

Sixty-Meter Dash

From a standing position, the athlete starts at will and two timers are positioned at 60 meters. The fastest of the two times is used, and is recorded to .1 second. Equipment needed is stopwatches.

Standing 30-Meter Dash

During the 60-meter dash (above), two timers are positioned at 30 meters. The fastest of the two times is used.

Flying 30-Meter Dash

This measurement is taken "on the fly," or from a moving start. The time from the above 30-meter dash is subtracted from the final 60-meter time and is recorded to .1 second.

Stride Frequency

The number of times a step is taken with a particular leg between 30 meters and 60 meters is ascertained, using two counters (one counter per leg). Add number of steps taken for each leg and divide total by flying 30-meter dash time.

For example, 8 with right leg + 7 with left leg = 15 strides.

15 strides divided by 5.0 seconds between 30 and 60 meters = 3.00 strides per second.

Case Study

To better understand the testing protocol, a hypothetical situation will be presented. John Doe of State University is being tested by the coaching staff to evaluate his potential. The following are the results of his testing:

Height: 6 feet, 3 inches = 75 inches

Weight: 200 pounds

Body Composition: subscapular: 12 millimeters, quadricep: 9 millimeters. Estimated body fat from tables = 10.2%

Standing Long Jump: Trial 1: 9 feet = 108 inches, Trial 2: 9 feet, 1 inch = 109 inches (use 109 inches)

Vertical Jump: Trial 1: 28 inches, Trial 2: 30 inches (use 30 inches)

Five Bounds for Distance: Trial 1: 50 feet, 1 inch = 601 inches, Trial 2: 49 feet, 10 inches = 598 inches (use 601 inches)

Sixty-Meter Dash: Trial 1: 7.5 seconds, Trial 2: 7.4 seconds (use 7.4 seconds)

Standing 30-Meter Dash: Trial 1: 4.0 seconds, Trial 2: 3.9 seconds (use 3.9 seconds)

Flying 30-Meter Dash: 7.4 seconds – 3.9 seconds = 3.5 seconds

Stride Frequency: 15 strides divided by 3.5 seconds = 4.29 strides per second

Stride Length: 30 meters divided by 15 strides = 2.00 meters = 78.75 inches

Stride Length

The stride length is taken from the flying 30-meter dash. It is the number of strides from 30 meters to 60 meters divided into 30.

For example, 8 with right leg + 7 with left leg = 15 strides.

30 meters divided by 15 strides = 2.00 meters = 78.75-inch stride length.

Calculations

The following formulas will help determine potential in track and field events for males and females.

Males

The basic formula for males follows:

Performance (in multi-event scoring points) = 205.55 + (2.12 × Height) + (1.79 × Weight) + (–3.31 × % Body Fat) + (2.46 × Vertical Jump) + (2.24 × Standing Long Jump) + (.63 × Five Bounds) + (–148.96 × Standing 30 Meters) + (–71.10 × Flying 30 Meters) + (41.74 × 60 meters) + (–.32 × Stride Length) + (17.87 × Stride Frequency).

For the John Doe in the case study the calculations would be:

205.55 + (2.12 × 75) + (1.79 × 200) + (–3.31 × 10.2) + (2.46 × 30) + (2.24 × 109) + (.63 × 601) + (–148.96 × 3.9) + (–71.10 × 3.5) + (41.74 × 7.4) + (–.32 × 78.75) + (17.87 × 4.29) = 205.55 + 159 + 358 – 33.76 + 73.8 + 244.16 + 378.63 – 580.94 – 248.85 + 308.88 – 25.2 + 76.66 = 915.93 points = 915 points.

Once a point total is generated, multi-event tables are used to estimate performance in the selected event. These tables are used for scoring the decathlon, heptathlon, and other common track and field events. If John Doe is a long jumper, that point total would equate to a predicted performance of 7.42 meters. You simply go to the decathlon tables (or heptathlon tables for women) and look up the event for which the athlete is being evaluated. (See table 2.1.) In this case, the coach would look at the long jump category and find John Doe's test score of 915 points. The performance next to that score is the predicted performance for the athlete—7.42 meters. Statistically, one can be confident that the true potential is ±110 points and 90% confident that John Doe's potential lies within 141 points. In other words, one can be 90% confident that Doe can jump between 6.83 meters and 7.98 meters.

The formula just explained obviously is unwieldy. A more efficient but less accurate equation for male athletes is the following:

359.22 + (6.42 × Vertical Jump) + (3.58 × Standing Long Jump) + (.61 × Five Bounds) + (–113.49 × Standing 30 Meters).

This equation yields a 68% confidence level of ±118 points and a 90% level of ±151 points.

TABLE 2.1 SAMPLE DECATHLON TABLE

Men
Long Jump

Meters	Points	Meters	Points	Meters	Points	Meters	Points	Meters	Points
8.99	1323	8.49	1188	7.99	1058	7.49	932	6.99	811
8.98	1320	8.48	1186	7.98	1056	7.48	930	6.98	809
8.97	1317	8.47	1183	7.97	1053	7.47	927	6.97	807
8.96	1314	8.46	1180	7.96	1050	7.46	925	6.96	804
8.95	1312	8.45	1178	7.95	1048	7.45	922	6.95	802
8.94	1309	8.44	1175	7.94	1045	7.44	920	6.94	799
8.93	1306	8.43	1172	7.93	1043	7.43	918	6.93	797
8.92	1304	8.42	1170	7.92	1040	7.42	915	6.92	795
8.91	1301	8.41	1167	7.91	1038	7.41	913	6.91	792
8.90	1298	8.40	1164	7.90	1035	7.40	910	6.90	790
8.89	1295	8.39	1162	7.89	1033	7.39	908	6.89	788
8.88	1293	8.38	1159	7.88	1030	7.38	905	6.88	785
8.87	1290	8.37	1157	7.87	1027	7.37	903	6.87	783
8.86	1287	8.36	1154	7.86	1025	7.36	900	6.86	781
8.85	1285	8.35	1151	7.85	1022	7.35	898	6.85	778
8.84	1282	8.34	1149	7.84	1020	7.34	896	6.84	776
8.83	1279	8.33	1146	7.83	1017	7.33	893	6.83	774
8.82	1276	8.32	1143	7.82	1015	7.32	891	6.82	771
8.81	1274	8.31	1141	7.81	1012	7.31	888	6.81	769
8.80	1271	8.30	1138	7.80	1010	7.30	886	6.80	767
8.79	1268	8.29	1136	7.79	1007	7.29	883	6.79	764
8.78	1266	8.28	1133	7.78	1005	7.28	881	6.78	762
8.77	1263	8.27	1130	7.77	1002	7.27	878	6.77	760
8.76	1260	8.26	1128	7.76	1000	7.26	876	6.76	757
8.75	1258	8.25	1125	7.75	997	7.25	874	6.75	755
8.74	1255	8.24	1123	7.74	995	7.24	871	6.74	753
8.73	1252	8.23	1120	7.73	992	7.23	869	6.73	750
8.72	1250	8.22	1117	7.72	990	7.22	866	6.72	748
8.71	1247	8.21	1115	7.71	987	7.21	864	6.71	746
8.70	1244	8.20	1112	7.70	985	7.20	862	6.70	743
8.69	1241	8.19	1110	7.69	982	7.19	859	6.69	741
8.68	1239	8.18	1107	7.68	980	7.18	857	6.68	739
8.67	1236	8.17	1104	7.67	977	7.17	854	6.67	736
8.66	1233	8.16	1102	7.66	975	7.16	852	6.66	734
8.65	1231	8.15	1099	7.65	972	7.15	850	6.65	732
8.64	1228	8.14	1097	7.64	970	7.14	847	6.64	729
8.63	1225	8.13	1094	7.63	967	7.13	845	6.63	727
8.62	1223	8.12	1092	7.62	965	7.12	842	6.62	725
8.61	1220	8.11	1089	7.61	962	7.11	840	6.61	723
8.60	1217	8.10	1086	7.60	960	7.10	838	6.60	720
8.59	1215	8.09	1084	7.59	957	7.09	835	6.59	718
8.58	1212	8.08	1081	7.58	955	7.08	833	6.58	716
8.57	1209	8.07	1079	7.57	952	7.07	830	6.57	713
8.56	1207	8.06	1076	7.56	950	7.06	828	6.56	711
8.55	1204	8.05	1073	7.55	947	7.05	826	6.55	709
8.54	1201	8.04	1071	7.54	945	7.04	823	6.54	707
8.53	1199	8.03	1068	7.53	942	7.03	821	6.53	704
8.52	1196	8.02	1066	7.52	940	7.02	818	6.52	702
8.51	1194	8.01	1063	7.51	937	7.01	816	6.51	700
8.50	1191	8.00	1061	7.50	935	7.00	814	6.50	697

Females

For female athletes, the most efficacious formula is the following:

$$(-1155.92) + (2.17 \times \text{Weight}) + (5.95 \times \text{Standing Long Jump}) +$$
$$(8.99 \times \text{Stride Length}) + (97 \times \text{Stride Frequency}).$$

The 68% confidence level for this equation is ±113 points, and the 90% level is ±145 points. Athlete Jane Doe has achieved the following test performances: 135 pounds in Weight, 96 inches in the Standing Long Jump, a Stride Length of 75 inches, and a Stride Frequency of three strides per second. The results would be 673 points. If Jane Doe is a long jumper, her predicted performance would be 5.40 meters, or 17 feet, 8.5 inches. Her 68% range would be from 5.00 meters to 5.79 meters, and her 90% range would be from 4.88 meters to 5.89 meters.

Explosive Event Performance

Regarding the formulae, it is apparent that the most effective way to improve performance in explosive events is by increased dynamic leg power (dynamic power being the ability to generate large amounts of muscular force while moving). This is evident by the fact that stride length, stride frequency, and five bounds for distance factor into the equations significantly. Likewise, research in the development of these formulae suggests that improvements in speed result primarily from increases in stride length rather than from improvements in stride frequency. Since increases in speed at 30 meters and 60 meters were found to be accompanied by improvements in vertical jump, standing long jump, and five

TABLE 2.2	EXPLOSIVE PERFORMANCE SUMMARY			
	Males		**Females**	
	13-14 yrs.	**15-16 yrs.**	**13-14 yrs.**	**15-16 yrs.**
Percent body fat	7.0-8.5	7.0-8.0	14.0-16.0	14.0-15.5
Standing long jump	2.40-2.55 m	2.50-2.65 m	2.09-2.21 m	2.11-2.22 m
Vertical jump	.56-.61 m	.61-.69 m	.43-.50 m	.46-.52 m
Five bounds	11.30-11.80 m	12.20-12.70 m	9.80-10.40 m	10.20-10.80 m
60 m	8.0-7.6 sec.	7.8-7.4 sec.	8.7-8.3 sec.	8.5-8.1 sec.
Standing 30 m	4.5-4.3 sec.	4.4-4.2 sec.	4.7-4.5 sec.	4.6-4.4 sec.
Flying 30 m	3.5-3.3 sec.	3.4-3.2 sec.	4.0-3.8 sec.	3.9-3.7 sec.
Stride frequency	4.3-4.7 strides/sec.	4.3-4.7 strides/sec.	4.0-4.4 strides/sec.	4.1-4.5 strides/sec.
Stride length	2.09-2.15 m	2.13-2.20 m	1.90-1.95 m	2.05-2.13 m

bounds, it would appear that increased explosive strength and the subsequent increase in stride length are the best means to greater running speed. As an example, if Jane Doe improved her stride frequency from 3.0 to 3.5 strides per second, her predicted long jump performance would improve approximately six inches (about 15 cm).

Table 2.2 indicates exceptional performance in the explosive tests for ages 13–16 (see page 27). Athletes achieving these marks should rank in the top 10 percent for these age groups. This type of ranking would indicate a strong possibility for future success in track and field events requiring speed and explosiveness.

Summary

Regardless of the size and diversity of the United States, it is possible to create the kind of predictive testing programs that have made other countries much more competitive. The program outlined in this chapter was created in an effort to stop youngsters with exceptional physical talent from going unnoticed. It enables coaches to recognize potential Olympic athletes at a young age and predict their performance in track and field events. Time has shown that such a program is essential to remaining competitive.

APPENDIX BODY FAT ESTIMATION TABLES
FEMALE

Iliac crest	5	6	7	8	9	Tricep 10	11	12	13	14	15	16	17
5	12.1	12.4	12.7	13.0	13.4	13.7	14.0	14.4	14.7	15.0	15.3	15.7	16.0
6	12.4	12.7	13.0	13.4	13.7	14.0	14.3	14.7	15.0	15.3	15.6	16.0	16.3
7	12.7	13.0	13.3	13.6	14.0	14.3	14.6	14.9	15.3	15.6	15.9	16.3	16.6
8	13.0	13.3	13.6	13.9	14.3	14.6	14.9	15.3	15.6	15.9	16.3	16.6	16.9
9	13.3	13.6	13.9	14.2	14.6	14.9	15.2	15.6	15.9	16.2	16.6	16.9	17.2
10	13.6	13.9	14.2	14.6	14.9	15.2	16.1	15.9	16.2	16.5	16.9	17.2	17.5
11	13.9	14.2	14.5	14.9	15.2	15.5	15.8	16.2	16.5	16.8	17.1	17.5	17.8
12	14.2	14.5	14.8	15.2	15.5	15.8	16.1	16.5	16.8	17.1	17.5	17.8	18.1
13	14.5	14.8	15.1	15.5	15.8	16.1	16.5	16.8	17.1	17.4	17.8	18.1	18.4
14	14.8	15.1	15.4	15.8	16.1	16.4	16.8	17.1	17.4	17.7	18.1	18.4	18.8
15	15.1	15.4	15.7	16.1	16.4	16.7	17.1	17.4	17.7	18.1	18.4	18.7	19.1
16	15.4	15.7	16.0	16.4	16.7	17.0	17.4	17.7	18.0	18.4	18.7	19.0	19.4
17	15.7	16.0	16.3	16.7	17.0	17.4	17.7	18.0	18.3	18.7	19.0	19.3	19.7
18	16.0	16.3	16.7	17.0	17.3	17.6	18.0	18.3	18.6	19.0	19.3	19.7	20.0
19	16.3	16.6	17.0	17.3	17.6	18.0	18.3	18.6	19.0	19.3	19.6	20.0	20.3
20	16.6	16.9	17.3	17.6	17.9	18.2	18.6	18.9	19.3	19.6	19.9	20.3	20.6
21	16.9	17.2	17.6	17.9	18.2	18.6	18.9	19.2	19.6	19.9	20.3	20.6	20.9
22	17.2	17.5	17.9	18.2	18.5	18.9	19.2	19.6	19.9	20.2	20.5	20.9	21.2
23	17.5	17.8	18.2	18.5	18.9	19.2	19.5	19.9	20.2	20.5	20.9	21.2	21.6
24	17.8	18.2	18.5	18.8	19.2	19.5	19.8	20.2	20.5	20.8	21.2	21.5	21.9
25	18.1	18.5	18.8	19.1	19.5	19.8	20.1	20.5	20.8	21.2	21.5	21.8	22.2
26	18.4	18.8	19.1	19.4	19.8	20.1	20.5	20.8	21.1	21.5	21.8	22.2	22.5
27	18.7	19.1	19.4	19.8	20.1	20.4	20.8	21.1	21.4	21.8	22.2	22.5	22.8
28	19.1	19.4	19.7	20.1	20.4	20.7	21.1	21.4	21.8	22.1	22.4	22.8	23.1
29	19.4	19.7	20.0	20.4	20.7	21.1	21.4	21.7	22.1	22.4	22.8	23.1	23.4
30	19.7	20.0	20.3	20.7	21.0	21.4	21.7	22.0	22.4	22.7	23.1	23.4	23.8

(continued)

BODY FAT ESTIMATION TABLES *(continued)*

FEMALE

Iliac crest	Tricep												
	18	19	20	21	22	23	24	25	26	27	28	29	30
5	16.3	16.7	17.0	17.3	17.7	18.0	18.3	18.7	19.0	19.3	19.7	20.0	20.3
6	16.6	17.0	17.3	17.6	18.0	18.3	18.6	19.0	19.3	19.6	20.0	20.3	20.7
7	16.9	17.3	17.6	17.9	18.3	18.6	18.9	19.3	19.6	19.9	20.2	20.6	21.0
8	17.2	17.6	17.9	18.2	18.6	18.9	19.3	19.6	19.9	20.3	20.6	20.9	21.3
9	17.6	17.9	18.2	18.6	18.9	19.2	19.6	19.9	20.2	20.6	20.9	21.3	21.6
10	17.9	18.2	18.5	18.9	19.2	19.5	19.8	20.2	20.5	20.9	21.2	21.6	21.9
11	18.2	18.5	18.8	19.2	19.5	19.8	20.2	20.5	20.9	21.2	21.5	21.9	22.2
12	18.5	18.8	19.1	19.5	19.8	20.1	20.5	20.8	21.2	21.5	21.8	22.2	22.5
13	18.8	19.1	19.5	19.8	20.1	20.5	20.8	21.2	21.5	21.9	22.2	22.5	22.8
14	19.1	19.4	19.8	20.1	20.4	20.8	21.1	21.5	21.8	22.1	22.5	22.8	23.2
15	19.4	19.7	20.1	20.4	20.8	21.1	21.4	21.8	22.1	22.5	22.8	23.1	23.5
16	19.7	20.0	20.4	20.7	21.1	21.4	21.7	22.1	22.4	22.8	23.1	23.5	23.8
17	20.0	20.4	20.7	21.0	21.4	21.7	22.1	22.4	22.8	23.1	23.4	23.8	24.1
18	20.3	20.7	21.0	21.3	21.6	22.0	22.4	22.7	23.1	23.4	23.7	24.1	24.4
19	20.6	21.0	21.3	21.7	22.0	22.3	22.7	23.0	23.4	23.7	24.1	24.4	24.7
20	21.0	21.3	21.6	22.0	22.3	22.7	23.0	23.4	23.7	24.0	24.4	24.7	25.1
21	21.3	21.6	21.9	22.3	22.6	23.0	23.3	23.7	24.0	24.3	24.7	25.0	25.4
22	21.6	21.9	22.3	22.6	22.9	23.3	23.6	24.0	24.3	24.7	25.0	25.4	25.7
23	21.9	22.2	22.6	22.9	23.3	23.6	23.9	24.3	24.6	25.0	25.3	25.7	26.0
24	22.2	22.5	22.9	23.2	23.6	23.9	24.3	24.6	25.0	25.3	25.6	26.0	26.3
25	22.5	22.9	23.2	23.5	23.9	24.2	24.6	24.9	25.3	25.6	26.0	26.3	26.7
26	22.8	23.2	23.5	23.9	24.2	24.6	24.9	25.2	25.6	25.9	26.3	26.6	27.0
27	23.2	23.5	23.8	24.2	24.5	24.9	25.2	25.6	25.9	26.3	26.6	27.0	27.3
28	23.5	23.8	24.2	24.5	24.8	25.2	25.5	25.9	26.2	26.6	26.9	27.3	27.6
29	23.8	24.1	24.5	24.8	25.2	25.5	25.9	26.2	26.6	26.9	27.3	27.6	28.0
30	24.1	24.4	24.8	25.1	25.5	25.8	26.2	26.5	26.9	27.2	27.6	27.9	28.3

MALE

Thigh	Subscapula												
	4	5	6	7	8	9	10	11	12	13	14	15	16
4	3.6	4.1	4.6	5.1	5.6	6.1	6.7	7.2	7.7	8.2	8.7	9.2	9.7
5	4.1	4.6	5.1	5.6	6.1	6.7	7.2	7.7	8.2	8.7	9.2	9.7	10.2
6	4.6	5.1	5.6	6.1	6.7	7.2	7.7	8.2	8.7	9.2	9.7	10.2	10.8
7	5.1	5.6	6.1	6.7	7.2	7.7	8.2	8.7	9.2	9.7	10.3	10.8	11.3
8	5.6	6.1	6.7	7.2	7.7	8.2	8.7	9.2	9.7	10.2	10.8	11.3	11.8
9	6.1	6.6	7.2	7.7	8.2	8.7	9.2	9.7	10.2	10.7	11.3	11.8	12.4
10	6.6	7.2	7.7	8.2	8.7	9.2	9.7	10.3	10.8	11.3	11.8	12.4	12.9
11	7.2	7.7	8.2	8.7	9.2	9.7	10.3	10.8	11.3	11.8	12.4	12.9	13.4
12	7.7	8.2	8.7	9.2	9.8	10.3	10.8	11.3	11.8	12.4	12.9	13.4	14.0
13	8.2	8.7	9.2	9.8	10.3	10.8	11.3	11.8	12.4	12.9	13.4	14.0	14.5
14	8.8	9.3	9.8	10.3	10.8	11.3	11.8	12.4	12.9	13.4	14.0	14.5	15.0
15	9.3	9.8	10.3	10.8	11.3	11.8	12.4	12.9	13.4	13.9	14.5	15.0	15.5
16	9.8	10.3	10.8	11.3	11.8	12.4	12.9	13.4	13.9	14.5	15.0	15.5	16.1
17	10.3	10.8	11.3	11.8	12.4	12.9	13.4	13.9	14.5	15.0	15.5	16.1	16.6
18	10.8	11.3	11.8	12.4	12.9	13.4	13.9	14.5	15.0	15.5	16.1	16.6	17.2
19	11.3	11.8	12.4	12.9	13.4	13.9	14.5	15.0	15.5	16.1	16.6	17.2	17.7
20	11.9	12.4	12.9	13.4	13.9	14.5	15.0	15.6	16.1	16.6	17.2	17.7	18.2
21	12.4	12.9	13.4	13.9	14.5	15.0	15.6	16.1	16.6	17.1	17.7	18.2	18.8
22	12.9	13.4	13.9	14.5	15.0	15.6	16.1	16.6	17.1	17.7	18.2	18.8	19.3
23	13.4	13.9	14.5	15.0	15.6	16.1	16.6	17.1	17.7	18.2	18.8	19.3	20.0
24	14.0	14.5	15.1	15.6	16.1	16.6	17.1	17.7	18.2	18.8	19.3	20.0	20.4
25	14.5	15.1	15.6	16.1	16.6	17.1	17.7	18.2	18.8	19.3	20.0	20.4	20.9
26	15.1	15.6	16.1	16.6	17.2	17.7	18.3	18.8	19.3	19.9	20.4	21.0	21.5
27	15.6	16.1	16.6	17.2	17.7	18.3	18.8	19.3	19.9	20.4	21.0	21.5	22.1
28	16.1	16.6	17.2	17.7	18.3	18.8	19.3	19.9	20.4	21.0	21.5	22.1	22.6
29	16.6	17.2	17.7	18.3	18.8	19.3	19.9	20.4	21.0	21.5	22.1	22.6	23.1
30	17.2	17.7	18.3	18.8	19.4	19.9	20.4	21.0	21.5	22.1	22.6	23.1	23.7

(continued)

BODY FAT ESTIMATION TABLES *(continued)*

MALE

Thigh	Subscapula											
	17	18	19	20	21	22	23	24	25	26	27	28
4	10.2	10.8	11.3	11.8	12.3	12.8	13.4	13.9	14.4	15.0	15.5	16.0
5	10.8	11.3	11.8	12.4	12.8	13.4	13.9	14.4	15.0	15.5	16.0	16.6
6	11.3	11.8	12.4	12.9	13.4	13.9	14.4	15.0	15.5	16.0	16.6	17.1
7	11.8	12.4	12.9	13.4	13.9	14.4	15.0	15.5	16.0	16.6	17.1	17.7
8	12.4	12.9	13.4	13.9	14.4	15.0	15.5	16.0	16.6	17.1	17.7	18.2
9	12.9	13.4	13.9	14.4	15.0	15.5	16.0	16.6	17.1	17.7	18.2	18.8
10	13.4	13.9	14.4	15.0	15.5	16.0	16.6	17.1	17.7	18.2	18.8	19.3
11	14.0	14.4	15.0	15.5	16.0	16.6	17.1	17.7	18.2	18.8	19.3	19.9
12	14.5	15.0	15.5	16.0	16.6	17.1	17.7	18.2	18.8	19.3	19.9	20.5
13	15.0	15.5	16.1	16.6	17.1	17.7	18.2	18.8	19.3	19.9	20.5	21.0
14	15.5	16.1	16.6	17.1	17.7	18.2	18.8	19.3	19.9	20.5	21.0	21.6
15	16.1	16.6	17.1	17.7	18.2	18.8	19.3	19.9	20.5	21.0	21.6	22.1
16	16.6	17.1	17.7	18.2	18.8	19.3	19.9	20.5	21.0	21.6	22.1	22.7
17	17.2	17.7	18.2	18.7	19.3	19.9	20.5	21.0	21.6	22.1	22.7	23.2
18	17.7	18.2	18.7	19.3	19.9	20.4	20.9	21.6	22.1	22.7	23.2	23.8
19	18.2	18.7	19.3	19.9	20.4	20.9	21.5	22.1	22.7	23.2	23.8	24.3
20	18.7	19.3	19.9	20.4	20.9	21.5	22.1	22.7	23.2	23.8	24.3	24.9
21	19.3	19.9	20.4	20.9	21.5	22.0	22.6	23.2	23.8	24.3	24.9	25.4
22	20.0	20.4	20.9	21.5	22.0	22.6	23.2	23.8	24.3	24.9	25.4	26.0
23	20.4	20.9	21.5	22.0	22.6	23.1	23.8	24.3	24.9	25.4	26.0	26.5
24	20.9	21.5	22.0	22.6	23.1	23.7	24.3	24.9	25.4	26.0	26.5	27.1
25	21.5	22.0	22.6	23.1	23.7	24.3	24.9	25.4	26.0	26.5	27.1	27.6
26	22.1	22.7	23.2	23.8	24.3	24.9	25.4	26.0	26.5	27.1	27.6	28.2
27	22.7	23.2	23.8	24.3	24.9	25.4	26.0	26.5	27.1	27.6	28.2	28.7
28	23.2	23.8	24.3	24.9	25.4	26.0	26.5	27.1	27.6	28.2	28.7	29.3
29	23.8	24.3	24.9	25.4	26.0	26.5	27.1	27.6	28.2	28.7	29.3	29.8
30	24.3	24.9	25.4	26.0	26.5	27.1	27.6	28.2	28.7	29.3	29.8	30.4

RUNNING EVENTS

3

100 and 200 Meters

Curtis Frye

To make the switch from merely running to running fast times in the 100 and 200 meters, both coaches and athletes must understand the objectives they are shooting for. The primary goal for all sprinters should be to improve their capacity to handle the increasing muscular demands of faster running. This chapter holds that conditioning and mechanics are important but that both factors are secondary to speed development. All athletes have speed potential—some more than others based upon their genetic makeup—but no athlete uses all of his or her potential. Coaches can no longer just prepare workouts. To actualize their athletes' potential and improve their performance, coaches must now oversee every aspect of their athletes' training.

Sprinting Mechanics

Understanding proper sprinting mechanics, however, will help contribute to speed development. Mechanics has to do with the effects of energy and forces on the body. For sprinters, muscle power, neurological innervation, and length of limbs are the most important factors to consider. These factors influence the two main components that affect speed: stride length and stride frequency.

Stride length is governed by the power the sprinter puts into the stride, or the ground contact time. Stride length also has an effect on the angle of the force to the ground. When athletes overstride, or place the landing foot too far forward of their center of mass, they create braking forces that slow them down. While trying to lengthen their stride, by overstriding athletes may actually cause their stride to shorten. The best way to improve stride is not by changing technique but rather by improving the ability to produce power (i.e., speed and strength). Natural increases in stride length occur when greater power is applied to the ground due to improvements in stride frequency.

Stride frequency is limited by the physiological makeup of each athlete. It is governed by the firing ability of the nerves stimulating the muscles, the fiber type the muscles are made up of, and the length of the limbs. The more fast-twitch fibers one has, the greater stride frequency one can attain. Shorter limbs rotate with greater frequency. Longer limbs have a lower stride frequency. Short sprinters therefore typically run with a very powerful stride and on average run the short races (60 to 100 meters) faster. Tall sprinters run faster in the longer sprint races in which both speed and endurance are needed.

Technique

An athlete's mechanical potential is measured by the ability to place each body segment in certain required positions to reduce ground time, improve stride frequency and stride length, and reduce the air time of each stride. All of this, in turn, will contribute to faster speeds. Coaches must develop a technical model for each of their athletes that displays their stride pattern. Coaches must then work

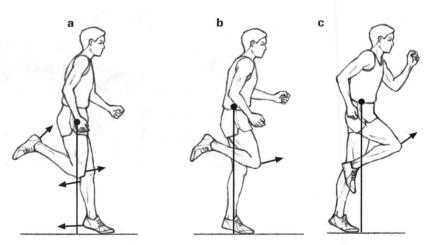

Figure 3.1 Sprint striding technique.

(continued)

on modifying each athlete's movement patterns to help the athletes improve their sprinting technique (thus improving their technical model).

Sprint Striding Phase

Analysis of an athlete's technical model will reveal aspects of the stride that show good technique or that need improvement. Here are some good striding techniques to look for:

1. A foot that is moving backward under the body upon landing (sometimes referred to as active foot plant or negative foot speed). See figure 3.1a.
2. High heel recovery as the drive foot leaves the ground (figure 3.1a).
3. A support foot landing that touches down as close as possible to a point under the center of mass (figure 3.1b).
4. The ankle of the forward swinging leg should cross the support leg above the knee (figure 3.1c).
5. A very tall posture with a slight forward lean from the ground, not from the waist (lean will be directly proportional to acceleration; the greater the acceleration the greater the lean, so once top speed is achieved forward lean should not be very noticeable).
6. Arms that swing backward as if reaching for the hip pocket (figure 3.1c).
7. Arms bent at the elbows (bent less than 90 degrees on the upswing but greater than 90 degrees on the downswing). (See figure 3.1d).
8. Relaxed hands (some coaches advocate extended fingers to create a longer lever of the moving forearm. This longer lever creates a larger moment of inertia of the moving forearm that helps to put more force into the ground as the athlete drives off. Be sure not to create tension, however.)
9. Arms that swing forward to a chin high position into the midline of the torso but do not cross the midline (figure 3.1d).
10. Relaxed shoulders, neck, jaw, and face.
11. A dorsally flexed ankle joint (toe up) just prior to the foot landing (figure 3.1e).

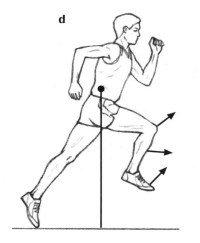 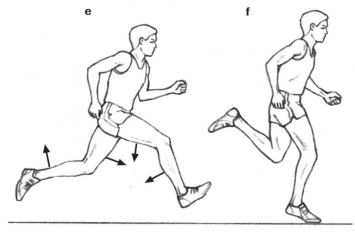

Figure 3.1 *(continued)*

12. Head is erect and eyes are focused on the finish line (figure 3.1f, page 37).

13. Sprinter runs in a straight line throughout the race with very small amount of lateral movement.

Acceleration Phase

The technical model during the acceleration phase of the sprint, including the start, should have the following characteristics:

1. Acceleration is achieved by driving or pushing with the drive leg. This requires a good forward lean—from the ground up, not the waist. Remember that the amount of lean an athlete exhibits will be directly proportional to acceleration. Also remember that acceleration does not mean speed but the rate of increasing speed. If a line is drawn from the foot of the drive leg through the center of mass, that line also should extend through the shoulder joint and head (figure 3.2a). That line should be at approximately a 45-degree angle from the ground.

2. The free leg will drive low and fast to place the foot down under the body and may even fall behind the center of mass depending on how quickly the athlete accelerates. Without proper acceleration the athletes will stumble since they are leaning so far forward.

3. The heel recovery of the drive leg will be very low coming out of the blocks in order to get the foot down fast in order to drive again and overcome inertia.

4. With each succeeding drive step, the athletes' speed grows until they reach their top speed. As speed increases acceleration decreases, so you should observe a continuous lessening of body lean. (See figure 3.2b.) Upon reaching top speed, posture should be very erect.

5. Along with the stride-by-stride decrease in acceleration, you should observe the athletes' heels rise higher as they get into their normal sprint stride.

6. The arm action during the acceleration phase is similar to the sprint striding phase. However, in the early phases of the start the hands will be driven very high and forward relative to the athlete's torso. The arms play a very important role in maintaining balance, rhythm, and relaxation, so you should have the athlete consciously work them vigorously.

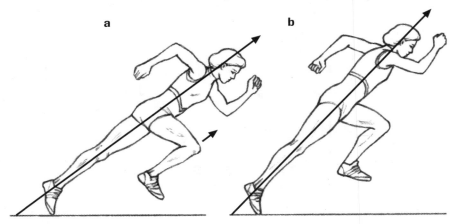

Figure 3.2 Acceleration mechanics: the greater the acceleration, the greater the lean.

7. As the athlete moves from the acceleration phase into the normal stride, you will want to focus upon the technical model for the sprint striding phase discussed above.

Finish Phase

The proper technique for a sprint finish requires concentration and timing. A mistimed lunge at the finish line is likely to cause the athlete to lose a close race. Here are examples of proper finishing technique:

1. The athlete maintains good sprint posture and a normal stride action through the finish line.

2. The athlete maintains the same sprint stride as in the middle of the race (it's common for sprinters to break down and start overstriding at the finish of a race when fatigue causes them to lose the ability to maintain good stride frequency; if athletes overstride, they will create braking forces that will cause them to slow down).

3. Good ankle dorsal flexion is maintained.

4. The landing foot is moved backward under the center of mass.

5. The athletes keep their strides quick, not long. Speed endurance allows the athletes to be able to maintain the best stride frequency they have. Whenever a sprinter has low speed endurance, stride frequency is diminished as fatigue sets in regardless of limb length.

6. The athlete continues to vigorously drive the arms.

7. As the athlete reaches the finish line, he or she lunges forward in order to lean at the tape. This is an effective technique, but it must be done just as the athlete takes his or her last stride through the finish line. There are two types of leaning models:

   • The athlete steps onto the finish line with the head lowered and both arms thrust backward to create a forward falling action. (See figure 3.3.)

   • The athlete drives the forward moving arm through the line and drives the opposite arm back and around to rotate the trunk. This technique turns the shoulder forward fast, helping the athlete to accelerate forward.

Figure 3.3 The lean at the finish.

Developing Strength, Power, and Speed

Conditioning is what strengthens sprinters, and power is the most important component of sprinter strength. To get the most out of conditioning, work during the season must proceed from low volume to high volume and from low intensity to high intensity before finally returning to low volume and low intensity before major competitions.

Young athletes require more overall body conditioning than do their adult counterparts. Their bodies must get accustomed to lower intensities and volumes of training before they are physiologically prepared to train harder and do more. Bringing young athletes along slowly allows them to fully and properly develop. You should therefore emphasize overall physical development rather than specific sprint training. As the young athlete matures and her or his sprinting ability becomes more apparent, you and the athlete will then be able to decide which events the athlete is best suited for—short sprints like the 100 and 200 meters or endurance sprints like the 400 meters. But keep in mind that when training young athletes, the less specialization the better. Wait until they are physically and mentally ready to do more specialized work. Only then should they spend the bulk of their training time specifically on speed components.

General conditioning entails improving strength and flexibility in all muscle groups and improving lung and heart capacities. Examples of strength training include bounding weight training, towing, hill running, and resistance running. Respiratory and cardiovascular capacities are increased using runs of longer distances with low intensity. More specific conditioning involves developing strength and power in the muscle groups primarily used in sprinting: gluteals, hamstrings, quadriceps, gastrocnemius and soleus (Achilles complex), dorsi-flexors or ankles, flexors or toes, and shoulder joint development for arm action. Advanced conditioning also involves acclimating the body to the specific energy requirements sprinters need. They are as follows:

100 meter—95% anaerobic

200 meter—90% anaerobic, 10% aerobic

Table 3.1 lists various types of training exercises based on the energy demands of sprinters. It can be used as a guide when preparing workouts for each part of the season. Column one lists the type of training. Column two gives the length of the run (in meters) to achieve that type of training. The third column defines the energy system that is challenged by the type of training. Column four gives the amount of intensity needed to achieve the desired effect for the training type. The intensity is given in percentage of maximum speed. The fifth column gives the amount of rest recovery needed before attempting another repeat in order to accomplish the training objectives of that type of training. Column six gives the total amount of distance to be run in a workout of the stated type. The total volume of distance is calculated by adding up all the distances of the repeats run. This is the recommended volume of training for the 100-meter sprinter. Column seven provides the same information as column six but for the 200-meter sprinter.

Weight Training

It is crucial that a strength base be in place prior to speed work and plyometric training. This is especially important for younger athletes. The work in the weight room tends to be more general, yet has some specific carryover. Proper equipment is important in weight training, including barbells, dumbbells, squat rack, Olympic platforms, and free weight apparatus equipment. Types of lifts that sprinters should do include power cleans, snatches, squats, single-leg squats, step-up lunges, lunges with weights, hang cleans, and bench press (athletes should be able to squat one and a half to two times their body weight prior to high-intensity training). It is also important to do the right amount of these exercises with the right intensity at the right time of the year.

For the early part of the year, it is important to work on endurance, starting with light weights at three sets of 10 to 15 repetitions and over time increasing the weight and reducing the number of repetitions. This allows the muscles to work at a higher rate, thus developing a larger work capacity throughout the season.

Muscle endurance should also be developed as the year goes on. A good form of training to improve muscle endurance is circuit training. This involves working

TABLE 3.1	CATEGORIES OF TRAINING RUNS AND HOW THEY ADDRESS THE ENERGY SYSTEMS					
Type of training	Length of run (multiple reps)	Energy system trained	Percent of max. speed	Recovery	Total distance for 100 m sprinters	Total distance for 200 m sprinters
Extensive tempo	>100 m	Aerobic	69-70%	30-90 sec.	1400-3000 m	1800-3000 m
Extensive tempo	>200 m	Aerobic	70-79%	30 sec.-2 min.	1400-2000 m	1800-2500 m
Intensive tempo	>80 m	Aerobic and anaerobic mixed	80-90%	30 sec.-5 min.	800-1800 m	800-2000 m
Speed	20-80 m	Anaerobic	90-95%	3-5 min.	300-800 m	300-800 m
Speed	20-80 m	Alactic	95-100%	3-5 min.	300-500 m	300-600 m
Speed endurance	30-80 m	Anaerobic	90-95%	1-2 min.	300-800 m	300-800 m
Speed endurance	30-80 m	Alactic	95-100%	2-3 min.	300-800 m	300-800 m
Speed endurance	80-150 m	Anaerobic	90-95%	5-6 min.	300-900 m	600-1200 m
Speed endurance	80-150 m	Glycolytic	95-100%	6-10 min.	300-600 m	400-800 m
Special endurance I	150-300 m	Anaerobic	90-95%	10-12 min.	600-900 m	600-1200 m
Special endurance I	150-300 m	Glycolytic	95-100%	12-15 min.	300-900 m	300-1000 m
Special endurance II	300-600 m	Lactic acid tolerance	90-95%	15-20 min.	600-900 m	600-1200 m

the muscles when they are in oxygen debt. It can be done with weights, medicine ball exercises, or with isometric exercises, which involve placing maximum force against immovable resistance. Apply effort for four to eight seconds during 5 to 10 exercises. Rest for two to three minutes in between sets.

Dynamic strength is developed predominantly through ballistic/explosive weight training, so it should likewise be incorporated into the athlete's training regimen throughout the season. This form of training enhances explosive strength, the ability to mobilize muscular force very quickly. Explosive lifting is done with a lower volume but at a higher speed. It is important to continue explosive lifting

TABLE 3.2	SAMPLE WEIGHT-TRAINING PLAN		
Phase	**Day 1**	**Day 2**	**Day 3**
Preseason Do three sets of 10-15 reps. Add weight if you can do more than 15 reps. Lighten weight if you cannot execute at least 10 reps.	Squats Step-ups Bench press Dumbbell arm swings	Lunges Single-leg squats Military press Power cleans	Squats Step-ups Bench press Snatch
Early sason On days 1 and 2, do three sets of 8-10 reps of cleans and snatches. Do three sets of 3-5 reps for everything else. Don't overload—better to go too light than too heavy.	Power cleans Bench press Step-ups Dumbbell arm swings Abdominal exercises	Snatch Military press Single-leg squats Dumbbell arm swings Lunges with dumbbells	Squats (two sets of 3reps at 70% of max.) Bench press (three sets of 5 reps at 80% of max.)
Late season On days 1 and 2, do three sets of 3-6 reps with a heavier load than in early season. The last two weeks prior to peak meets, do two sets of 2-5 reps at 80% of max. Lift only two times during the week.	Power cleans Bench press Step-ups Dumbbell arm swings Abdominal exercises	Snatch Military press Single-leg squats Dumbbell arm swings Lunges with dumbbells	Rest

throughout the entire season, but athletes should reduce such training (one to two weeks recovery, depending on individual differences) before desired peak performance. The main emphasis in the peaking period is to maximize rest and recovery without losing strength development. Reduce load by cutting the number of sets and/or reducing the percentage of maximum weight.

Table 3.2 presents a sample weight-training plan for sprinters.

Plyometrics

Dynamic and explosive strength is also developed through plyometrics. Plyometric exercises involve having an athlete repeat a series of jumps of varying heights and distances, on and off boxes, up and down inclines, with single and double leg actions. This enhances the athlete's neuromuscular stretch reflex. Eccentric loading occurs while the muscle is lengthening, and concentric loading occurs while the muscle shortens. Jumps should be done with boxes ranging from 6 to 36 inches (about 15 to 91 cm) in height. You can vary the heights of the boxes and their distances apart and then have the athlete jump on, off, and/or over them. Bounding exercises include single- and double-leg jumps forward and backward.

Resistance running and assisted running are other forms of plyometric training. They can be done by running or jumping with a weighted vest or by having the athlete tow or pull a person (preferably a coach) 30 to 60 meters with rubber surgical tubing. Never stretch the tubing more than double its length.

As with other methods of training, it is important to know when to use plyometrics and how much to do. Jumping should start early in training. Specifically, in the second week of practice ground bounds need to start. (See figure 3.4.) For example, on Tuesdays and Fridays, have the athlete do the following five jumps five times each: double-leg forward, double-leg for height, single-leg standing forward for distance (five times each leg), and alternate-leg bounds (10 total takeoffs). Increase the weight, time, or distance of the jumps as the athlete matures. However, increase only one parameter—weight, time, or distance—at a time.

This type of work should follow the intensity and volume protocol used in the athlete's weight-training program. Change training loads throughout the season to shock the system. The body needs change every few weeks, and increases or

Figure 3.4 Ground bounds.

reductions of load will help the athlete avoid becoming stale and unable to improve their speed development. It also improves the athlete's ability to adapt to different types, volumes, and intensities of training. The same routine must be rehearsed at least six to eight practice sessions in order to allow the body to remember the action. For example, after two weeks of having the athlete train at a reduced load, you should have him or her return to an increased load. Thus, you might do six weeks at 90%, two weeks at 75%, and then three weeks at 98%. Reduce the training load as the athlete nears desired peak performance.

Speed Training

One of the most misunderstood concepts in training for sprinters is speed endurance. It refers to the ability of an athlete to move at their maximum rate for an extended distance. It does not have anything to do with how efficiently one uses oxygen.

First find athlete's maximum speed. A good way to do this is to time each for a full 60-meter dash. Be sure also to get an intermediate 30-meter split time. This divides the evaluation into acceleration (the first 30 meters) and speed (the last 30 meters). Time the first 10 meters and the last 20 meters; then time the first 20 meters, and the last 10 meters. You will then have the information you need to help the athlete improve each of their 10 meter splits. As the season goes on, work on improving the 20-meter splits. Finally, work on improving the 30-meter fly. To maximize speed potential, first increase the number of repetitions with low intensity. Later decrease the number of repetitions and increase the intensity.

Training Drills

The following drills will help promote and enhance your athletes' speed development.

Ins and Outs

Ins and outs at training distances of 20 to 60 meters are an outstanding way to develop speed and relaxation. Here are two examples of workouts:

> 20 meters fast + 20 meters easy + 20 meters fast = 60 meters total; repeat three times

After three weeks change to the following:

> 30 meters fast + 30 meters easy + 30 meters fast = 90 meters total; repeat five times

Block Starts

Full-speed block starts help develop reaction time at the start of a race. Starts should be run only 10 meters at first, then 20 meters, 30 meters, and finally 60 meters. Use a starting signal (e.g., a pistol shot or spoken word) or a rolling start. The athlete should maintain a high rate of acceleration throughout the run and should eventually train at the race distance(s) at race pace in order to get used to starting under these conditions.

Stick Drill

The stick drill is very effective in helping sprinters improve their stride frequency and decrease their ground contact time. You will need several 4-inch × 18-inch (about 10 cm × 46 cm) sticks.

1. For men, place the sticks five feet (about 1.5 m) apart. Start with four feet (about 1.2 m) for women and adjust downward for youths. Place up to 20 sticks on the ground for a total distance of approximately 30 yards (about 27.4 m) for men and 25 yards (about 22.9 m) for women.

2. From a running start, have the athlete run over the sticks, avoiding contact with them. Do this two times per week, four to five times per workout. As the season progresses—waiting at least four weeks—extend the length between sticks another six inches (about 15 cm). Maintain this length for another two to four weeks, then extend the distance another six inches (about 15 cm). If at any time the athlete has to reach out to cross the sticks, they are too far apart. The emphasis of this drill is on improving frequency, not stride length (although their stride length should naturally improve).

3. Time male athletes at 30, 34, and finally at 38 yards (about 27, 31, and 35 m); time female athletes at 25, 29, and then 33 yards (about 23, 26.5, and 30 m). The maximum distance the athlete should run for this drill is 38 yards (about 35 m) for men [when the sticks are at six-foot (about 1.8 m) intervals] and 33 yards (about 30 m) for women [when the sticks are at five-foot (about 1.5 m) intervals].

Continuous Acceleration Drill

The continuous acceleration drill is for good starters and poor finishers. Work on repeat 100s (perhaps three to five repetitions), timing the last 50 meters. Then after three to four weeks of timing the last 50 meters, increase the timed zone to 60 meters, then to 70 meters, and finally all the way to 90 meters. Emphasize to the athlete that they must make a conscious effort to increase speed in the later stages of the 100-meter dash.

Distance Drill

To train speed endurance in the early season, do a very relaxed 2 × 80, 2 × 100, 2 × 140, and 2 × 150. Increase the volume at midseason to 3 × 3 × 150, and after the second week at this volume change to 2 × 4 × 150. In late season, do 3 × 150 at about 98%, 5 × 50 easy, and 5 × 50 at 100%.

Keep in mind, though, that before focusing on speed endurance you should emphasize general speed development. This improves the athlete's overall racing ability.

After taking into consideration the various types of training that should be part of a sprinter's regimen, and factoring in the volume and intensity that is appropriate for each season, table 3.3 presents sample workouts for the preseason, early season, and late season. You can use them as is, or tailor them to meet the needs of your athletes.

Performance Factors

To avoid injury and meet the demands of training day after day, factors like diet, rest, and proper warm-up and stretching must come into play. Athletes will not be able to sustain a high level of performance throughout a long season without taking proper care of their bodies at, and away from, the track.

Flexibility

Flexibility is a component of sprint mechanics. It corresponds to the elasticity of an athlete's muscle, tendons, and joints. There are different ways to increase flexibility, including static stretching, resistance stretching, proprioceptive neuromuscular facilitation (PNF), and dynamic exercises. Ropes or rubber tubing are useful tools in stretching, and partner stretching is a great way to create resistance stretching.

Stress to the athletes that they need to stretch during their warm-ups. But be more adamant that they stretch during their cool-downs. Emphasize developing flexibility of the hip joints, ankles, and lumbar sacral joints by doing stretches involving the groin, hamstring, quadriceps, lower back, gastrocnemius, and anterior shin muscles.

TABLE 3.3   SAMPLE WORKOUTS FOR 100 AND 200 METERS

Preseason

Monday	Warm-up Sprint drills Speed development work Turn-around 40 m or 50 m sprints Falling acceleration starts Plyometric training Cool-down Stretch
Tuesday	Warm-up Interval training 4 × 400 m (jog curve, stride straights) 4 × 200 m @ 75-80% of max. (60-90 sec. recovery between sets) Circuit training Cool-down Stretch
Wednesday	Warm-up Sprint drills Technical practice (modeling-rotary running) Block starts and start drills to 30 m Stick drill running Cool-down Stretch
Thursday	Warm-up 15 min. aerobic run Circuit training Cool-down Stretch
Friday	Warm-up Sprint drills Technical practice Modeling Rotary running Speed development work Stick drill running Rollover starts 4 × 150 m ins and outs
Saturday	Warm-up 2 × 300 m @ 80-85% of max.

4-6 × 100 m uphill runs

Circuit training

Cool-down

Stretch

Early Season

Monday	Warm-up
	Sprint drills
	Speed development work
	Turn-around 40 m or 50 m sprints (either increase speed or increase distance to 100 m)
	Cool-down
	Stretch
Tuesday	Warm-up
	Sprint drills
	Technical practice (modeling-rotary running)
	Speed stick running
	4 × 60 m block starts
	4 × 30 m flying starts (work on finishing at tape)
	Bounding with a weighted vest
	Cool-down
	Stretch
Wednesday	Warm-up
	Technical practice
	4 × 100 m relaxation strides (easy pace, focus on good form)
	Cool-down
	Stretch
Thursday	Warm-up
	Sprint drills (emphasize rotary running)
	4 × 120 m (speed endurance)
	6 × 50 m weighted sled pulls
	Cool-down
	Stretch
Friday	Warm-up
	Sprint drills
	Rotary running
	3-4 × 20 m starts
	2 × 100 m smooth striding
	Cool-down
	Stretch

(continued)

(continued)

Saturday	Warm-up
	Early competition

Late Season

Monday	Warm-up
	For 100 m athletes: 5 × 200 m @ 90% of max.
	3 min. recovery between sets
	For 200 m athletes: 4 × 300 m @ 85-90% of max.
	10-12 min. recovery between sets
	Cool-down
	Stretch
Tuesday	Warm-up
	Sprint drills
	Technical practice (modeling-rotary running)
	Speed stick drill
	2 × 100 m continuous acceleration drill
	2 × 120 m (speed endurance)
	Plyometric training
	Cool-down
	Stretch
Wednesday	Warm-up
	6 × 100 m relaxation strides (easy pace, focus on good form)
	Cool-down
	Stretch
Thursday	Warm-up
	Sprint drills
	Technical modeling (emphasize rotary running)
	2-3 × 30 m block starts
	1 × 150 m @ 100% of max.
	Cool-down
	Stretch
Friday	Warm-up only
Saturday	Warm-up
	Most important competition

Diet

The athlete's diet affects his or her performance directly. Competitive athletes must eat a balanced diet containing all four food groups, and eating a variety of foods within each group is essential. For example, in the vegetable group it is beneficial to eat all of the different colors of vegetables in order to receive every type of vitamin and mineral, as well as antioxidants. Power athletes should follow a 40–40–20 ratio—that is, a diet composed of 40 percent protein, 40 percent carbohydrates, and 20 percent fats.

Rest and Recovery

Along with eating right, an athlete should rest and recover properly. There are different ways to help the body recover, and it's important to use a variety of recovery approaches in order to determine which ones each athlete responds to the best. Complete rest means not performing any physical activity, while active rest involves maintaining some level of physical activity that does not pertain to the athlete's event. Other techniques that help recovery include pool therapy, massage, acupuncture, chiropractic adjustments, and physical therapy. Ice massage and ice application, cold-hot contrast, and hydrotherapy are more specific recovery tools. Ice application is always a helpful way to flush the body after fatiguing exercise. Cold whirlpool treatments are another good option.

Competition

Being mentally ready for a competition is just as important as being physically ready. The two go hand-in-hand. Setting goals and practicing mental training techniques will help athletes compete at the level of their potential.

Goal Setting

An important part of competing is being able to set goals and accept challenges. Should you, the coach, set goals, or should goal setting be done together with the athlete? If the relationship between you and the athlete is strongly authority-oriented, you will most likely assign goals. On the other hand, if the athlete has personal experience that makes her or his input very valuable, an athlete and coach can set goals together. In either case, the goals must be challenging but realistic. If athletes see their goals as unattainable, they will reduce their effort, thus reducing their chances for success. Throughout the competitive season it is important to reevaluate the athletes' goals using their results in training and competitions.

Mental Toughness

Mental toughness enables your athletes to reach their goals. A strong mental disposition allows the athletes to accept challenges, handle stress, and assume responsibility for successes and failures. The best way to put your athletes in the right frame of mind and to reduce their stress is to adequately prepare them for every aspect of competition. The best ways for athletes to prepare include being in good physical shape, planning which competitions they will participate in and focus their training around, evaluating performance and progress, setting goals, creating training timetables, and learning to hold themselves accountable.

A large factor in the ability to cope with stress is self-confidence. This is developed through fitness preparation, skill development, and improved performance. You must play an important role in building up your athletes' confidence without creating overconfidence, which can lead to a total loss of confidence when unrealistic goals are not met. You must therefore work on building up athletes' confidence yet help them realize their present limitations. Then help set a path for each athlete to follow to gain the skills necessary to break through these limitations.

Imagery and Visualization

The athlete's psyche directly affects his or her performance, and coaches must learn how to utilize sport psychology techniques to benefit their athletes. Mental imagery and visualization techniques can help an athlete learn the necessary skills of sprinting. Mental imagery is assisted when the athletes can view film or video of correct technique. This helps to develop a mental picture for the athlete. A film or video will also help athletes recognize flaws in their technique. They can then visualize how to achieve the desired technical model. This process involves the athlete seeing themselves executing the correct technical model in their mind prior to attempting the skill in either practice or competition.

Before a practice session or competition, the athletes should take a few moments to mentally rehearse the technical model. The athletes should not only see the model in their mind but should sense the rhythm of the effort in their nerves. When an athlete does this effectively, you can see movements in the body that are responding to the mental process. Athletes should also rehearse the skills away from practice in a very quiet and undisturbed setting. They should close their eyes and concentrate on seeing themselves executing a perfect performance. Repeating this process greatly enhances their ability to perform well. Other aspects of competition should also be visualized, such as crossing the finishing tape and being on the award stand. This helps motivate and move athletes toward their goals.

Summary

My goal in this chapter has been to make you aware of and to help you understand the many significant training components that go into developing good sprinters. Coaches can no longer simply prepare workouts. They need to be part of every aspect of their athletes' training.

Yet this chapter is not intended to get everyone to agree on a single plan for developing all sprinters. It simply shows how preparation, consideration, discussion, and review can be used to construct an athlete's training program and how you can prevent problems before they occur. Preparation requires a plan. Consideration entails remembering that each athlete is a person with specific feelings, needs, beliefs, and opinions. Discussion-based communication with your athletes about their program, what works, and what needs to be changed is a necessity. And it is important to review and evaluate the program with your athletes and to assess their progress in order to help them improve their technique and performance. This includes developing a good start and acceleration pattern, good running mechanics for high-speed performance, and top-speed endurance that allows for the best finish possible. Each stage of your athletes' development necessitates careful review of their past training history. And your athletes' emotional, physical, and social development cannot be ignored. You may not have all the answers, and this is not wrong. But not consulting, reading, and investigating to find the answer is! Keep in mind that your athletes' well-being is in your hands.

4 400 Meters

Clyde Hart

The 400-meter dash is an endurance sprint incorporating the speed of the sprinter and the endurance of the half-miler. It is considered by many to be one of the most demanding and grueling of competitive events. Usually the 400-meter runner is one of two distinct types—the sprinter type or half-miler type. Both of these types have had their share of success over the years. Occasionally you will find an athlete who possesses some characteristics of both sprinter and half-miler.

Michael Johnson, a world and Olympic champion in both the 200 and 400 meters, is a prime example of the sprinter-type 400 runner. However, he has developed his strength and endurance over the years to the point that he can better maintain his superior speed over a longer distance than his competitors.

Distribution of Speed

The ability to distribute one's speed and energies in the most efficient manner over the total racing distance is the primary means of achieving success in the 400-meter dash. No one is capable of running the 400 meters all out from start to finish. Judging pace well in effort and distribution is a must. Remember, the 400 meters is not a full sprint. Outstanding speed at 100 and 200 meters can be a tremendous advantage to the 400-meter runners but only if they learn to distribute these energies properly. Generally, the outstanding 400-meter runner will have approximately a one-second differential between their best open 200 meters and the time it takes them to run the first 200 meters of the 400-meter dash. The less-experienced 400-meter runner has approximately a two-second differential.

A good formula for predicting the potential 400-meter time for 200-meter runners, provided they are willing to train and to give all they can to become a top 400-meter runner, is to double the time of their best open 200 meters, then add 3.5 seconds. Obviously the sprinter type has the advantage through the early stages of the 400 meters; however, if he or she is not trained properly, this advantage can melt away in a hurry toward the end of the race. The half-miler type will definitely have an advantage from the 300-meters mark to the finish. We are seeing more of the sprinter type succeed in the 400 meters today largely because stamina and endurance can be developed more effectively than can the sprinting abilities of the middle-distance runner.

Training

The 400 meters is an oxygen-deficient event. This means that the level of oxygen absorption is below that which is necessary to supply the ATP (adenosine triphosphate) requirement. The energy used during the 400-meter dash is derived from the breakdown of high-energy phosphate compounds and from the splitting of glycogen to lactic acid. This event will rely primarily on two anaerobic systems—the ATP-PC and lactic acid systems. Physiologists have not found a good way to measure anaerobic power, and this makes it very difficult to know if one is increasing the anaerobic reserves or not. We must rely on what we have learned from physiologists concerning the components of fatigue during the running of the 400-meter dash. This tells us what types of stress we must deal with during both 400-meter training and competition.

Proper training will help athletes learn to deal with the stress that they will face toward the end of the 400-meter dash. We know that severe exercising imposes great stress on the body, and it must learn to adapt to this stress or it will break down. We also know that when the body is gradually put under stress, it will do whatever is necessary for its own well-being to adjust to this new environment. When an organism is conditioned to the stress of athletic competition, it will be able to perform in that environment when called upon.

Training Segments

The training year of the 400-meter runner will be divided into four segments:

1. off-season (summer and September–December),
2. early competitive season (January–February),

3. midseason (March–April), and

4. late season (May–June).

Types of Workouts

Based on the demands of the 400-meter event, the following training workouts are recommended in varying degrees of emphasis during the training year. The time frame in which each workout is used in the course of the training year is of vital importance. To derive the most from any training program, the coach and runner must pay close attention to the proper introduction of a specific workout.

SPEED ENDURANCE

In speed-endurance running the runner incurs a high oxygen debt, and there is a definite lactic acid buildup. This type of workout is vital to good 400-meter running. The distances run can vary from 100 to 600 meters. The number of repetitions is figured by multiplying the race distance two and a half times; in the case of the 400-meter dash, this would be about 1000 meters. The recovery period will usually be around 10 minutes, which gives the runner almost full recovery so that there will be quality in the runs. The following speed-endurance workouts are designed to help the lactic acid energy system.

Reps × m	Rest (min.)
10 × 100	5-10
6 × 150	5-10
5 × 200	10
4 × 300	10
3 × 350	10
2 × 450	10

TEMPO ENDURANCE

Tempo endurance, an aerobic workout, will pay great dividends to 400-meter runners. Not only will it help them to increase their oxygen uptake, which will help to shorten their recovery time, but it will enable them to accomplish more and longer workouts. Since the runs are done at a slower pace, this workout helps the runners learn rhythm, and, as the name suggests, tempo. Another vital by-product of this workout is that it helps to train the body to increase production of phosphate, which is a primary energy source. The emphasis in the following workouts, as with speed-endurance workouts, should be on quantity and not on quality. The rest factor is generally kept short—usually two to three minutes.

Reps × m	Rest
8 × 200	2 min.
6 × 300	2 min.
50-100-150-200-300-350	Walk the same distance for rest

STRENGTH ENDURANCE

These strength-endurance workouts involve activities that will last longer than 10 seconds. Such activities will include resistance running, long-hill running, and stadium-step runs.

> 6 × 150 m uphill
>
> 6 × 60 stadium steps (figure 4.1)
>
> 6 × 15 sec. rope-resistance runs

Figure 4.1   Stadium-step runs.

ENDURANCE RUNNING

The endurance-running workout is pure aerobic running. It consists of continuous runs of 15 to 45 minutes at a steady-state speed. Although the 400 meters requires only about 5% aerobic running, it is important to 400-meter runners to get a good base of aerobic running to improve their oxygen uptake so that their recovery time between efforts is cut to a minimum.

> 15 min. at steady-state speed
>
> 30 min. of fartlek running
>
> 6 × 800 m on cross-country course with 3 min. recovery

POWER SPEED

The following power-speed workouts emphasize speed of muscle contraction. This is usually done with fewer than 10 repetitions and no more than 10 seconds per repetition.

> Short-hill runs of about 60 m
>
> 10 × 30 m harness runs
>
> 10 × 10 sec. fast rope jumps

EVENT RUNNING

The event-running workout does exactly what the name implies. The runner runs different distances at a predetermined race strategy in order to learn to work on different aspects of running the 400 meters. We also refer to this as segment running.

Workout	Description
3 × 300 m	First 50 m, run all out. Next 150 m, run with a relaxed, floating action. Run all out on the last 100 m. Time and record each run.
2 × 450 m	The first 200 m, 300 m, 400 m, and final 50 m are all timed and recorded.
1 × 350 m	Quality run, with each segment run as if in the 400 m race.

SPEED

Speed workouts will use distances varying from 30 meters to 150 meters. Work will be done at full speed either on the straightaway or curve. Rest between runs is usually long, allowing full recovery and quality performances. Relay handoff work will count as doing speed workouts.

> 6 × 40 m starts
>
> 6 × 60 m flying starts
>
> 6 × 60 m sprint-relay handoffs

STRENGTH

Strength workouts consist of both general and specific strength development. Our general strength development is done through the traditional weight-lifting programs of both free weights and machines. We also recommend the use of plyometric drills to give us our specific weight work.

> 30-min. traditional weight-lifting workout (1 set, 13 reps)
>
> Explosive jumps for the development of starting power and acceleration
>
> 3 sets of 10 hops, each leg
>
> Fast 50 m bounding runs with barbell

Table 4.1 indicates the percentage of emphasis, by segment of training year, to be given to the above workouts. Altering the emphasis of different workouts throughout training will enhance your athletes' performances when it comes time for competition.

In addition to the workouts presented thus far, table 4.2 presents various running exercises that will improve everything from endurance and speed to overall technique and running efficiency. The best training segment or season in which to practice these exercises is also given. Many of these running exercises are also found in the comprehensive sample workouts in table 4.3 (see page 57).

TABLE 4.1 PERCENTAGE OF MAX. EMPHASIS FOR WORKOUTS

Types of workouts	Fall	Early	Mid	Late
Speed endurance	75	90	100	100
Tempo endurance	100	100	100	75
Strength endurance	100	90	80	70
Endurance running	100	20	10	5
Power speed	20	60	70	80
Event runs	25	90	100	100
Strength	100	100	100	100

TABLE 4.2   RUNNING EXERCISES FOR SPRINTERS

Exercise	Description	Benefits	Season
Endless relay	Baton is kept moving, rest and run are controlled	Endurance, stamina, and exchange work	All
Australian pursuits	Sprints and slow jogging for total of 3 min.	Endurance, speed, and kicking drill	All
Long hill	100 m or more, slow runs	Endurance, stamina, and knee lift	Fall/early
600 m	Pace first 400, pick up last 200 m	Endurance and stamina	Fall/early
500 m	Pace first 400, pick up last 100 m	Endurance, stamina, and knee lift	Early/mid
350 m	Quality and training distance, all 5.5-7 sec. under 400 time	Mental preparation, endurance, and stamina	Early/mid and late
300 m event	200 m slow pace, last 100 m faster	Mental preparation, endurance, and running efficiency	Early/mid and late
450 m	Pace first 400 and pick up last 50 m	Mental preparation, endurance, stamina, and knee lift	Mid/late
Short hill	Less than 100 m fast runs	Speed, leg drive, and stamina	Mid/late
Flying bears	Repeat 100s with jogging	Speed, strength, and running efficiency	Mid/late
320 m	Quality distance, add 10-12 sec. for 400 time	Mental preparation, speed, and running efficiency	Mid/late
Speedmaker	Short 50 m sprints, jogging	Speed, strength, and running efficiency	Mid/late
150 m buildups	50 m at 1/2 speed, 50 m at 3/4 speed, 50 m at near full speed	Running efficiency, speed, endurance, and mental preparation	Early/mid and late

Designing a Training Program

Before coaches plan their 400-meter workouts, they should ponder several concepts:

- The basic concept of going from quantity to quality has not changed over the past several decades.

- All workouts should follow a progressive pattern; you should standardize your workouts so that speed of the running distance is progressively shortened and in some cases the amount of rest as well.

- The concept of overloading pays dividends. The following is an example: Have the 400-meter runner run 2 × 600s, coming through the 400 meters at a very slow pace. As the time of the first 400 meters is gradually lowered to the point that the runner has difficulty maintaining pace, the distance is lowered. At the next distance, 500 meters, the runners run at the same pace through the first 400 meters as if they were running at the previous distance. The athletes continue this workout drill until the distance is reduced to 450 meters. Try to reach this final distance by midseason and continue it to the end of the year. We suggest having the athletes do one run, rather than two, before a major competition. Although the runners are getting less distance, their effort has increased—with more stress being put on the body.

- Another factor to consider in planning 400-meter workouts is that it takes a hard run of around 40 seconds to incur a significant lactic acid buildup. This being the case, the ideal distance is 300 meters for women and 350 meters for men. Since most quality 400-meter runners will cover this distance in slightly over 40 seconds, they are working a couple of seconds into lactic acid buildup. By running this distance, the runner can accomplish several of these runs in a workout session.

Keeping these points in mind, a complete training program that features sample workouts for each season is presented in table 4.3.

TABLE 4.3 SAMPLE WORKOUTS FOR 400 METERS

These workouts can be applied to all levels of 400-meter runners, but performance times given in this sample are for a potential 46-second quarter-miler; so adjust accordingly.

The *Rest* times apply to each run. For example, 3 × 300. *Speed:* 50 sec. *Rest:* 1 min. means:

1. 1 × 300 2. Rest for 1 min. 3. 1 × 300
4. Rest for 1 min. 5. 1 × 300

Fall (September–December)	
Monday	1. Warm-up: 1-mile cross-country run
	2. Flexibility exercises
	3. 2 × 600 *Speed:* 90 sec. (60 sec./400 m pace) *Rest:* 15 min.
	4. 3 × 300 *Speed:* 50 sec. *Rest:* 1 min.
	5. 3 × 300 *Speed:* 40 sec. *Rest:* 5 min.
	6. Cool-down: 1-mile cross-country run
	7. Weights

(continued)

(continued)

Fall (September–December)

Tuesday	1. Warm-up: 1-mile cross-country run
	2. Flexibility exercises
	3. 10 × 200 *Speed:* 30 sec. *Rest:* 3 min.
	4. 6 × 150 long-hill runs. *Speed:* fast *Rest:* jog back
	5. Cool-down: 1-mile cross-country run
Wednesday	1. Warm-up: 1-mile cross-country run
	2. Flexibility exercises
	3. 4 × 350 (event run). *Speed:* 48 sec. *Rest:* 10 min.
	50 fast —150 relaxed (200 time of 28 sec.) — 100 picked up fast —
	last 50 steady and keeping good form
	4. 3 × 200 *Speed:* 30-29-28 sec. *Rest:* 3 min.
	5. Cool-down: 1-mile cross-country run
	6. Weights
Thursday	1. Warm-up: 1-mile cross-country run
	2. Flexibility exercises
	3. 600-400-200-400-600 *Speed:* 30-sec. pace *Rest:* 5 min.
	4. 6 × 100 strides. *Speed:* medium *Rest:* 1 min.
	5. Cool-down: 1-mile cross-country run
Friday	1. Warm-up: 1/2-mile cross-country run
	2. Flexibility exercises
	3. Two-mile cross-country timed run
	4. Weights
Saturday	No organized practice, encouraged to do 3 miles running.
Sunday	No organized practice, encouraged to do 20-min. fartlek.

Early Season (January–February)

Monday	1. Warm-up: 1 mile of in and outs (100 sprint/100 walk, 3 laps, faster each lap, 4th-lap run of 200 in 26 sec.)
	2. Flexibility exercises
	3. 2 × 500 *Speed:* 70 sec. (56 sec./400 m pace) *Rest:* 15 min.
	4. 3 × 200 *Speed:* 30-29-28 sec. *Rest:* 3 min.
	5. 8 × 10-sec. rope jumps. *Rest:* 10 sec. Repeat
Tuesday	1. Warm-up: 1 mile of in and outs
	2. Flexibility exercises
	3. 8 × 200 *Speed:* 28 sec. *Rest:* 3 min.
	4. 6 × 150 long-hill runs. *Speed:* fast *Rest:* jog back
	5. Weights
Wednesday	1. Warm-up: 1 mile of in and outs
	2. Flexibility exercises

	3. 4 × 300 (event run). *Speed:* 42 sec. *Rest:* 5 min.
	4. 3 × 200 *Speed:* 30-29-28 sec. *Rest:* 3 min.
	5. 6 × 10-sec. rope-resistance run. *Speed:* fast. *Rest:* 10 sec.
Thursday	1. Warm-up: 1 mile of in and outs
	2. Flexibility exercises
	3. 1 × 350 *Speed:* fast. *Rest:* 15 min.
	4. 4 × 200 *Speed:* 26 sec. *Rest:* 5 min.
	5. Weights
Friday	1. Warm-up: 1 mile of in and outs
	2. Flexibility exercises
	3. 3 × 200 *Speed:* 30-29-28 sec. *Rest:* 3 min.
	4. 1600-relay handoff work
Saturday	Meet
Sunday	No organized workout; encouraged to do some light cross-country running, about 20 min.
Midseason (March–April)	
Monday	1. Warm-up: 1 mile of in and outs
	2. Flexibility exercises
	3. 2 × 450 *Speed:* 58.5 sec. (52 sec./400 m pace). *Rest:* 15 min.
	4. 3 × 200 *Speed:* 28-27-26 sec. *Rest:* 3 min.
Tuesday	1. Warm-up: 1 mile of in and outs
	2. Flexibility exercises
	3. 6 × 200 *Speed:* 26 sec. *Rest:* 3 min.
	4. 5 × 20 sec. rope-resistance runs. *Speed:* slow. *Rest:* 3 min.
	5. Weights
Wednesday	1. Warm-up: 1 mile of in and outs
	2. Flexibility exercises
	3. 4 × 300 (event run). *Speed:* 42 sec. *Rest:* 5 min.
	4. 8 × 100 short-hill runs. *Speed:* fast. *Rest:* walk back.
Thursday	1. Warm-up: 1 mile of in and outs
	2. Flexibility exercises
	3. 3 × 200 *Speed:* 26–25–24 sec. *Rest:* walk 200.
	4. 3 × 150 (buildups). *Speed:* fast. slow–medium–fast. *Rest:* walk back.
	5. Weights
Friday	1. Warm-up: 1 mile of in and outs
	2. Flexibility exercises
	3. 3 × 200 *Speed:* 26 sec. *Rest:* walk 200.
	4. 1600-relay handoffs

(continued)

(continued)

Midseason (March–April)	
Saturday	Meet
Sunday	No organized practice; encouraged to do some cross-country running, about 20 min.

Late Season (May–June)	
Monday	1. Warm-up: 1 mile of in and outs 2. Flexibility exercises 3. 1 × 450 *Speed:* 50–sec. 400. *Rest:* 15 min. 4. 3 × 200 *Speed:* 26–25–24 sec. *Rest:* walk 200.
Tuesday	1. Warm-up: 1 mile of in and outs 2. Flexibility exercises 3. 4 × 300 *Speed:* 42 sec. *Rest:* 5 min. 4. 4 × 200 *Speed:* 28–27–26–25 sec. *Rest:* 3 min. 5. Weights
Wednesday	1. Warm-up: 1 mile of in and outs 2. Flexibility exercises 3. 1 × 320 (quality run). *Speed:* fast. *Rest:* 15 min. 4. 3 × 200 *Speed:* 26-25-24 sec. *Rest:* walk 200. 5. 8 × 80 short-hill runs. *Speed:* fast. *Rest:* walk back.

Thursday	1. Warm-up: 1 mile of in and outs
	2. Flexibility exercises
	3. 3 sets of speedmakers. *Speed:* fast. *Rest:* jog.
	    50-meter all-out sprint, 50-meter swing down, 50-meter slow jog.
	    Repeat until four all-out sprints are done. Three minutes rest between sets.
	4. Weights

Friday	1. Warm-up: 1 mile of in and outs 2. Flexibility exercises 3. 2 x 200 *Speed:* 26 sec. *Rest:* walk 200. 4. 1600-relay handoffs
Saturday	Meet
Sunday	No organized practice; encouraged to do some cross-country running, about 20 min.

Competition

The ideal race pattern consists of smooth deceleration, if the athletes have dispersed their energies properly, with as little tightening up at the finish as possible. Runners should try to cover the first 50 meters at near top speed. At this point they should relax the actions of the upper body while maintaining their leg speed. Their minds should settle into the rhythm of the race and get a feel for their

Inger Miller's competitive experience and effective race plan put her ahead of her opponents during the final curve.

competition. They should also begin thinking about the next big effort they will make, which will be at the 200-meter mark. They should be trained and conditioned to know that at this point in their race plan, they will make a determined effort to increase the actions of their arms and to begin driving and lifting their knees, trying to resume more of a sprinting action. The runners who learn to work the turn from the 200- to the 300-meter mark will usually find themselves in good position to win the race. It is a controlled pickup, one that should allow the runners to come off the final curve even or ahead of their opponents. During the final 100 meters of the race, the runners must stay relaxed while fighting the effects of fatigue. One of the best ways to do this is by concentrating on the proper running technique and good form they have been taught.

Summary

The coach must become more than just a trainer by becoming personally involved in the race strategy of the 400-meter runners. Time the different segments of workout runs as well as competitive races. Let the runners know beforehand what you expect their 200-meter split, or even 300-meter split, to be so that you and they know what kind of pace they are keeping. Oftentimes, the race will dictate what pace the runners will have to carry to be competitive, but this is no excuse for not having them mentally ready to perform at a certain level. If they know they have been through different checkpoints at a certain time in practice, they will not have a fear of doing this in actual competition.

5 100- and 110- Meter Hurdles

Ralph Lindeman
John Millar

Wanted: Highly motivated sprinters to attempt one of track and field's most dynamic events. Must be extremely rhythmic and highly coordinated to hurdle 10 barriers in a 110-meter sprint race. Competitive sprinting speed is a prerequisite. Explosive strength and dynamic flexibility required to sprint over hurdles 39–42 inches (about 99–107 cm) high. Tall stature can be an advantage during the developing years (but may cause problems at elite levels). Determination, mental toughness, and ability to concentrate necessary to learn the techniques and develop speed endurance. Terrific opportunities for success.

The coach who actively recruits athletes with these characteristics for the 110-meter hurdle event has a base of athletic individuals around which to develop his or her team. By these very qualifications, hurdlers have the versatility to compete in other explosive speed events (sprints, vertical and horizontal jumps, relays) and enhance the team.

Technique

Many coaches teach the high hurdles as a highly technical event, spending much of their time (and the athlete's energy) measuring and analyzing aspects of hurdling such as number of strides to the first hurdle, takeoff distance, landing distance, hurdle clearance techniques, and touchdown times, while neglecting the basic premise of the event—the 110-meter high hurdle race is a sprint event. The majority of the coach's (and athlete's) energy should be spent on teaching the concept of sprinting over the hurdles.

The athlete's speed is a function of his stride length and stride frequency. The hurdler's stride length is for the most part predetermined by the set distance from the starting line to the first hurdle, in between each of the 10 hurdles, and then to the finish. Ideally, there are eight strides to the first hurdle and three strides in between. This means that the young high school hurdler takes the same number of strides as the elite international-caliber hurdler. The difference between them is the hurdler's stride frequency. The coach, then, needs to develop the athlete's stride frequency, and does this by training him with fast rhythmic repetitions over the hurdles so as to adapt the athlete's speed to hurdling.

Start and Approach to First Hurdle

The starting position and block clearance are the same for the hurdler as for the 100-meter sprinter. The hurdler makes a transition to erect sprinting posture ("running tall") more quickly than the sprinter to prepare for takeoff over the first hurdle.

The high hurdler should strive for eight strides to the first hurdle. Eight strides will give the hurdler a stride length during the three strides prior to the hurdle that will be similar to the stride length that will be required on the three strides between each of the subsequent hurdles. To effect eight strides to the hurdle, the hurdler must have the lead leg in the back block at the starting line.

Takeoff

As the hurdler plants on the eighth step from the blocks, he must drive the lead knee of the free leg linearly toward the hash mark on the lead leg side of the hurdle. (See figure 5.1a and b.) *A fast lead knee is critical to hurdling efficiency.*

Figure 5.1   The athlete must drive the lead knee of the free leg at takeoff.

The takeoff distance from the hurdle depends on the hurdler's horizontal velocity at takeoff. If the hurdler takes off too close to the hurdle, the result will usually be excessive clearance height over the hurdle. The center of mass should be raised only as high as needed for the athlete to clear the hurdle efficiently (figure 5.1c).

The head leads the body over the hurdle. This results in lean of the upper body into the hurdle. The trunk lean makes it possible to minimally raise the center of mass for effective hurdle clearance.

The takeoff leg, which will serve as the "trail leg," must fully extend at takeoff. This is sometimes referred to as a "delayed trail leg," although it happens naturally if the drive of the lead knee is sufficient.

The hips and shoulders must stay "square" to the hurdle. The hurdler should coordinate lifting the elbow of the lead arm with driving the lead knee. The lead arm comes up to a position where the hand is in front of the sternum. The hurdler should never "reach" the lead arm too far in front of the body or across the midline of the body—this results in excessive rotation as the hurdler clears the barrier.

Hurdle Clearance

Proper leg and arm action is essential to fast and efficient hurdle clearance.

Lead Leg

When the thigh of the lead leg drives up to a position parallel to the track, momentum is transferred to the lower leg, which extends naturally. The foot of the lead leg reaches its apex of the flight curve prior to clearing the hurdle. The foot is always dorsiflexed with the toe up. (See figure 5.2a.) The hurdler should never "swing" the lead foot up and toward the hurdle.

The hurdler "paws" the lead foot down to the track after clearing the hurdle, with the foot still dorsiflexed. Never "snap" the lead leg down—this jerks the trunk back (action-reaction) and out of good sprint position. The hurdler should "hold the lean" of the trunk throughout hurdle clearance (figure 5.2b).

Trail Leg

Immediately after takeoff, the foot of the trail leg should "tuck in" or "fold up" behind the hip and follow the knee over the hurdle as in figure 5.2c. The hips

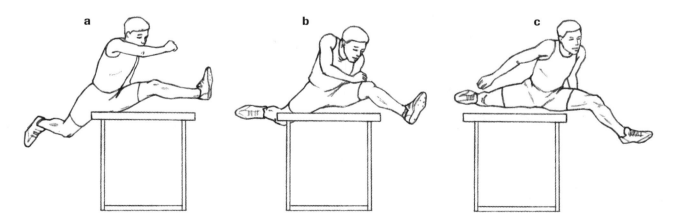

Figure 5.2 Proper lead and trail leg positions during hurdle clearance.

precede the knee over the hurdle, and the hurdler should "pull" the trail leg through over the hurdle in a continuous accelerating motion (with no "posed" position).

Arm Action

The lead arm should "sweep" back in a wide arc. This is necessary to increase the moment of inertia of the arm to balance the greater mass of the trail leg moving in the opposite direction. As soon as the lead arm passes the trail leg, the radius shortens to resume sprinting action. The trail arm stays relaxed with the hand near the hip (on the lead leg side). It should deviate as little as possible from normal sprinting action.

Landing

The hurdler should strive for an "active" landing, with the lead leg pawing back at the ground with the foot still dorsiflexed as in figure 5.3a. The foot of the lead leg should land directly beneath the hurdler's center of mass (figure 5.3b and c). A fast getaway stride is the result of high and effective trail leg technique.

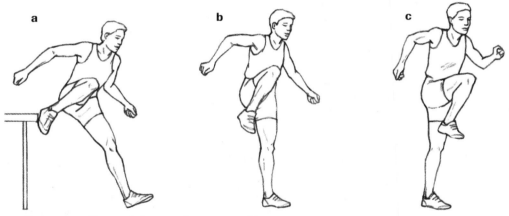

Figure 5.3 The touchdown and getaway stride.

Correcting Common Faults

In analyzing hurdlers' technique, it is often advantageous to view the hurdler, either actively or via videotape, from a head-on position. Most of the faults listed below can be spotted from such a viewing position.

Fault: Taking off too far from the first hurdle.

Causes:

    a. Blocks may be too bunched.

    b. Initial strides are too short.

Corrections:

    a. Space the blocks farther apart.

    b. Accelerate more explosively.

Fault: Excessive height over the hurdle.

Cause: Taking off too close/jumping over the hurdle.

Correction: Use lower hurdle heights in practice.

Fault: Locking the lead knee.

Cause: Swinging the foot up instead of driving the knee.

Correction: Perform skipping drills on the sides of and over the hurdles.

Fault: Off-balance landing.

Cause: Excessive rotation around the vertical axis.

Correction: Avoid reaching the left elbow of the lead arm.

Fault: Landing on heel.

Cause: Snapping lead leg down; straightening trunk.

Correction: Hold the lean throughout hurdle clearance.

Fault: Serpentine stride pattern between hurdles.

Cause: Excessive rotation around the vertical axis.

Correction: Drive the knee at takeoff; keep hips and shoulders square.

In addition to troubleshooting technique visually, the coach can also analyze touchdown times to evaluate performance both in training and competition. The coach can manually (or by viewing videotape played at actual speed) time the touchdown of the lead foot over each hurdle, and by plotting the data, have an effective model of each repetition and race.

Drills

Sequences of progressive drills can be used both to teach hurdle technique in introductory sessions as well as to prepare the hurdler for training or competition as part of a warm-up. Drills may be done at lower than standard heights to increase efficiency. For example, high school boys may do the drills over 33–36-inch (about 84–91 cm) hurdles and advanced hurdlers over 36–39-inch (about 91–99 cm) hurdles.

A-March

With the hurdles set 4–6 feet (about 1.2–1.8 m) apart, the athlete steps in a marching rhythm over the tops of the hurdles, exaggerating knee-up/toe-up/heel-up action and erect posture. This is illustrated in figure 5.4.

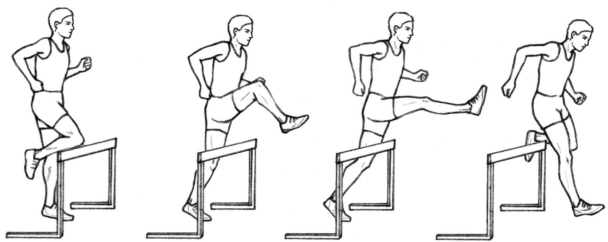

Figure 5.4 A-march drill.

A-Skips

With the hurdles set 6-8 feet (about 1.8-2.4 m) apart, the athlete skips over the top of the hurdles, again emphasizing knee-up/toe-up/heel-up action in the skipping rhythm.

B-Skips

With the same setup and same skipping rhythm, the athlete casts his lead leg out and over the hurdle on every other skip, pawing the lead leg back to the ground after clearing the hurdle.

C-Skips

With the same setup and same skipping rhythm, the athlete raises his trail leg laterally on every other skip, clearing the side of the hurdle.

Fast-Leg Drill

With several hurdles set 8.5-8.8 meters apart, the athlete performs a fast-leg drill over the lead-leg side of hurdle—that is, pulling the heel tightly to the butt in an accelerating motion, simulating a sprint stride at maximum velocity on every fourth stride.

Half-Hurdling—Lead Leg

With same setup, the athlete sprints over the lead-leg side of the hurdle, executing the lead-leg action. Efficient execution may require setting the hurdles as much as 9 inches (about 23 cm) below standard hurdle height.

Half-Hurdling—Trail Leg

With same setup, the athlete sprints over the trail-leg side of the hurdle, executing the trail-leg action. This requires an "air-step," with the lead leg coordinated with trail-leg action. To avoid overrotation around vertical axis, the lead leg should land 6-12 inches (about 15-30 cm) beyond the hurdle.

Although this sequence of drills is not a complete list of drills, performing these drills in sequence prepares the athlete for hurdling at faster velocities. Additional drills that produce strength and dynamic flexibility in the range of motion used in hurdling include the following:

Ground Hurdling

Seated on the ground, the athlete imitates the arm action, leaning his trunk forward on every fourth arm pump and lifting the elbow of the lead arm, then sweeping it back while keeping the shoulders square.

Wall Hurdling

The athlete leads with the knee while lifting the elbow of the lead arm and "landing" the dorsiflexed foot of the lead knee against the wall.

Fence Drill for Trail Leg

While balancing by bracing with the arms against a fence or another hurdle to support a leaning trunk, the athlete repetitiously circles the trail leg continually over the hurdle, as demonstrated in figure 5.5.

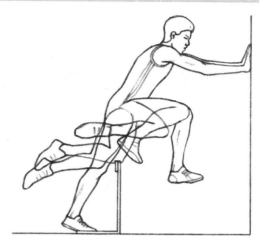

Figure 5.5   Fence drill for the trail leg.

Resisted Trail Leg

In the same position as the previous drill, the athlete circles the trail leg against the resistance of a partner holding the foot of the trail leg.

In teaching the beginning hurdler, don't hesitate to lower the hurdles or move them closer. The objective should be to teach efficient hurdle clearance technique at a fast rhythm, and not necessarily to negotiate the hurdles at their standard height and distances.

It can also be advantageous to teach the beginning hurdler to take four steps between hurdles. This will allow the hurdler to maintain efficient sprint technique without "reaching" for the hurdles, and will force him or her to develop ambidextrous hurdling ability, an advantage if the athlete will also compete in the 300-meter or 400-meter hurdle race.

100-Meter Hurdles

John Millar

The women's 100-meter hurdles emerged from the 80-meter hurdles when, in 1968, the IAAF changed the event to its present distance. The 100-meter event was first contested the following year. The change was made because of increases in the speed and strength of female athletes, along with improvements in track surfaces and equipment.

The event consists of 10 hurdles spaced at 8.5 meters, with a starting distance of 13.0 meters and a finishing distance of 10.5 meters. The height of the hurdles is 33 inches (.84 meters). These segments determine the number of strides taken by the athlete. The starting distance to the first hurdle is usually covered in eight strides, with three strides taken between hurdles.

Much of the technique described for the 110-meter high hurdles can be applied to the 100-meter hurdle race. However, there are distinct technical differences in the women's

(continued)

hurdle event based on the lower hurdle heights and the decreased distances between hurdles. The most evident differences between the events are the hurdle clearance and trail-leg mechanics.

Hurdle Clearance

The lower hurdle height in the 100-meter hurdle race affects the clearance stride, or the distance the hurdler travels from takeoff into the hurdle until touchdown over the hurdle. An aggressive lead leg resulting from a shortened takeoff stride allows the athlete to attack the hurdle more quickly, thereby minimizing the loss of horizontal velocity over the hurdle. This action and the lower hurdle height enable the hurdler to keep the flight path of the center of gravity as flat as possible, allowing her to touch down closer to the hurdle than her male counterpart and resulting in a shorter clearance stride over the hurdle.

Trail-Leg Mechanics

The trail leg of the female hurdler is brought through in a much less pronounced manner than the "ascending knee under the arm" position used in the men's 110-meter hurdles. The trail-leg foot is folded tightly against the buttock as the trail leg is pulled across the hurdle (see figure 5.6). The lower hurdle height permits women hurdlers to allow the thigh of the trail leg to hang down as it crosses the hurdle rail—the degree of hang depends on the height of the athlete. Shorter female hurdlers will also bend the trail leg away from the pelvis more than their taller counterparts.

Drills

To master hurdling technique, athletes learn a number of specific drills that not only isolate the various hurdle movements but also teach the different phases and eventually the whole movement. Stationary drills are the main source of teaching beginners the basic hurdle movements, as these drills isolate the different positions of the legs, arms, and body as well as help to develop specific hurdling flexibility. Once the various stationary drills have been mastered, the individual moves on to the more complex walking, skipping, and running drills.

The following teaching progression can be used in developing the hurdling technique and rhythm of the novice 100-meter hurdler.

Figure 5.6 Trail-leg position during hurdle clearance for 100-meter hurdlers. The lower hurdle height allows for the thigh of the trail leg to hang down as it crosses the hurdle.

Marching and Skipping Exercises

Six low hurdles are placed 1.5 meters apart. The athlete begins by isolating the trail leg and lead leg over their respective sides of the hurdle, and finally combines both actions over the center of the hurdles.

One-Step Hurdling

The hurdles are now placed 3.0-3.5 meters apart. The same sequence is used as in the previous drills, beginning with the trail leg, except that the athlete now takes one step between hurdles.

Three-Step Hurdling

The hurdles are moved out to a distance of 6.5 meters, allowing the athlete to begin to establish the three-step rhythm that is so critical to success in the 100-meter hurdle race. Once again, the trail-leg and lead-leg actions are done in isolation before the whole technique is established over the center of the hurdle.

Training

Drills can be of value for teaching hurdling technique, and as a warm-up method, but the majority of practice time and energy should be spent on fast hurdling. Repetitions over hurdles can be done using several different methods to accomplish varied training objectives, sometimes within the same workout (see table 5.1).

The primary objectives during the preseason should be developing explosive strength and learning hurdle technique. Explosive strength can be increased by doing exercises like hill running, bounding drills, and plyometrics. Technique can be learned with drill progressions and video analysis. The early part of the season should focus on improving speed endurance. This can be done with a high

TABLE 5.1 HURDLE REPETITIONS

Method	Objectives
Starts over 2-3 hurdles	Starting mechanics; acceleration pattern
Reps over 4-6 hurdles	Transition from acceleration phase to maintenance
Reps over 8-12 hurdles	Speed endurance
Reps over 6-10 hurdles, 8.5-8.8 m apart for men, 6.5-7 m apart for women	3 strides in reduced distance forces faster stride frequency; quick rhythm between hurdles
Reps over 4-6 hurdles, 12.5-13 m apart for men, 11.5-12 m apart for women	5 strides over increased distance allows athlete to sprint over hurdles at faster velocity

volume of repetitions at longer distances. During the midseason, the main objective should be on gaining racing experience. A high volume of races will help hurdlers gain the experience they need to compete consistently and intelligently. During the peak season, the focus should switch to refining speed. This is when high-intensity repetitions and quality races come into play. Keeping these objectives in mind, the following table (table 5.2) separates the hurdler's training year into preseason, early season, and late season, and presents a sample weekly training plan for each.

TABLE 5.2   SAMPLE WORKOUTS FOR 100- AND 110- METER HURDLES

Preseason

Monday	Warm-up 6 × 100 m easy strides Hurdle flexibility exercises 5 × 30 m bound uphill Cool-down
Tuesday	Warm-up 15 min. continuous run Circuit training
Wednesday	Warm-up 2 × 5 × 100 m @15-16 sec. with 45-sec. recovery 6 × 50 m uphill runs Cool-down Stretch
Thursday	Warm-up 6 × 100 m @ 80% Relaxation strides Hurdle flexibility exercises Walking hurdle drills Cool-down Stretch
Friday	Warm-up 6 × 300 @ 45-50 sec. 3-5 min. rest Plyometric jump training Cool-down Stretch

Saturday	Warm-up
	Hurdle flexibility drills
	Harness sled pulls for 50 m
	Circuit training
	Cool-down
	Stretch

Early Season

Monday	Warm-up
	Hurdle drills
	Low hurdle technique practice (gradully working up to competitive heights)
	1 × 300 m
	1 × 250 m
	1 × 200 m
	1 × 150 m
	Cool-down
	Stretch
Tuesday	Warm-up
	Hurdle drills
	Sprint drills over adjusted heights and spacings
	Plyometric training
Wednesday	Warm-up
	No hurdling
	Flexibility drills
	15-20 min. aerobic run
Thursday	Warm-up
	Hurdle drills
	Technique practice
	Starts over 3-4 hurdles (adjust heights and spacing) while developing 4 x 120 m speed endurance
	Cool-down
	Stretch
Friday	Warm-up
	Hurdle drills and flexibility
	3-4 starts over 3 hurdles
	2 × 100 m relaxed striding
	Cool-down
	Stretch
Saturday	Early competition

(continued)

(continued)

Late Season	
Monday	Warm-up Hurdle flexibility drills Hurdle technique drills 3 × 8 hurdles, plus run all the way to 150 m Cool-down Stretch
Tuesday	Warm-up Hurdle flexibility drills Speed hurdle training (move hurdles close together to emphasize fast frequency) Plyometrics Cool-down
Wednesday	Warm-up No hurdles Flexibility drills 6-8 × 100 m easy striding
Thursday	Warm-up Hurdle flexibility drills Technique practice 3-4 starts over 5 hurdles 3 × 120 m with 11 hurdles spaced 1 ft. (about 30.5 cm) closer than normal Cool-down
Friday	Warm-up only
Saturday	Most important competition

Summary

Despite the fine technical differences between the 110-meter high hurdles and the 100-meter hurdles, they both demand the fundamental qualities of explosive strength and dynamic flexibility. Attention must also be given to the proper technique for each phase of the race. Drills that accentuate the above essentials, along with a well-thought-out training program, are paramount for achieving success in both races.

6

400-Meter Hurdles

Gary Winckler

The 400-meter hurdles is a distinctive and challenging event. The 400-meter hurdler needs the strength abilities of an 800-meter runner, the hurdling ability of the sprint hurdler, and the visual steering ability of the horizontal jumper. Successful competitors in the event have come from the sprint, hurdle, jump, and middle-distance ranks.

The event itself is composed of 10 hurdles spaced at 35 meters, with a starting distance of 45 meters and finishing distance of 40 meters. The hurdles are 30 inches (about 76 cm) high for women and 36 inches (about 91.5 cm) high for men. In selecting athletes for the event, one should look for the following:

- Sprint ability—Speed is always the primary limiting factor in any speed and power event.
- Aggressive mental attitude and concentration—By the nature of the event, hurdlers must be aggressive and be able to concentrate on negotiating the barriers.
- Competitive nature—Any athlete must be competitive to succeed.

- Strength—High levels of both maximal strength and strength endurance are requisite for good performances. Not only must athletes be fast over 400 meters, but they must be able to perform the powerful action of hurdling in a highly fatigued state.
- Dynamic mobility—Mobility within the hips to efficiently perform the hurdling motion will be critical over the course of a 10-hurdle event of 400 meters.

The coach should attempt to ingrain the following performance qualities (in order of importance).

1. *Ability to apply force at takeoff to move through the hurdle and minimize deceleration.* Application of the right kind of forces at takeoff ultimately determines the efficiency of one's hurdling skills. This application requires strength, power, and speed as well as good technique.

2. *Ability to perform effective and efficient hurdling skills with both legs.* The best hurdlers today and certainly the champions of tomorrow will be athletes who can master the skill of hurdling with either leg.

3. *Ability to maintain a consistent rhythm for 10 hurdles.* The best hurdler in the long run has the special strength and consistent technique to run over 10 hurdles with the least amount of technical decrement from start to finish.

4. *Ability to manage race distribution efficiently.* Knowledge and experience of 400-meter racing builds a solid foundation of race management skills, which can be carried over to the hurdles event.

Technique

Particular importance should be placed on executing precise technique during different phases of the 400-meter hurdles.

Start and Approach to First Hurdle

A stride pattern of 22–25 steps is typically used to the first hurdle for women and 20–23 steps for men. This is predicated by the speed and strength of the athlete and by which leg they prefer to use at the first hurdle. Most hurdlers will use the left leg for hurdles on the curve, as this allows them to run on the inside of the lane without fear of pulling the trail leg over the inside of the hurdle during clearance. A right-leg lead on the curve must allow for the trail leg to clear the hurdle without being off to the inside of the lane, as this results in disqualification. (See figure 6.1a). An athlete who uses the right lead on the curve should run toward the middle to outside portion of the lane to allow space for the trail leg to clear over the hurdle

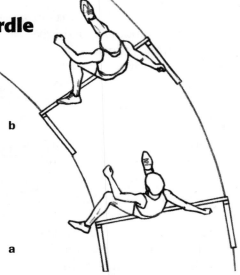

Figure 6.1 *(a)* Pulling the trail leg over the inside of the hurdle during clearance will result in disqualification. *(b)* Athletes who use a right lead on the curve must instead run toward the middle or outside part of the lane.

(figure 6.1b). This also means that the athlete will run farther than if he or she were on the inside of the lane.

1. Attack the first four to five strides with the characteristic inclination of the body found in the normal acceleration from blocks.
2. Attack the hurdle from about 10 meters away. This will ensure an aggressive run, which will minimize the deceleration that normally occurs at this point. Minimize height and increase speed over the hurdle by "sprinting through the hurdle" as shown in figure 6.2.

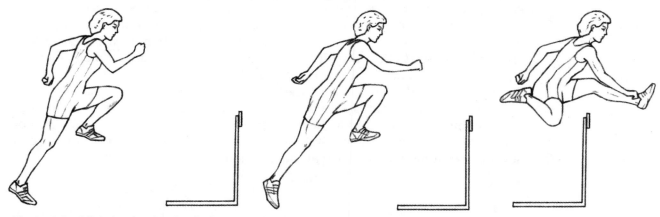

Figure 6.2 Minimize deceleration by "sprinting through the hurdle."

Takeoff

The term *takeoff foot* will refer to the trail-leg foot. This is the foot from which the hurdler will propel himself or herself into the hurdle. The placement of this foot to the track should be active (i.e., pulling backward from the hip with the foot in dorsiflexion and the ankle joint strong and stable). By *active landing* we mean an active, quick placing of the trail leg into the takeoff position somewhat faster than in the previous running stride. This active landing action will "cut" or shorten the last stride, preventing planting or braking action and minimizing loss of velocity going into the hurdle. (See figure 6.3.) This placement should be on the forefoot and occurs approximately 2.0 meters from the hurdle. Anthropometrics must be considered in determining correct distance from the hurdle.

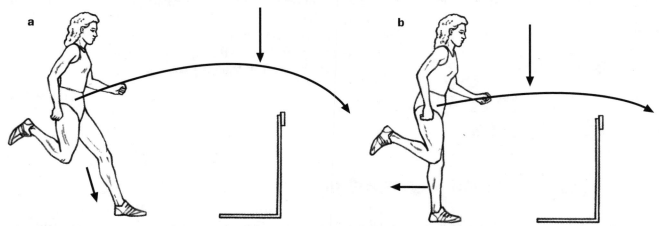

Figure 6.3 Planting action on the takeoff: *(a)* too much planting action, which increases the height over the hurdle. *(b)* Active foot plant and good sprinting action into the hurdle, which keeps the momentum moving forward.

Hurdle Clearance

To achieve efficient hurdle clearance, the athlete must comprehend the interplay of the lead leg, trail leg, and arm actions.

Lead Leg

To a great extent, the lead leg initiates and controls the hurdle clearance. *Efficient clearance begins in the strides before the hurdle.* Once the lead leg finishes its last ground contact before the hurdle, it immediately is recovered, heel to butt, as the knee is driven up to a point over the hurdle rail. This requires flexion at the hip and the knee. The lower part of the lead leg remains tucked under the thigh until the thigh has reached parallel to the ground or above. When the thigh reaches its apex, momentum is then transferred to the lower leg by relaxing the hamstring and allowing the knee joint to open. The knee does not lock. (Another reason for flexing the hip and then extending the lower leg as a two-step sequence is that the rectus femoris and hamstring muscles are multiple-jointed muscles that cross over the hip and knee, and a characteristic of such muscles is that they do not permit complete movement in both joints simultaneously.) It is not a mistake to not fully straighten the lead leg at the knee joint.

Arm Action

The lead leg and its opposing arm must move in a parallel manner. If the arm is directed inward toward the leg, then the leg will also move inward, crossing toward the arm, and the forward motion of the body will be disturbed. The velocity of both arms must coincide with that of the lead leg.

Trail Leg

The trail leg must work in concert with the lead-leg and lead-arm actions. The trail leg should be active throughout its range of movement. As the trail foot leaves the ground, the leg is drawn vigorously forward and upward, tucking the heel tightly to the butt and thereby shortening the trail-leg lever as much as possible. (See figure 6.4.) This enables the leg to pass over the hurdle with greater speed and reduces the degree of compensating rotation in the rest of the body. The foot of the trail leg should never rise higher than its knee. The trail leg is kept tightly folded until the knee has reached the front of the body and is ready to accelerate downward to the track once again. The athlete should attempt to sprint off the hurdle, with the trail leg coming down quickly and grabbing the track.

Figure 6.4 The trail leg should be kept tightly folded toward the body during hurdle clearance.

Sequencing of Actions

Problems for the coach and athlete aspiring to elite levels arise largely from established motor and neural patterns within the athlete. Especially with athletes who have been hurdling for many years, there is an ingrained rhythmic pattern, which may ultimately be the greatest hindrance to breakthrough performances. The athlete must be able to do the following:

- Adapt to performing sequences of hurdling actions at varied speeds.
- Anticipate the hurdle coming up more quickly.
- Break ingrained mental and physical rhythms from past races that were not of a high performance standard.

• Understand the interplay of the lead leg, trail leg, and arm actions in hurdle clearance and running between. Because balance is a key ingredient in hurdling, these levers must work at highly corresponding velocities that are well coordinated. When an athlete is airborne, the lead leg cannot be forced to come to the track if the trail leg is not coming through at the same time. The trail leg should not come through until the lead leg is at the point where the hurdler wants it to come back to the track.

Correcting Common Faults

Fault: Takeoff is too far from the first hurdle.
Causes:

a. Sprint strides during initial acceleration from blocks are too short.
b. Arm action in acceleration to first hurdle may be too passive.

Corrections:

a. Athlete lacks contractive strength necessary to drive from the blocks with sufficient stride length.
b. Lengthen arm action and increase the amplitude of arm movement during the run to the first hurdle and attack the last 10 meters prior to the hurdle.

Fault: Clearance is too high over the hurdle.
Causes:

a. Too close to the hurdle at takeoff.
b. Takeoff foot planted on heel too far ahead of center of mass.
c. Nonexistent or nonactive takeoff.
d. Lead leg not folded tightly until thigh reaches parallel or above.
e. Athlete afraid of hurdle.

Corrections:

a. Keep athlete in sprint acceleration posture longer. This keeps strides shorter and helps the athlete attain higher velocity. Make sure the athlete is accelerating in a pattern and not overstriding. If the athlete is planting the takeoff foot like a long jumper, this will make the last stride before the hurdle too long and result in placement too close to the hurdle.
b. Practice a tall posture, making the takeoff step active and on the front of the foot.
c. Again, practice a tall posture.
d. Rehearse proper lead-leg mechanics and body posture going into hurdle. Also examine what the takeoff foot is doing. If it is planted on the heel, then the lead leg will tend to open up too soon.

e. In practice use hurdles constructed of soft, flexible materials or constructed to be forgiving. If the hurdle is not a threat to life and limb, the athlete will gain the necessary confidence to run through the hurdle with the velocity necessary to perform efficient technique.

Fault: Hitting trail knee on the hurdle.
Causes:

a. Rushing takeoff (jumping through the hurdle rather than running off the ground).

Corrections:

a. Focus on an active takeoff step and do not rush the force application of the trail leg. Also, leave the trail leg back until feeling a push-off of the toe. This will cause a stretch in the thigh muscles that will snap the trail leg through with little or no effort.

Fault: Off balance coming off the hurdle.
Causes:

a. Lead leg and opposite arm are driven inward and not parallel to the direction of travel.

b. Trail leg opening up too soon as it clears the hurdle.

Corrections:

a. Work on keeping the lead-leg mechanics as described above to enable the athlete to more easily keep actions in line with the direction of the run. Use sprint arm action into the hurdle and not across the body. Also, the athlete may be too close to the hurdle.

b. Do a significant amount of work on trail-leg mechanics to keep the leg folded until the thigh has reached a position where the knee is pointing in the direction of travel before opening up toward the ground. This problem often occurs when the athlete is trying to rush the trail leg to the ground.

Fault: Hitting hurdles late in the race.
Causes:

a. Loss of rhythm.

b. Too close to hurdles.

c. Loss of concentration.

Corrections:

a. Athlete fails to maintain a hips-tall position, which may cause him or her to sit and thereby not maintain good sprint mechanics.

b. Make eye contact with the next hurdle at least 15 meters away and run aggressively to the hurdle.

c. Think of the hurdle race as 400 meters long and 48 inches wide. Learn to limit attention to what's happening in your own lane and to concentrate on your own rhythm.

Training

Training for the 400-meter hurdles event will have many of the same characteristics as the training for the 200-meter and 400-meter dashes. Refer to those chapters for specific suggestions about energy system training. What I list below are event-specific considerations in designing the training program for the 400-meter hurdler.

Program Priorities

The priorities of this 400-meter hurdle training program are listed in order of importance.

Performance Approach

The first priority is to acquire the proper kinesthesis of force application through a performance approach. In the traditional approach taken by many coaches and athletes, much time is spent on drills where the athlete walks, skips, or runs over hurdles spaced very close together or at spacings that are greater than or equal to competitive spacings and heights. This approach improves conditioning more than technique. It emphasizes limb movement skills, which is good from the standpoint of dynamic mobility; but from a technical standpoint, it emphasizes vertical velocity. This is a poor emphasis, since most hurdle athletes already generate too much vertical velocity at takeoff. Such training results in longer flight times over the hurdle and in greater ground time on touchdown off the hurdle. All of these factors result in slower performances.

The performance approach uses drills and exercises designed to call into play the same muscles and forces used in the actual event. These exercises involve using hurdles of reduced height and spacings, which allow for speeds that are 90–110% of race speeds. For example, hurdle heights should be 24–30 inches (about 61–76 cm) for women and 30–36 inches (about 76–91 cm) for men, and spacing of hurdles should allow for 8–11 strides between. To figure these spacings, use the race stride pattern of the athlete and multiply the stride length used in the race by the number of strides between the hurdles you desire. Add three meters to this distance for the hurdle stride and you have your interhurdle spacing. Examples follow:

$$17\text{-stride pattern} = (35 \text{ meters} - 3 \text{ meters})/17$$
$$= 32/17$$
$$= 1.88 \text{ meters/stride}$$

Thus, for the spacing to be 11 strides, you would use $11 \times 1.88 + 3$ meters, or 23.68 meters.

$$16\text{-stride pattern} = (35 \text{ meters} - 3 \text{ meters})/16$$
$$= 32/16$$
$$= 2.00 \text{ meters/stride}$$

Thus, for the spacing to be 11 strides, you would use $11 \times 2.00 + 3$ meters, or 25.00 meters.

$$15\text{-stride pattern} = (35 \text{ meters} - 3 \text{ meters})/15$$
$$= 32/15$$
$$= 2.13 \text{ meters/stride}$$

Thus, for the spacing to be 11 strides, you would use $11 \times 2.13 + 3$ meters, or 26.43 meters.

$$14\text{-stride pattern} = (35 \text{ meters} - 3 \text{ meters})/14$$
$$= 32/14$$
$$= 2.29 \text{ meters/stride}$$

Thus, for the spacing to be 11 strides, you would use 11 × 2.29 + 3 meters, or 28.19 meters.

$$13\text{-stride pattern} = (35 \text{ meters} - 3 \text{ meters})/13$$
$$= 32/13$$
$$= 2.46 \text{ meters/stride}$$

Thus, for the spacing to be 11 strides, you would use 11 × 2.46 + 3 meters, or 30.06 meters.

Use exercises that are effective and to which the athlete can relate. Only then will faster and more effective learning occur.

Core Strength

The body is limited in its ability to apply force by the "pillar" or "core" strength of the trunk. The core must be developed well and maintained to improve performance through greater power output. Abdominal and back muscles, which maintain the posture necessary for good performance, must especially be developed.

Sprinting Ability

Speed is ultimately the greatest limiting factor in any running event. Although valuable training time must be expended on refining technique, speed development should be addressed throughout the entire training year, not just at the very end.

Rhythm

Rhythm must be a focus throughout all phases of training. A consistent rhythm should be established before the major competitive season; in fact, it must be honed earlier, in the preparation phases, so that it can be continually improved. Lactacid power and capacity are important abilities for any athlete running the 400-meter distance. Distribution of energy and proper management of the race are critical to optimal performance.

Steering

Steering is the ability of the athlete to visualize where the hurdle is and to make adjustments so as to negotiate the hurdle without sacrificing speed and hurdling efficiency.

Strength and Power

Strength and power is an important biomotor ability for all speed and power athletes. Maximum strength must be developed for starting ability as well as for power conversion to maintain speed and rhythm throughout the race.

Speed and Speed Endurance

Enhance speed and speed endurance qualities to establish a baseline for 400-meter improvement. An athlete's best 400 meters should be approximately 2 × (best 200 meters) + 3.5 seconds. To this you can add 3–4 seconds for a predictor of best 400-meter hurdle performance.

It is also important to learn the proper distribution of effort. Use 4 × 400-meter relays with inexperienced athletes to build confidence. It gives athletes additional competitive experience at the given distance, which enhances their confidence to run 400 meters.

Teaching Strategies

The following teaching strategies should be a part of your overall training program.

1. *Fast runs* over hurdles at reduced height and spacing.
2. Emphasize preparation for takeoff and takeoff mechanics.

   - Put athlete in positions to feel force application on ground and hip displacement through the hurdle.
   - Contrast resistance to speed with the normal state and with assistance to speed.
   - Control the pattern of stride length to the first hurdle to enhance takeoff position and regulate takeoff distance.
   - Control takeoff distance from the hurdle by use of coaching markers (approximately two meters from hurdle)
   - Don't rush the trail-leg recovery. "Leave it back."

3. Approach 400-meter hurdle event from the perspective of rhythm and distribution.

   - Acceleration goal should be for the first two hurdles.
   - Use rhythmic units in training and in competition to provide feedback and motivation. (Rhythmic units are segments or portions of the race that have repeated running patterns. For example, the stride frequency from touchdown of hurdle one to touchdown of hurdle two is a rhythmic unit.)

     Between each hurdle, the athlete runs a specific number of strides to accommodate his or her most efficient stride length to get to the next hurdle without having to speed up or slow down. Figure 6.5 on page 84 illustrates the evaluation of each hurdle segment (rhythmic unit) for a world-class hurdler. The rhythmic units (RU) are measured in seconds. The steps are the number of strides from the landing of one hurdle through the landing of the next.

     The given distance of 35 meters between hurdles, 45 meters to the first, and 40 meters from the last hurdle to the finish line makes it possible to calculate the velocities for each rhythmic unit.

   - First, seek consistent rhythm throughout the race.

     Training example: 6–10 hurdles at reduced spacing (19–21 meters) using a smooth transition to, over, and off of each hurdle, developing a consistent rhythm throughout.

   - Second, challenge the established consistent rhythm to break through to faster times by preparing to deal with adverse conditions such as wind.

     Training example: 6–10 hurdles at reduced spacing (19–21 meters) spaced at varying distances to promote the development of a "steering mechanism."

Tonja Buford: 400H Analysis

World Championships—Final, August 11, 1995

Lane 3

Hurdle	Total	RU	Lead	Steps	Velocity
1	6.47		L	23	6.96
2	10.50	4.03	L	15	8.68
3	14.60	4.10	L	15	8.54
4	18.77	4.17	L	15	8.40
5	23.07	4.30	L	15	8.14
6	27.47	4.40	L	15	7.95
7	32.17	4.70	R	16	7.45
8	36.97	4.80	L	16	7.29
9	41.94	4.97	L	17	7.05
10	47.00	5.06	L	17	6.91
Finish	52.62	5.62			7.12

(H10–H9)–(H2–H1): 1.03

H(5–10)–H5: 0.86

H8–H5: 13.90

H9–H6: 14.47

H10–H7: 14.83

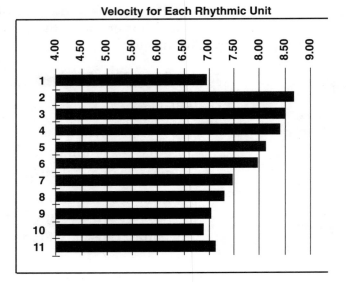

Velocity for Each Rhythmic Unit

Figure 6.5 Evaluation of each hurdle segment for athlete Tonja Buford.

Table 6.1 provides hurdle spacings to advise specific step patterns in practice at various speeds. For example, at 100 percent race speed, a 13-step hurdler has hurdles at 35 meters. To practice using 11 steps at 100 percent, move the hurdles to 30.06 meters. If you want to slow the pace down to 90 percent of race pace, put the hurdles at 31.50 meters to achieve a 13-step pattern. Thus, you are able to figure out various hurdle spacings, which allows greater amounts of hurdle training at proper rhythmical units without getting too fatigued to accomplish those rhythms.

4. Develop qualities in parallel.
   - Develop flat speed, hurdle acceleration, and specific hurdle endurance simultaneously. This is necessary to ensure integrity of technique.
   - Develop strength in conjunction with speed. This will maintain the delicate balance between muscle strength and coordination.

Drills

Technical exercises or drills serve to correct deficiencies in mechanics, to teach and ingrain proper motor patterns, and to promote local muscle and specific hurdle conditioning. Some basic exercises should be reviewed and used even with the most advanced hurdler. The basis of most hurdling exercises should be sound sprinting exercises. Hurdle training is by nature very specific—to improve as a hurdler, you must hurdle. Training sessions must be geared toward the specific rhythm necessary in hurdling. For advanced hurdlers, special hurdle endurance should be emphasized in training.

TABLE 6.1 SPACINGS FOR VARIED PRACTICE STEP PATTERNS

Hurdle spacings (in meters) for 100% of race speed.

	9 steps	10	11	12	13	14	15	16	17
13-step pattern	25.14	27.60	30.06	32.52	35.00				
14	23.61	25.90	28.19	30.48	32.77	35.00			
15	22.20	24.33	26.47	28.60	30.73	32.87	35.00		
16	21.00	23.00	25.00	27.00	29.00	31.00	33.00	35.00	
17	19.94	21.82	23.71	25.59	27.47	29.35	31.24	33.12	35.00

Hurdle spacings (in meters) for 98% of race speed.

	9 steps	10	11	12	13	14	15	16	17
13-step pattern	24.64	27.05	29.46	31.87	34.30				
14	23.14	25.38	27.63	29.87	32.11	34.30			
15	21.76	23.85	25.94	28.03	30.12	32.21	34.30		
16	20.58	22.54	24.50	26.46	28.42	30.38	32.34	34.30	
17	19.54	21.39	23.23	25.08	26.92	28.77	30.61	32.46	34.30

Hurdle spacings (in meters) for 96% of race speed.

	9 steps	10	11	12	13	14	15	16	17
13-step pattern	24.13	26.50	28.86	31.22	33.60				
14	22.67	24.86	27.06	29.26	31.46	33.60			
15	21.31	23.36	25.41	27.46	29.50	31.55	33.60		
16	20.16	22.08	24.00	25.92	27.84	29.76	31.68	33.60	
17	19.14	20.95	22.76	24.56	26.37	28.18	29.99	31.79	33.60

Hurdle spacings (in meters) for 94% of race speed.

	9 steps	10	11	12	13	14	15	16	17
13-step pattern	23.63	25.94	28.26	30.57	32.90				
14	22.19	24.35	26.50	28.65	30.80	32.90			
15	20.87	22.87	24.88	26.88	28.89	30.89	32.90		
16	19.74	21.62	23.50	25.38	27.26	29.14	31.02	32.90	
17	18.74	20.51	22.28	24.05	25.82	27.59	29.36	31.13	32.90

Hurdle spacings (in meters) for 90% of race speed.

	9 steps	10	11	12	13	14	15	16	17
13-step pattern	22.63	24.84	27.05	29.27	31.50				
14	21.25	23.31	25.37	27.43	29.49	31.50			
15	19.98	21.90	23.82	25.74	27.66	29.58	31.50		
16	18.90	20.70	22.50	24.30	26.10	27.90	29.70	31.50	
17	17.95	19.64	21.34	23.03	24.72	26.42	28.11	29.81	31.50

(continued)

(continued)

Hurdle spacings (in meters) for 88% of race speed.

	9 steps	10	11	12	13	14	15	16	17
13-step pattern	22.12	24.29	26.45	28.62	30.80				
14	20.78	22.79	24.81	26.82	28.84	30.80			
15	19.54	21.41	23.29	25.17	27.05	28.92	30.80		
16	18.48	20.24	22.00	23.76	25.52	27.28	29.04	30.80	
17	17.55	19.20	20.86	22.52	24.17	25.83	27.49	29.14	30.80

Hurdle spacings (in meters) for 86% of race speed.

	9 steps	10	11	12	13	14	15	16	17
13-step pattern	21.62	23.74	25.85	27.97	30.10				
14	20.30	22.27	24.24	26.21	28.18	30.10			
15	19.09	20.93	22.76	24.60	26.43	28.27	30.10		
16	18.06	19.78	21.50	23.22	24.94	26.66	28.38	30.10	
17	17.15	18.77	20.39	22.01	23.62	25.24	26.86	28.48	30.10

High-Knee Routines (Mach Drills)

Exercise is performed with high-knee action, pulling heels to butt. Posture is tall. Ankle joint is kept dorsiflexed and weight bearing is on forefoot. Progress down the track is slow, with all foot contacts under center of mass.

The three high-knee variations are:

> Marching
>
> Skipping
>
> Running

Fast-Leg Routines

This exercise is very difficult and demands good coordination and timing. The objective is to isolate the proper motion of the sprint stride into left- and right-side movements, teaching the proper mechanics of the leg through the recovery cycle. Speed of movement is the ultimate objective, although most athletes will learn this exercise at slow speeds and progress to faster speeds.

The following cues will help with this drill:

- Hips tall.
- Active action with toe-up, heel-up, knee-up sequence.
- Try to place the support foot under the center of mass at ground contact.
- The recovery leg should cycle, with the ankle passing above the knee of the support leg.

The two types of fast-leg routines are:

1. Single-Side Actions—From a jog the athlete attains a tall posture. In concert with the arms, one leg is quickly cycled through the recovery cycle, following the sequence of actions described above and accelerating the foot back to the track again. Performance of the movement is alternated with two to three jogging steps. When

performed properly, the athlete senses an acceleration upon each contact of the foot with the track. Emphasize the following:

- Full and proper range of motion
- Acceleration of thigh and heel *upward* during recovery
- Acceleration of thigh *downward* in preparation for support
- Active cycling culminating in a clawing action of the foot in preparation for contact with the ground again
- Lower leg kept folded tightly to the thigh until full thigh lift is complete
- Quick actions of the hands and arms in proper sprint arm motions

2.   Dual-Side Actions—The dual-side form of the fast-leg routine is performed in the same way as the single-side form, except the movement alternates from left side to right side following the two to three jogging steps between movements. When athletes become accomplished with this exercise, they can accelerate quickly and perform its actions at near top speed. The ultimate objective is to improve speed of movement, neuromuscular timing, and coordination, and thus be able to perform an efficient movement on each and every stride in full-flight sprinting.

The following exercises may also be appropriate.

Fence Drill for Trail Leg

The hurdle (30 inches or about 76 cm high) is placed about two feet (about 61 cm) from a fence or other immovable object and parallel to it so that the athlete is facing the fence and the hurdle in the normal orientation. (See figure 5.5 on page 69.) Standing on the side of the hurdle the athlete inclines the body toward the fence and puts one or both hands on the fence. The athlete then performs the trail-leg action over the side of the hurdle. The exercise develops specific dynamic mobility as well as teaches correct mechanics of the trail leg. This is more of a beginner's exercise, but it may be useful to more advanced athletes as well. The action should be quick, and the trail leg should never be allowed to open up at the knee once it has cleared the hurdle. The action coming off of the hurdle should be an acceleration of the thigh toward the ground.

Partner Drill for Trail Leg

This exercise is performed similarly to the previous drill, except the hurdle is placed on the track and the athlete uses a partner in place of the fence. The partner actively pulls the athlete by the hand as the athlete performs the trail-leg movement. In this way the athlete feels what it is like to move quickly over the hurdle and can begin coordinating a fast, uninterrupted movement of the trail leg with good horizontal velocity over the hurdle. Figure 6.6 illustrates this drill.

1. Keep trail foot tight to the butt and knee moving forward and upward.

Figure 6.6   Partner drill for improving trail-leg action.

2. Thigh lift should continue until trail foot has once again come in alignment under the thigh.

3. Trail-leg thigh should be accelerated downward with foot under center of mass.

4. Hips should move through the hurdle, and athlete should feel the fast horizontal displacement of the hips forward. Maintain hips in tall position throughout.

Fast-Leg Lead Leg Over Hurdles

In this exercise the fast-leg action is performed with the lead leg over the side of four to six hurdles spaced at 7–8.5 meters apart for three-stride rhythm and 9–11.5 meters apart for five-stride rhythm. The hurdle height used can vary from 12 inches to 30 inches (30.5 cm to 76 cm).

You can perform this drill:

1. With a normal stride pattern and heel recovery between hurdles.

2. Using a fast-leg action on every lift of the lead leg, thus placing more emphasis on local muscular endurance.

Make sure you maintain hips in tall body posture throughout, and adhere to principles prescribed earlier for fast-leg routines.

Running Hurdle Skills

The title for this group of exercises refers to a variety of skill drills that could be performed over half or whole hurdles. Usually 3–5 hurdles are used, with spacings of 7.5–8.2 meters and heights of 27–30 inches (about 68.5–76 cm). The exercises are individually oriented in the sense that each may be used to emphasize very different technical points. The speed of the run is usually quite fast because the primary objective is to increase one's ability to perform correct technical or mechanical movements at high velocity.

The two variations of this exercise are:

1. Half-hurdle lead leg

On each run the emphasis may differ:
- Maintaining distance of takeoff foot from hurdle
- Active takeoff step going into hurdle
- Heel of lead leg to butt going into hurdle.
- Fast-leg action of lead leg.
- Active downward action of lead leg coming off hurdle.
- Performance of lead-leg action while accelerating over five hurdles.

2. Half-hurdle trail leg

On each run the emphasis may differ:
- Draw heel to butt actively and as soon as takeoff foot leaves ground.
- Keep trail leg continuously in motion from start of movement until touchdown.

- Keep trail toe up and leg folded until completion of action to the front of the body.
- Perform the lead-leg action on the outside of the hurdle. This aids in keeping balance and in being able to perform the trail-leg and associated arm actions in a coordinated fashion.
- Actively accelerate trail leg to the ground under the center of mass and in position to sprint into next stride.
- Have the athlete imagine that the lead leg and trail leg are racing each other to the ground. This encourages quick action off of the hurdle and helps the athlete anticipate the touchdown.

Designing a Training Program

Establishing a training plan is important for systematic and continuous progress. Variety is important but only to the point that it keeps the athlete fresh and does not become variety for variety's sake. Table 6.2 on page 90 contains an outline of the general objectives for the 400-meter hurdler throughout the training year. Some specific examples are given for the fall preparation. Remember, to be the most effective coach you must use what your environment provides. Samples of what other programs do are only as effective as you are in adapting your coaching style and ideas to the athletes and the environment in which you both work.

Competition

Preparation for competition is what training is about. If the specific preparation for a major competition is not begun during the earliest stages of preparation, competitive readiness will be difficult to attain. Everything discussed in this chapter to this point is important to the performance on the big day. Only minor planning details, such as adapting to wind, track, and other environmental conditions, should be left for the day of the race. The athlete's diet should be very similar to the diet during the regular training year, and rehearsal of what to eat and when to eat should occur during training sessions leading up to the competition season. In general, the diet should be high in carbohydrates, with plenty of water intake. Hydration should be emphasized at all times of the training year.

Summary

In summary, the 400-meter hurdle event is one of beauty, endurance, grace, speed, and power. Once a dumping ground for athletes who could not achieve high levels of success in the 400-meter dash or 800-meter run, it has grown into a highly specialized event. The primary reason for its continued growth has been the improved technical prowess of participating athletes. Skill in hurdling, once nearly nonexistent, has become the most important ingredient in recent record performances. And it is in this area where the most can be gained for future record performances.

TABLE 6.2 SAMPLE WORKOUTS

Fall Preparation

Monday	**Circuit training** Field circuit: such as 30 push-ups, 10 tuck jumps, 100 m run, 30 lunges, 40 crunches, 200 m run, 10 pull-ups, plus other exercises of your choice, including medicine balls and jump ropes. The circuit is performed with 0-30 sec. rest between stations and should last 15 min. per circuit.
Tuesday	**Bounding, core training** Long alternate-leg bounding on grass: 8 × 60 m Core: push-ups, sit-ups, and so on for the trunk.
Wednesday	**Hill running** 2 × 4 × 200-250 m hill, with walk back recovery.
Thursday	**Sprint development, hurdle skill** Rollover starts (start by leaning over until you lose your balance forward and go) High-knee running Butt kicks Fast-leg exercise Marching and skipping over hurdles Runs over 4 hurdles set at 27 in. (about 68.5 cm) and spaced at 20 m: 6–8 runs
Friday	**Acceleration, circuit training** Rollover starts Block starts over 2 hurdles Circuit work as on Monday
Saturday	**Aerobic running** Tempo runs over 100-200 m with 50 m walk between Continuous run at varied pace for 15 minutes.
Sunday	**Rest**

Indoor Preparation

Monday	**Sprint development, power development**
Tuesday	**Hurdle skill, weights, multi-jumps**
Wednesday	**Hill running, strength endurance**
Thursday	**Weights, core training, swimming**
Friday	**Acceleration, lactacid power**
Saturday	**Tempo running, core training**
Sunday	**Rest**

Indoor Season

Monday	**Sprint development, power development**

Tuesday	Hurdle skill, weights
Wednesday	Lactacid power, strength endurance
Thursday	Weights, core training, swimming
Friday	Acceleration
Saturday	Competition
Sunday	Rest

Outdoor Preparation/Season

Monday	Hurdle skill, weights, core training
Tuesday	Lactacid power, 400-meter hurdle distribution
Wednesday	Core training, tempo running
Thursday	400-meter hurdle starts, weights
Friday	Core training, tempo running
Saturday	Competition
Sunday	Rest

7 800 Meters to Mile

Mike Poehlein

The middle-distance events include the 800-meter run, the mile run, and all distances in between—including the 1500 meters. That the 800-meter world record is now 1:41 indicates that races of these distances are very demanding, requiring a mixture of speed, strength, and endurance. The athletes who succeed can give it their all on race day, but also can really let it hang out on key practice days.

Besides the physical skills that are needed to perform successfully in this event category, mental strength is essential to run at high speeds for the duration of the race. You must have courage to keep going while your body is telling you it's going to be painful to continue at such intensity. That courage is developed during training. Practices are aimed at not only building the necessary stamina for these races, but developing the confidence to persevere as well. Middle distance racing is some of the most challenging in track and field. It requires preparation that develops all the essential biomotor abilities as well as mental toughness.

Selection Process

The middle distances have always been among my favorite of the track events to coach. I always felt I could influence the existing talent pool somewhat, especially when I was coaching in high school. Since I enjoyed the middle-distance events, I would in some cases try to move the sprinters and 400-meter runners to the 800 meters and mile at an early age. Then, I would convince them to try cross-country in the fall—as a way of establishing contact and, more importantly, to get them to make the tough mental adjustment from the sprints to the middle distance. With this task accomplished, I usually had a pool of athletes that was significantly faster than most of our opponents.

When selecting candidates for the middle-distance races, be sure to take into consideration the athletes' work ethic. If your chosen candidates don't truly love running and enjoy hard training, they will not survive in the middle distances.

Physical Traits

Another consideration is the physical traits of middle-distance runners. It is believed that the successful middle-distance runner will have a ratio of fast-twitch to slow-twitch muscle fibers of about 50:50, with a 5 to 10% deviation either way. For example, the ideal 800-meter prospect would probably be at 60% fast twitch and 40% slow twitch. A miler might be 60% slow twitch and 40% fast twitch. A good, stable team of middle-distance runners will all fall somewhere in between these 60:40 or 40:60 ratios.

The problem is how to know an athlete's muscle fiber type. College coaches get their athletes into the university physiology lab for a muscle biopsy. However, this may not be available to you. In this case, the vertical jump test may help.

Vertical Jump Test

A simple but fairly accurate gauge in determining aptitude for middle-distance running is a vertical jump test. Once the athletes are in pretty good shape, have each one take a two-inch piece of chalk and stand flatfooted against a wall; they are to reach as high as possible and make a mark on the wall. Next, while starting from a flatfooted position with both feet on the floor, they are to jump up and make a mark above the original mark. Have them do this three times. Measure the distance between the standing mark and the jumping mark, and average the three marks.

After you have the results of all your team members, divide the group. The third with the highest marks will make up the sprinters. The middle third are likely to be most successful at the middle distances. The long-distance group will likely come from the last third. If you have a large group, there is a lot of validity in this test.

This is only a quick guide and should not alter other selection criteria established by the coaching staff, but it is a good indicator of your athletes' muscle fiber type. In the final analysis, however, your candidates must also have good body flexibility and good speed.

Types of Middle-Distance Runners

There are basically three types of 800-meter runners. (The same profiles will also be used to identify 1500-meter and mile runners.)

1. Those possessing exceptional speed for 400 meters who move up to the longer distance.

2. Those that are gifted with better than average 400-meter speed and also compete successfully in the mile.

3. Runners with average 400-meter speed who are mainly the miler type, but yet because of superior conditioning are able to compete quite well at 800 meters. They are especially effective in championship meets where several rounds of qualifying are required.

Technique

Postural and mechanical considerations for the middle distances will vary slightly between the 800- and 1500-meter runner/miler. Both will run with a very erect posture. The head should be level with the eyes focused 50-100 meters down the track. Make sure athletes do not look down at their feet.

The rhythm of the stride cycle is similar to that of a sprinter, except that since running economy dictates a short stride, the heel recovery after the drive foot lifts from the ground will not raise all the way to the hips. It will recover to only about three-fourths of that distance for the miler when it starts to descend forward. The 800-meter athlete will look more like the 400-meter sprinter with fairly high heel recovery. Both athletes will swing the free leg forward and downward, and move the foot back under the body's center of mass upon landing. Since the middle distance runner is moving at a slower rate than the sprinter, the body doesn't pass over the support foot as quickly and the foot can land almost directly under the center of mass. (See figure 7.1, pages 96–97.)

Dorsal flexion of the ankle joint is still an important issue to keep the athlete rolling off the ball of the foot. As the athlete's foot lands nearly flat-footed for the 1500-meter runner/miler, the athlete should propel forward off the ball of the foot. The 800-meter athlete will land higher on the ball, but then drop the foot flat at the point of midsupport just before propelling off the ball of the foot again.

The arm carriage for the 800-meter athlete is very similar to that of the sprinter. The hands should be relaxed and swing forward to the midline of the body, but without crossing the midline. The hand will swing about chin high with the elbow bending to less than 90 degrees. On the downswing, the hand moves back toward the hip pocket as the elbow opens to about 120 degrees.

The miler, on the other hand, will have a shorter arm stroke due to a shorter stride. The motion should be in the same direction to the midline but not crossing it.

In both races, the shoulders should remain level and perpendicular to the direction of the run. No twisting back and forth of the torso should be observed. When watching the motion of the athlete's body at the top of the head, you should not see much up and down motion (vertical displacement).

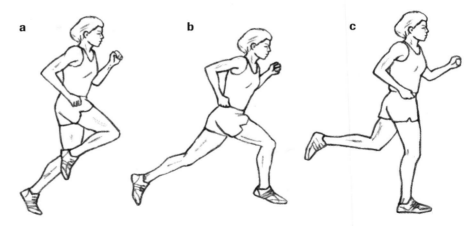

Figure 7.1 Distance running technique. Note the way the free leg swings forward and downward then moves under the body's center of mass upon landing. *(continued)*

Training Philosophy

We must always guard against training absorbing too much of an athlete's competitive fire. Some athletes become workout centered, so that workouts take on more importance than actual racing.

For this not to happen, we must address all facets of the athlete. People are tridimensional: with a physical side, a mental and emotional side, and a spiritual side. A proper training program must include components of all three dimensions.

Training itself must be multifaceted. Keep in mind that everyone can dramatically improve his or her relative running speed, power, flexibility, endurance, strength, self-image, and self-confidence. Just think what the result would be if all of the components were improved.

Finally, as in most physical activities, middle-distance training is a learning process. This learning comes from event-specific training, from training that involves all of the energy systems, and from training that teaches the mental aspects of toughness and competitive spirit.

The Physical Side

The physical dimension involves not only proper training but understanding the race and the tactics specific to that race.

When planning race tactics, the following factors should be considered:

- Distance of the race
- What you know about the opponents in the race
- Condition of the racing surface
- Weather
- Current physical condition
- Level of training of rivals
- Personal ability, strengths, and weaknesses, including pace judgment and ability to lead or follow
- Number of competitors in the race

d   **e**   **f**

Figure 7.1   *(continued)*

Remind your athletes of the following: Save about 40% of your energy for the last one-quarter of the race. Expect the unexpected. Never take the lead unless you want to do something with it. You might wish to increase the pace, decrease the pace, or to gain tactical position. It is also critical to maintain contact if you are not leading. Contact refers to your effective striking distance or believable passing distance.

Other key components of training are recovery and proper rest. When training loads are applied, there must be sufficient recovery time for the body to adapt, resulting in greater fitness. Insufficient recovery will lead to physical breakdown, injury, or illness.

The Mental and Emotional Side

On the mental and emotional side of training, you and your athletes must always have a plan or a road map of where you want to go. This should be supported by a set of vivid goals that provide for immediate, short-range, midrange, and long-range planning. Remember, the greatest motivation is a series of achievements or accomplishments.

The higher your athletes' performance goals are, the more subsidiary goals they must have. For example, if the goal is to increase training load by 10%, then you need a series of goals that provide the athlete with more sleep, more recovery, improved diet, and rehydration. You must also address the habits that help your athletes reduce and manage stress, and your athletes need a refocusing plan in case the unexpected happens.

Your athletes have to expect the unexpected. If it does occur, how are your athletes going to prepare themselves mentally and physically?

Ask them to think about how they would deal with the following:

- Pre-event hassle
- Delay in start
- Loss of focus
- Poor performance
- Nonideal conditions
- Poor start
- Mistake in event

These things happen; so there must be a plan to handle them.

During the race it is important to stay within passing distance of the leader. Sara Thorsett (right) works hard to maintain contact with the leading runner in this 1500-meter competition.

Remember that the ability to concentrate is one of the final pieces to the complex jigsaw puzzle we are trying to piece together. The ability to focus on the complete task is critical for ultimate success. If your athletes don't have the ability to concentrate or focus on the assigned task, they run the risk of wasting all their previously learned skills.

The Spiritual Side

The spiritual side of training deals with the intangible qualities the athlete may or may not possess. For example, drive, desire, belief, confidence, and commitment are vital to succeed. Roger Bannister said, "The battle for the first sub 4 minute mile was fought in the mind, not in the body."

The spiritual side of athletics finally comes down to the competitive spirit the athlete can muster in important situations. Of all traits, this is the most internally generated. The athlete must have an inner resolve that sparks this dimension. It is also fed by the enthusiasm, emotion, and inspiration of previous achievements and future conquests. This spirit is continually fueled by the energy the athlete can draw from those around him or her. With awareness and understanding of this spirit, it can be heightened and improved. The correct belief system and environment can improve the overall strength of the soul.

Training Cycles

Regardless of whether your athletes are in middle school, high school, or college, most American track and field programs reach their peak competitive seasons during late March, April, and May. Some competition extends into early June. At this time competitive track ends for about 90% of participating Americans (though it is just getting started for the rest of the world).

Because this is the peak time of the year, for training cycle purposes, we shall work from these tentative guidelines:

>Preseason workouts: February and March

>Midseason workouts: April to mid-May

>Late-season workouts: mid-May to mid-June

What you do during these periods will vary according to the length of the indoor season, and the age, previous background, and mental, emotional, and physical health of the athletes. Regardless of these variables, however, you can still use the training percentages in table 7.1 as a general guideline from which to build your workouts. Table 7.1 is broken down into the preseason and late season and gives suggested training percentages based on the physical demands of the 1500-meter runner/miler and 800-meter runner.

TABLE 7.1	TRAINING PERCENTAGES FOR MIDDLE-DISTANCE RUNNERS	
	1500 m/mile	**800 m**
Preseason	Speed 10% Anaerobic endurance 10% Aerobic endurance 80%	Speed 10% Anaerobic endurance 30% Aerobic endurance 60%
Late season	Speed 30% Anaerobic endurance 40% Aerobic endurance 30%	Speed 40% Anaerobic endurance 30% Aerobic endurance 30%

Preseason Workouts

Emphasis will slowly switch from quantity to quality. Progression of training requires you to consider longer series of intervals with shorter rest periods from preseason to midseason. As you approach the late season, the volume will drop and repetitions will increase in quality.

Time Trial

I suggest doing the bulk of preseason work at 3K or 5K racing pace. If you aren't certain of this, give your athlete a 3K time trial, either outdoors or indoors. Subtract 30 seconds from that time. For example, if the athlete's 3K time is 11:00, use 10:30 as your reference. This time breaks down to 3:30 per 1000 meters. So a good workout might be

5 × 1000 at 3:30, with a two-minute rest interval,

repeat 1200s at pace, or

3 × 1200 at 4:12, with three minutes rest.

As the athlete gets stronger, these times should drop. Give your athletes a goal for these workouts. After they reach these time goals, take 30 to 45 seconds off the recovery interval. A word of caution, though: change only one variable at a time. I prefer to lower the time of the running interval first because this is a strength workout based on the time of the athlete's 3K, and we assume that time will drop as the season progresses. Also bear in mind that, although it isn't practical to do a specific 3K evaluation for all your middle-distance runners, you might at least divide them into two or three groups, based on their 3K time trial results.

The workouts described above should be considerably harder than the aerobic runs that are done during all phases of training, but they should be significantly slower than race pace.

Practice Runs

In order to determine the athlete's fitness at each stage of training, I would suggest an occasional workout involving a series of practice runs that would mirror the estimated race pace of an untrained middle-distance runner. This is best done by doing a time test or time trial at three-fourths of the racing distance—that is, 600 meters for the 800-meter prospect, and 1200 meters for the 1500/mile candidates.

For example, let's assume the candidates ran 1:33 for a 600. That means they are covering each 200 at 31 seconds. We could do many different workouts, but I suggest not dropping below 300 meters during this stage of the athlete's cycle. I also like doing one workout every 10 days at slightly faster than current race pace. So the following are two possible workouts:

5 × 400 at 62 seconds, with two minutes rest

4 × 500 at 78 seconds, with two minutes rest

(62 seconds and 78 seconds represent the same paces as in the 600-meter time trial.) These workouts would satisfy the race pace requirements.

Speed Training

To satisfy the speed requirement, again probably not more than once every 10 days during this premeet segment, you could have the athletes do the following:

6 to 8 × 300 at 45 seconds, with two to three minutes rest

When practicing, repetition at near race pace is the proper time to look at the athlete's mechanics. When running slower paces you cannot evaluate the athlete due to the changes that occur in slower runs.

Each athlete will respond differently to those workouts; so you can change either the speed of the workout, or length of rest (but not both).

Workouts similar to these should not be repeated too many times during this period because while they significantly raise the fitness level of the athlete, they may reduce the athlete's ability to improve at the end of the season.

Midseason Workouts

During the midseason, continue to emphasize quality, and focus on event-specific training. Following the principles listed below will enable athletes to continue to improve.

- The best runners train closer to race pace more often.
- The best runners are capable of racing off a high-mileage base.
- The best runners show a very high rate of consistency in training.
- The best runners build a recovery plan that ensures they remain injury free.
- Most training sessions must be done under calculated pressure. Training not done under pressure is of no real value.
- The best runners look forward to and thrive on pressure. Fatigue and time are your opponents.

During the early part of midseason, shift the emphasis gradually from training to racing. The number of competitions your team has per week and the number of races your athletes have per competition will be factors in some types of training.

All successful middle-distance coaches follow what is called bracketing, or the over-under theory. Simply stated, in the early season an 800-meter runner competes only occasionally in that event. About 60% of the time he or she competes in a race beyond 800 meters. This could be a 1200 in a distance-medley relay or the 1500 meters. The idea here is to develop the athlete's staying power and specific endurance for later on when he or she needs to run more than one race or needs to run more than one round of qualifications in championship meets. It is also good for concentration and it cuts down on the likelihood of injury.

Occasionally it is good to have your athletes run events of less distance, or "below" their normal event. If you have a lot of "less important" meets, consider having your middle-distance runners run the 400 and 4 × 400-meter relay. Do the same with your miler group.

Bracketing is useful in other ways as well. It can create excitement because it gives athletes a break from the norm. It also provides indicators on training. For example, if the athlete competes successfully below the chosen event, but not above it, that indicates that the training has been too speed oriented. If the athlete competes well above the racing event, but not below it, that indicates the need for more speed work in the training.

The ideal is to be able to compete both above and below the event. All national-level and international-level athletes can do this. We also use these methods to diagnose one more thing. If the athlete runs the first 75% of the race well but can't finish, he or she probably needs a few longer races (or training). If the athlete finishes strong but can't find that kick or one more gear, perhaps a little speed work, or some shorter races, will eliminate that weakness.

The training workouts during this segment will be determined somewhat by what the race results tell you. In the latter stages of this cycle you will need to remove some of the training that is too far removed from the running rhythms of your athletes' racing. For example, you might replace a 6- to 10-mile run at seven minutes per mile with a 3- to 4-mile run at a significantly quicker pace.

This is also the perfect time to reintroduce resistance training involving uphill and downhill training. Also useful are bounding hurdle hops (figure 7.2), rope jumping, and natural methods of increasing flexibility and developing much needed lower leg strength.

Figure 7.2   Bounding hurdle hops.

During this segment of your training racing cycle, it would be wise to add one workout of pure speed, such as one of the following:

8–10 × 100 meters at 95% maximum, with a 100-meter slow walk

6–8 × 200 meters at 90% of full speed, with a 200-meter recovery

Such a workout should not be used more than once every 10 days.

Although at this point in the season speed is starting to become important, it is best to get it through hill runs and by racing below one's normal event. The last type of workout to consider using during this period consists of either 400s or 500s at two to three seconds below current race pace. Use a moderate pace without full recovery for these.

For 800-meter athletes, you may want to use 2–3 × 1000, or 1–2 × 1200, at two seconds slower than race pace, with a complete recovery. If the athlete has been experiencing a slump in performance, this may help bring her or him out of it.

Late-Season Workouts

As with all training, there is a progression. If your athletes aren't on schedule for reaching racing goals, there are several ways to get them on schedule. One way is to give them several days of easy running or complete rest. Back down on hard anaerobic training. Work low volume, high intensity runs with full recovery.

We have deliberately held off on speed training. When we mix speed with rest and back off strength training, we usually see improved speed. For our speed workouts, it is acceptable to use longer rest periods as we try to influence the explosive qualities of our athletes.

Rest and recovery become a prime consideration late in the season. They, along with high-level competition and significantly better weather, are the final catalysts for the breakthrough athletes are expecting.

Keeping the above training strategies in mind, table 7.2 presents a sample weekly training plan for each part of the season.

TABLE 7.2 SAMPLE WORKOUTS FOR 800 METERS TO MILE

Preseason

Monday	10-15 min. warm-up run
	Stretching
	4 × 100 m @ strides
	4 × 1200 m @ date pace*
	5 min. recovery between sets
	10-15 min. cool-down run
	Stretching
Tuesday	6 mile run at a steady-state pace
	Mostly aerobic
Wednesday	10-15 min. warm-up run
	Stretching
	6 × 500 m @ date pace
	400 m walk recovery between sets
	10-15 min. cool-down run
	Stretching
Thursday	45 min. aerobic run
	6-8 × 100 m @ race pace
	10 min. cool-down
	Stretching
Friday	10-15 min. warm-up run
	Stretching
	4 × 100 m buildups
	2 × 150 m buildups
	6-8 × 300 m @ date pace
	200 m recovery walk between reps
	10-15 min. cool-down run
	Stretching
Saturday	45-75 min. long aerobic run @ conversational pace

Early Season

Monday	10-15 min. warm-up run
	Stretching
	4 × 100 m strides
	4 × 1000 m @ 3 sec. faster than date pace
	15 min. cool-down run
	Stretching

*Date pace—the pace of the interval to be run that is equal to the pace of the best performance that the athlete is currently able to achieve for the event that he or she is preparing for.

(continued)

(continued)

Tuesday	10-15 min. warm-up run
	Stretching
	2 × 3 mile loop @ 80% of max.
	10 min. rest between reps
	Circuit training
	10 min. cool-down run
	Stretching
Wednesday	10-15 min. warm-up run
	Stretching
	4 × 100 m strides
	4 × 150 m @ buildups
	4 × 500 m @ 2 sec. faster than date pace
	Full recovery
	10 min. cool-down run
	Stretching
Thursday	45 min. aerobic run
	8 × 100 m slightly faster than race pace
	10 min. cool-down run
	Stretching
Friday	30 min. run @ easy pace
	4 × 100 m relaxed strides and/or baton exchanges
	10 min.cool-down run
	Stretching
Saturday	Some racing at distances above major event

Late Season

Monday	10-15 min. warm-up run
	Stretching
	6 × 100 m strides
	2 × 1200 m @ goal pace**
	6 min. rest between reps
	10 min. cool-down run
	Stretching
Tuesday	10-15 min. warm-up run
	Stretching
	2 × 2 mile loop @ 80% of max. or 30 min.
	10 min. cool-down run
	Stretching

**Goal pace—the pace of the interval to be run that is equal to the pace of the performance that the athlete is striving to achieve by the end of the season.

Wednesday	10-15 min. warm-up run
	Stretching
	4 × 100 m strides
	4 × 150 m buildups
	4 × 600 m @ 2 sec. faster than 3/4 of race distance
	10 min. cool-down run
	Stretching
Thursday	10-15 min. warm-up run
	Stretching
	4 × 100 m buildups
	2 × 150 m buildups
	6 × flying 50 m sprints
	15 min. cool-down run
	Stretching
Friday	30 min. aerobic run
	4 × 100 m easy strides
	10 min. cool-down run
	Stretching
Saturday	Some racing at distances below major racing event.

Competition

When preparing for a competition, it is important to keep the following strategies in mind. These tactics should all be practiced months in advance, so that when race day rolls around, they have already become somewhat second-nature.

Practicing Race Tactics

A runner who plans on changing tempos or taking the lead should rehearse those things in practice. Fartlek workouts where there are a variety of speed changes can be very helpful. Practice runs that incorporate increases and decreases in speed are very taxing but help the athlete prepare for those stresses in competition.

The 2% Margin

There is a margin of 2% that the runner must respect. This means that athletes may run 2% above or below their best race pace and still be able to stay on their target pace. A runner who gets out of this margin will likely crash and burn. In every good race, there is a short period of time when the outcome is in balance. All races are won or lost at this time; the person who recognizes that exact moment often wins.

The Success Segment

This "success segment," as it is called, usually occurs in the last 25% of the race. The person who controls the success segment will win the majority of the races.

You must recognize this segment, and understand the tendencies of the better runners in the race. This is the portion of the race that is the most difficult mentally to maintain a strong pace when the athlete is tired. Some superior athletes will take off at this point and challenge you to go with them. Others may sit a while and delay their kick. You must understand your own abilities, established through training.

Reserving Energy

You must also plan for this segment by saving about 40% of your energy for the last 25% of the race. You must learn to race early, but to not expend all of your energy. You don't want to leave the last quarter of the race to will and determination only. Determination is a wonderful quality, but of little value on an empty tank. Try to have the mindset of a pit bull, but also conserve a little fuel.

Effects of Heat

Depending on the area of the country you live in, your athletes may be racing in hot conditions. Many things can go wrong in the late stages of a race run in severe heat. One is that the runner's body mechanics break down. This will happen to all runners, but to different degrees and at slightly different times. The longer an athlete can hold off this breakdown, the greater his or her chances of success.

Mentally Preparing for Fatigue

Have your runners do very difficult exercises when they are extremely tired, so they can at least be mentally prepared for and delay this shutdown during a race. For example, run a strong tempo distance run of five to six miles and come back to the track and run repeat short intervals in a state of fatigue.

Leading Versus Following

It is more tiring to lead than to follow, since there is usually a wind condition and the front runner will catch all of the wind. At some point in the race, leading is obviously critical, because if you never lead you never win. I usually tell my runners to never take the lead in the middle stages of a race unless they want to do something with it, such as force their opponents to race early to eliminate their late race kick. Or, if the pack is well below your ability, cause the pace to be more to your own race strategy.

In this race Regina Jacobs takes the lead while her opponents struggle to keep up.

Avoiding a Box

A critical aspect of middle-distance running, especially the 800, is to avoid getting boxed in. One can usually avoid a box by running in the second or third position just off the right shoulder of the leader. Always know where the competitors in the race are. This is not a difficult skill to master.

Maintaining Touch Contact

Try to impress on your runners to never let a race string out. If it does, they should react immediately and fill the gap to maintain what is called touch contact. Touch contact is the feeling that you can physically reach out and touch the runner in front of you. As long as the runner has touch contact, he or she is still in the race.

Anticipating the Move

If, in the last quarter of the race, there are several runners still in contention, it is just a matter of time until somebody tries to make a move. The athlete should anticipate this move, and then respond to it. This is the success segment of the race. Remind your athletes: Be there, be accountable, and you will be successful. Being accountable means taking responsibility for yourself to be ready to react to others. Maintain your mental concentration of your running as well as those around you.

Summary

It is critical to lay out a yearly training scheme. We need blueprints of where we want our athletes to go and how they can get there. Much of our success depends on how accurately we assess the athletes' abilities and how we plan on developing those talents over the year. The plan will help athletes maintain their energy and enthusiasm, and a balance between their personal life and their athletic life.

The old saying goes: Plan your work and work your plan. Not bad advice.

8

3000 to 10,000 Meters

Lance Harter
Harry Groves

To train a distance runner, one must understand and have the ability to implement a program that abides by scientific principles that govern physical and mental responses to training. Basic biomechanical, physiological, and psychological factors must be applied progressively, systematically, and intelligently to each individual athlete. Success then becomes a matter of planning rather than random physical and psychological challenges. With this in mind, the following parameters need to be considered.

1. All training programs are individualized, yet a common approach can be used to provide team continuity.

2. Each individual needs to identify an ideal blend of various training schemes to develop his or her specific strengths and reduce weaknesses, using the following physiological principles as guidelines:
   - Specific stresses must be applied.
   - The stress cannot be too great.
   - The body will adapt to the stress during the rest/recovery phase.

The application of training loads stresses the body so that as the body adapts to those loads it becomes stronger and increases its physical capacity. If those training loads are too great or too frequent, the body will not adapt and may break down. Adequate recovery is the key to physical development.

3. All training is designed to physiologically and psychologically enhance the athletes' potential to function as close as possible to his or her maximum potential in racing—that is, we train athletes to race.

4. Training must be consistent and progressive.

5. Coach and athlete open a direct line of communication by establishing and discussing the athlete's season and career goals. This gives athlete and coach a clear and positive direction in training and racing.

6. A conscious effort is made to create a holistic stress awareness and management program.

7. Each athlete's running mechanics in both "fresh" and "fatigued" state are evaluated, and a daily routine of "form drills" is implemented.

Technique

A distance runner's stride, like that of any other track athlete, is composed of three phases:

1. Push-off or drive
2. Recovery
3. Support

During the push-off phase, the body is propelled forward via the support foot and finally the toes. The recovery phase is that period when the body is in the air with neither foot in ground contact. The support phase is when the foot recontacts the ground. As the body's center of gravity passes over the supporting foot, the drive phase of the next stride begins. As each leg is propelled forward, the opposite arm opposes all phases of the runner's stride. In other words, the left leg is forward at the same time the right arm is forward, and vice versa.

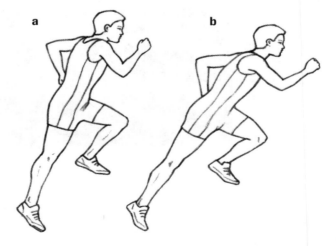

Figure 8.1 *(a)* A tall running posture, and *(b)* a greater body lean due to increased acceleration.

Factors to consider in instructing running mechanics include the following:

- Individual differences in running styles must be respected while basic principles of mechanics must be obeyed.
- Stride length (the distance between each foot) and stride frequency (the strides per second) are the basic components of running speed.
- Good running posture is produced by "running tall," with the runner's shoulders being square to the runner's hips, and weight centered over the hips and respective support foot. (See figure 8.1a.)
- The greater the acceleration, the greater the body lean forward (figure 8.1b). Do not lean forward at slow speeds, as this results in an inefficient running style. (The forward leaning action causes the body to reach out with the foot to prevent falling. This results in braking, which slows the athlete and requires much physical effort to overcome the braking. Also, it leads to shorter stride length.)
- Distance runners should seek a running style that is efficient for the majority of the race, yet leaves them effective for specific challenges in a race, such as when they decide to catch an opponent or kick at the end of a race.
- Arm action should be a "comfortable forward and back swing," with the angle between forearm and bicep at less than 90 degrees (figure 8.2a), until a sprinting action is required and the optimal arm angle changes to approximately 90 degrees. (See figure 8.2b.) During the arm action swing forward and back, the runner should avoid an arm carry that crosses the body's midline, as this ultimately causes a decrease in stride length.
- The arms control running, as the arms' cadence supports the runner's frequency in stride revolutions.
- The optimal footstrike is a "midfoot" strike, in which the athlete lands on a relatively flat foot in a supporting position under the hips, while the body's weight continuously moves forward to the ball of the foot as the respective leg straightens and finally into a push-off phase from the toes.

Figure 8.2   Angle between forearm and bicep at: *(a)* less than 90 degrees for the majority of the race, and *(b)* 90 degrees during sprinting action.

Running Cues for Coaches and Athletes

Posture:

Run tall with your hips underneath you.

Chest out as shoulders stay square to your hips.

Toe up, heel up, knee up.

Arm Action:

Keep your shoulders loose and relaxed.

Arms swing forward and back from hip to shoulder level as a single efficient motion.

Keep hands cupped and fingers relaxed—no excess tension.

Footstrike:

Land in a flat-foot action, with a continuous active footstrike/pawing motion.

Acceleration:

Quicken arms by shortening the arm angle to 90 degrees.

Quickly paw the ground and effectively push off forward.

Training

"An effective training program results from efficient planning, the judicious use of rest and recovery days, and gradual increases in training intensity and duration."

Dr. Jack Daniels

There are a myriad of training methods, each varying in purpose, format, intensity, and duration. Yet we must remember that the physiological demands of distance races require various aerobic activity levels, with the remainder being anaerobic. So the thrust of an athlete's program should be built upon these physiological parameters, while the coach and athlete adjust the training scheme to complement innate strengths and improve upon areas of weakness. In any scheme chosen, specific seasonal and long-term training and racing goals need to be determined.

The following are samples of specific training methods:

Steady-Pace Runs

Steady-pace runs are those that can be maintained for an hour or more at a pace equivalent to 70% of an individual athlete's $\dot{V}O_2max$ (approx. one and a half minutes per mile slower than 5K race pace). Workouts of 30 to 60 minutes at this effort ideally develop the cardiovascular system, improve capillarization, and improve running efficiency.

Anaerobic Threshold Training

Anaerobic threshold (AT) tempo running trains athletes to sensitize, tolerate, and buffer the increase in lactic acid accumulations and greater running intensities. Most successful runners target their training to this specific threshold, plus or minus 5%. Threshold runs can be sustained for roughly 20 minutes at a pace that is approximately 15–20 seconds per mile slower than 10K race pace, or 90% of maximal effort.

Cruise Intervals

Cruise intervals (CI) are efforts performed at approximately 88–90% of $\dot{V}O_2$max. Efforts are 3–10 minutes each, with recoveries limited to one minute or less. The benefits of cruise intervals are similar to those of AT tempo running, yet allow one to incorporate more quality per total work sessions. Total work can equal a maximum of 8% of total working miles.

Pace-Surge Training

Similar to fartlek training (i.e., speed play), pace surging alternates steady-pace runs with bouts of "pickups" or "surges." For example, a mile steady run paced at 6:00 might include 30–60-second bursts at the two- and four-minute mark. Through pace-surge training, athletes develop a mental/physical racing weapon that prepares them for adjusting to the competition's pace shifts and for executing their own pace shifts.

Pace-surge and speed-endurance training gives this athlete the ability to surge ahead of his opponents during competition.

Repetition Training

Ideal repetition training consists of efforts from 15 seconds to 2 minutes of fast-paced (3–5 seconds/400 faster than race pace) running, with a 1:4–5 run:recovery ratio—numbers supported by physiologists. The intensity of effort is usually at or slightly faster than race pace to develop the athlete's pace consciousness and efficiency at maintaining race pace. Repetition efforts totaling up to 20 minutes of "quality work," or 5% of the weekly total mileage, are maximal.

Interval Training

Interval-training efforts last one to five minutes, with recoveries equal to or less than the effort—that is, a 1:1 work/rest ratio. Individual efforts are approximately 95% to 100% $\dot{V}O_2$max (i.e., 5K race pace) and can total 8% of total weekly mileage per session, with a maximum of two per week.

Speed Endurance

Speed-endurance training consists of submaximal to near-maximal efforts of 30 to 90 seconds, with complete or near complete recovery between repetitions (10–16 minutes). This system generally prepares the athlete to finish strongly, and to better handle "surging" during competitions.

Speed Drills

In speed training, sprints of 7 to 20 seconds are performed at near maximal effort, with recoveries of two to five minutes.

Rest and Recovery

Any training format will result in stress to the body. Follow a bout of stress with rest, and the body will adapt to the stress and be ready for an even greater stress load. Athletes who are not allowed, or do not allow themselves, proper rest will usually suffer increased illness or injury.

Designing a Training Program

Each runner has natural strengths or "weapons"—those tools that give a runner his or her unique competitive abilities. Each runner also has weaknesses. The weaknesses should be the focus in early season training. The strengths should always be addressed but primarily in the later stages of training.

First, one must determine the length of the training and competition season, or the macrocycle. Second, determine the date of the "summit" competition, and divide the total number of weeks from "start to summit" into three phases: preparation, base, and competition.

Preparation Phase

Phase I, known as the preparation phase, lasts three to six weeks and is devoted to the athletes' entry or reentry into training. It primarily includes aerobic running, flexibility, and introduction to basic dynamic drills.

During this phase, the volume per week should be increased no more than 15 percent per week to minimize the chance of injury or illness.

Training Terms

The terms used to describe specific periods of training can seem an infinite litany. Below is a simple list of periodization terminology.

Training year—the period of time a specific athlete trains during a single calendar year.

Macrocycle—a term that describes an extended training regime. For example, cross-country, indoor, and outdoor seasons accumulatively would be a single macrocycle.

Cycle—a period for which workouts with a specific purpose are planned. This is a subset of a macrocycle; terms such as mesocycle, monocycle, bicycle, and tricycle refer to various types of cycles.

Microcycle—a specific and integral part of a cycle, lasting 7 to 21 days.

Phase—another subset of a cycle. A period may divide into three basic phases: preparation—base—competition, leading to a *peaking* process.

Session—a single day's workload.

Unit—a specific part of a single workout.

Base Phase

Phase II, known as the base phase, is the time between the preparation and competition phases. Given that it takes a minimum of three to six weeks to enter or reenter training and that the competition phase begins and ends with the season's races, the length of the base phase must be adjusted to each athlete's length of season. If the base phase is longer than 12 weeks, it can be divided into early and late phases, each with its specific work.

No matter the duration, during the base phase the training priority shifts from volume to intensity. In other words, the volume can and will change, but more subtly than in phase I. Volume should be increased no more than 10 percent per week. Intensity is increased through a shift in training systems, with a greater emphasis on preparing for race tempo.

Competition Phase

Phase III, the competition phase, is predetermined by the first race date and the summit race of the season. Like the base phase, phase III can be divided into two phases—in this case, a competition phase and a peak phase—if the total number of weeks exceeds 12. Each subphase will have unique training requirements specific to the athlete's racing needs and abilities. Also as in phase II, there is a gradual shift in training emphasis toward adaptation to race pace. As this phase progresses, the volume gradually tapers while the intensity increases.

As the coach and athlete design the macrocycle, the various training phases can be identified, for one, by primary and secondary training priorities and also by specific workouts that suit the individual athlete.

Referring back to the various training systems, one then simply matches the specific need with the specific system. The "dos and don'ts" of specific workouts is your decision, and will always be right when you can answer the question, "Why are we doing this workout and how will it make this athlete race better?" Remember to not include too much quantity or quality in a single workout; the athlete should always be able to have done more.

Workout recovery times vary according to the specific athlete's age, ability, experience, and so on and the specific type and duration of the training session. A general approach to training is the hard-easy model, in which a hard session is followed by one or more easy days during which recovery and regeneration occur. The athlete is then ready for another hard workout bout.

Table 8.1 on pages 116–118 contains sample workouts for each phase. It can be used as a guide when creating workouts that fit each athlete's needs during different parts of the season.

Peaking for the Summit

If one has carefully planned and then executed a periodized plan of training, the final three weeks can be the most critical. By this time, the physiological work has been accomplished; so now the psychological work, or emphasis on confidence building, is paramount. Assuming that the training has gone according to plan, a simple formula for tapering volume is as follows:

Three weeks from summit: reduce by 15% from the highest training volume.

Two weeks from summit: reduce by another 15%.

One week from summit: reduce by a final 20%.

TABLE 8.1 SAMPLE WORKOUTS FOR 3000 TO 10,000 METERS

PREPARATION PHASE

Objectives:

Aerobic development; speed/pace adaptation; introduce threshold training/pace training (goal pace[1]/date pace[2])

Weekly Workout	Veteran	Novice
Monday	20 min. AT[3] run Buildups Cool-down	Easy run (aerobic pace)
Tuesday	Easy run	Easy run
Wednesday	Negative split run[4] Buildups	AT run
Thursday	6 × 150 @ RP[5], or 6 × 300 @ RP	Easy run Buildups
Friday	Easy run Accelerations	Fartlek (short ON[6], long OFF[6])
Saturday	3-4 × 600 @ best avg., or 3 × 1000	Interval 150s with equal rest
Sunday	Off or long run	

BASE PHASE (EARLY)

Objectives:

Threshold development; aerobic tolerance; lactate tolerance; speed/pace adaptation

Weekly Workout	
Monday	Rep hills Interval runs
Tuesday	Easy run
Wednesday	AT run: accelerations
Thursday	Speed (Rep 60, 80s), or Speed endurance
Friday	Warm-up/cool-down
Saturday	Competition
Sunday	Off or long, easy run

BASE PHASE (LATE)

Objectives:

Lactate tolerance; threshold training; aerobic development; speed/pace adaptation

Weekly Workout	
Monday	3-4 × 1000 m intervals with 1:1 rest
	Twist
Tuesday	AT run, accelerations
Wednesday	Easy run
Thursday	Intervals: 600, 600, 250, 250, 250
Friday	Easy run
Saturday	Test workout
	Long cool-down
Sunday	Off or long run

COMPETITION PHASE

Objectives:

Lactate tolerance; speed/pace adaptation; aerobic maintenance; race simulation—tactics/strategy

Weekly Workout	
Monday	2 × 500/150 @ GP Hit (achieve goal pace), or
	2 × 700 @ CZ[7] pace
Tuesday	Easy run
Wednesday	Repetition 150s with 1:5 rest (rest period is 5 × the intensity period)
Thursday	Easy run
	Accelerations
Friday	Pre-race prep.
Saturday	Competition (summit race)
Sunday	Off or easy run

COMPETITION PHASE (PEAK PERFORMANCE LEVEL)

Objectives:

Fine-tune; speed/pace adaptation; race simulation—tactics/strategy; aerobic maintenance

Weekly Workout	
Monday	1000 @ GP
	2 × 300 or 500 @ GP

(continued)

Weekly Workout *(continued)*	
Tuesday	AT run Accelerations
Wednesday	Easy run
Thursday	Easy run Accelerations
Friday	Pre-race prep. Cool-down
Saturday	Competition
Sunday	Off or easy run

1. Goal pace (GP)—a workout pace that corresponds to summit performance pace.

2. Date pace (DP)—the corresponding workout pace that reflects present race-pace efforts.

3. Anaerobic threshold (AT)—the running pace at which the accelerated production of lactate occurs (usually around 160-170 BPMs).

4. Negative split—a steady run or pace-surge effort where the first part of the workout is completed at a specific pace and the return or balance of the run is completed at a faster effort.

5. Race pace (RP)—the average per segment pace that will achieve what you are capable of running at the current date. Same as "date pace."

6. ON/OFF—another description of a pace-surge effort (fartlek) where the ON effort is the up-tempo of the run and the OFF effort is the recovery part of the run—e.g., 3 min. ON with 1 min. OFF x 5 sets.

7. Critical zone (CZ)—the specific finishing-effort pace needed to maximize the athlete's ability to "outkick" the opposition. As in any other phase of training, the critical zone (or finishing-effort ability) must be rehearsed repeatedly to introduce and then buffer the athlete to this training zone.

Blends—mixing one or two specific types of workouts is a common training axiom. One must remember that the sum of these parts must be considered, and that more than two types of workouts should not be blended.

While the volume component is described mathematically, the intensity factor can be best characterized verbally, as "aggressive yet controlled." This is not the time to leave one's best race effort in a training session.

By tapering the training volume, the athlete is able to regenerate physically. Using the overload principle of training, the athlete will be ready for an even greater physical challenge. (Overload refers to the unit of training, but done with a decreased volume.) The athlete needs to use the final three weeks to focus on positive accomplishments and to anticipate the upcoming challenge with a fighting spirit and renewed confidence.

Lifestyle Rules for Successful Distance Running

by Harry Groves

Athletes need to look at what they could be and then at what they really are. At that point, they must begin to implement the proper mechanics "to close the gap." Distance runners must have the proper active lifestyle to become even a good (let alone great) runner.

The following are 10 absolute lifestyle covenants for your athletes:

Exercise Every Day

Run (or do some type of cardiovascular exercise) every day, unless you are ill. Of course, illness requires a common sense approach of no running (or complete rest) in order to recover as quickly as possible. Proper running is done because you enjoy the development toward top competition. When you run out of compulsion, you are working on a losing mental state—not the winning one.

When running, train in all your energy systems:

• *Aerobic condition* is developed with runs requiring 140–160 heartbeats per minute and composing 60% of total weekly mileage. For collegiate runners, this means runs from 30 minutes to 2 hours at 6:00 to 6:10 mile pace. The pace goes down a little with long-term development and up slightly with longer runs. (The heart rate in training may vary individually but those given here are representative of the general index.)

• *Anaerobic condition* is developed with runs requiring 160–180 heartbeats a minute and composing 20% to 10% of the total weekly mileage. For collegiate athletes these runs could be 3–4-mile runs at 3K or 5K pace, with 3:00 jog recovery, or tempo runs of three to five miles for 5 to 25 minutes at faster than marathon pace but slower than 10K pace. These are anaerobic (lactate threshold) runs. You could also use a 15–25-minute fartlek run at paces similar to tempo runs, with very short recovery jogs.

• *Aerobic capacity* is developed with runs requiring 180–195 heartbeats per minute and composing 15% to 5% of the total weekly mileage. For collegiate athletes, workouts would be 10–12 × 400 meters (200 jog) at mile pace, 5–6 × 800 meters (200 or 400 jog) at 3K pace, short fartlek (speed play) at mile pace or faster. These workouts develop running economy (improved gas mileage). Along with aerobic conditioning and anaerobic conditioning, this directly improves the $\dot{V}O_2$max.

• *Anaerobic capacity* is developed with runs requiring a 100% training heart rate of over 195 beats per minute and composing 5% to 3% of the total weekly mileage. These runs could be repeated hard 400s at faster than mile race pace, or hard 800s at mile pace, or 200s at 800 pace or faster, with full recoveries between runs. The heart rate must drop below 120 beats per minute before the next run. Although this energy system is trained largely with short speed runs, time trials and racing could be put in this category. In the late season, the runner should add 100–150-meter speed bursts, with full recovery, to training to ensure good speed mechanics as well as to add to anaerobic capacity.

Should your athletes run twice a day or once? How much daily and weekly mileage should they do? Answers must vary. In high school and college, our runners obviously do not train enough. The precompetitive phase of training is not long enough. It should consist of at least six to seven months each year, with a slow progression in mileage and intensity up to the competitive phase. College seniors should be hitting some 100-mile weeks, with two-a-day runs at least four or five days per week. The morning of a meet, one to two miles should be commonplace. Morning runs have to be part of the lifestyle.

Strength Train Three Times a Week

Work on upper- and lower-body strength three times a week.

- Weights (free weights are preferable to machines)
- Manual resistance exercise
- Water resistance
- Plyometrics
- Uphill running or walking. Downhill running has value but requires caution to avoid injury.
- Manual labor. This strength developer was in vogue before weights were invented. Many good athletes in the past built a very high general strength level by farm work, construction work, and so on.

All strength-training methods involve proper technique, number of sets, and repetitions. Consult a strength coach who can interpret strength buildup for the distance runner.

Work on Flexibility Before and After Exercise

Before and after workouts, train the flexibility of joints for a full range of movement. Flexibility, like strength, requires a knowledgeable selection of proper muscle groups to be flexed, duration of exercise, static or ballistic methods, the stretch-contract-stretch-contract antagonist stretch method, and ranges of flexibility. The best results are gained with flexibility training prior to and after running.

Develop Good Rest and Relaxation Habits

These habits constitute a large part of the physical and mental regeneration of the human body and spirit. Regularity of bedtimes and rising times, with eight hours sleep, is advisable.

Practice Good Nutrition

For best results, consult with a certified nutritionist. Approximately 65% of your total diet should be carbohydrates, 20% fat, and 15% protein, with vitamin, mineral, and water intake all important parts of the nutritional cycle. When to eat in relation to training and competition, what to eat, and how to eat when you are on the road—these too are important nutritional considerations. It is essential that hard-training distance runners have the caloric intake needed for the performance level of their sport in training and competition. You and the nutritionist can work together in this entire area.

Prevent Injury by Doing Lower-Extremity Exercises

This includes incorporating strength exercises for the ankle and foot, with supplemental drills, natural activities such as hiking and biking, or explosive games using legs and feet. Barefoot drills in the grass or sand will contribute to strength if done in moderation on a regular basis. Maintaining calf strength by toe walking and toe step climbing can pay big dividends by preventing lower-extremity injuries. Off the wall calf stretching should also be a daily ritual.

Develop a Positive State of Mental Health

This comes through balanced lifestyle habits in the areas of work, love, play, and spiritual life. Balance is individualized but certainly does not entail a constant or even allotment of time in each area. Enjoyment of ourselves and other human resources is essential for the balance. A balance helps us live with our emotions, which is the secret to healthful living.

Achieving balanced lifestyle is sometimes difficult for collegiate distance runners. With the pressure of academic demands, many athletes develop an "unquenchable thirst" for social interaction and sexual gratification that upsets the balance in all four areas. Although athletics, or for that matter, even academics, can be overindulged, oversocialization is one of the biggest pitfalls for collegiate athletes. In addition, society and biology place athletes in a vulnerable position. They are pressured to "grow up" or "be an adult" and "fit in." Unfortunately, the bombardment of these forces somehow comes down to a can of beer or the great hormonal push. Alcoholic consumption and sexual gratification accelerate to the point that other pursuits are secondary. Frankly, it takes a real adult to be a great distance runner and to be able to work one's way through the traps of society and biology to achieve balanced lifestyle and to put everything in its proper order.

Despite the high ratio of success of some foreign athletes, we cannot remove American athletes from the American social structure and replace their lifestyle with that of foreign athletes. However, we must learn from both cases—ourselves and our opponents—and move forward to a high level of performance based on common sense and logic. The very first step is getting off the rationalization trail. In other words, don't make excuses. Focus becomes easier, which leads to more positive results and more attainable running goals.

Live Truthfully and Honestly

Face the truth directly. Success and rationalization are the antithesis of each other. If you didn't reach your goal, was it because you failed to commit yourself to the necessary effort? Were you willing to train more than once a day? Did you make an effort in the weight room? Did you lose rest or training because you wasted time? Be honest with yourself. Making excuses takes you backward in your athletic, as well as personal, development. Avoid using psychological ploys to adjust to failure or frustration.

Enjoy Your Personal and Social Life

Have fun; but remember that fun and dissipation are not partners. Physical and mental abuse of one's self retards growth.

Use Mental Training to Improve Performance

Understand the psychological aspects of distance running and use mental techniques for positive results. For best results, consult a sports psychologist for useful mental training drills such as visualization and self-talk. You are probably already using many positive psychological techniques in your training and competition. Try to become more aware of them.

In the final analysis, there is no magical way to gain success. For great distance runners, there is mileage, there is effort, and there is the proper application of these 10 guidelines of proper lifestyle.

Summary

As athletes prepare for the culmination of yet another season, they should take time to recheck their physical and mental focus, considering each of the following:

- Think realistically and keep your poise.
- Accurately analyze and critique the season thus far, eliminating any negative aspects and emphasizing the positive. Continue to build confidence in your ability to perform well.
- Evaluate upcoming opportunities and prepare pace, race strategy, tactics, and so on.
- Understand each workout's purpose and application to racing.
- Remember your flexibility training—twice daily.
- Take advantage of every opportunity in workouts.
- Do not insert any unknown variables into your daily routine. No radical changes.
- Think! And think positive!
- Stay healthy and rested.
- Believe in yourself and your program. Don't finish your season or career with "I wish I had...."

Relays

Rob Johnson
Karen Dennis

The sport of track and field places a strong emphasis on individual participation and individual performance. However, relays are an integral part of the sport. Relays generate great excitement among the spectators and are fun and exciting for the participants as well. Relay running requires the cooperative effort of four individuals. The relays are the true team events of track and field, and may provide opportunities for talented, and sometimes slightly less talented individuals to collectively produce great performances. In some regions, relays are so popular that colleges and high school teams devote at least one or more meets a season for competing at huge relay carnivals such as the Drake Relays and Penn Relays. These carnivals and similar smaller versions serve as good opportunities to showcase great relay competitions. Some of the 50 state championships held at the high school level run as many as four different relays in their respective meets. The relays most frequently run at the various state championships are the 4 × 100 meters,

4 × 200 meters, 4 × 400 meters, and 4 × 800 meters. Some states will also include a sprint medley as one of the relays at their championship. College championships, and international championships such as the Pan-American Games, World Championships, and Olympic Games, include only the 4 × 100 and 4 × 400 relays.

Sprint Relay

by Rob Johnson

The 4 × 100-meter sprint relay is the fastest and the most technically difficult of all the relays. In order for a sprint-relay squad to be successful, it must display speed and skill, combined with excellent teamwork. Because of the technical, timing, and tactical demands, developing a consistent, cohesive quartet can be challenging for even the most accomplished coach. However, to see well-timed and well-executed 4 × 100 exchanges made under pressure and in stiff competition make this a truly beautiful event to watch. It is also a sterling example of synergy, where a combined effort can produce a faster time than the sum of the individual times. (If you add the best 100-meter times of each runner together, you should be able to produce a relay faster than the total of their individual 100-meter times due to the flying start of three of the legs.)

Team Selection

The decision of which athletes run the various relay legs can be a critical factor in the success of a sprint relay. A sprint relay is not just the sum of its parts. The ability to pass, receive, and adjust under pressure affects the speed of the relay exchanges as well as the energy distribution of the athletes.

Lead-Off Leg

The lead-off leg requires an experienced athlete who is capable of good starts from the blocks and has acceleration ability. The athlete should have good balance and the ability to run the curve. The only exchange technique necessary is to be able to focus on the receiver's target hand and attack the end of the run well into the exchange zone. When considering who to have run the legs with the curves, look to athletes trained in the 110 or 100 hurdles. These athletes work a good deal on stride frequency rhythm, which is conducive to running on the curves. Their coordination and balance also helps make them good candidates for the curves.

Second Leg

The second leg of the relay runs the backstretch, with very little or no curve running. This permits the use of a very fast runner who does not need to be a good curve runner. However, the athlete does need to develop both passing and receiving skills to be effective in this leg. Good relay experience is very helpful for this athlete, as he or she must be able to adjust quickly to errors in timing by teammates.

Many coaches choose to place their best sprinter here, with the intention of getting the baton into this runner's hand early and passing it late in order to maximize his or her speed. Excellent speed and speed endurance is very important for this leg. Being a quick accelerator is not as critical, since the acceleration zone allows more time to build speed into the first handoff. In looking for athletes who have good power and speed endurance, consider 400-meter runners or long jumpers for the second and anchor legs.

Third Leg

The runner of the third leg of the relay will be a complete curve runner. Therefore balance and leaning ability while sprinting is a priority. This runner must have the ability of the second leg to both pass and receive. It is wise to use an athlete on this leg who has good relay experience, since passing lane adjustments are needed sometimes on both ends of the leg. A good curve runner who may not have sprint starting skills can be a good candidate for this leg. This athlete must be a strong sprinter and have good speed endurance to attack the zone of the final exchange.

Fourth Leg

Often coaches will put either their fastest or second fastest athlete in this position. The fourth leg has some of the same requirements as the second leg. It also requires a very competitive athlete who can finish the event by either catching or holding off other challengers into the finish line. This athlete needs only to be able to receive the baton well, not pass it. Since the run is done completely on the straight, curve running ability is not needed either. All you need here is a good, fast competitor, allowing you to place other athletes in strategic positions.

Technique

The ultimate goal of the relay is to move the baton around the track and across the finish line in the fastest legal way possible. Since the acceleration phase is so critical for baton speed through the exchange zone, the blind exchange has proven to be the most effective and fastest method of passing the baton in the 4×100 relay. With the blind exchange, once the outgoing runner starts to accelerate, he or she must not look back, but anticipate and be ready to receive a high-speed, nonvisual pass.

There are several methods for executing a fast, blind 4×100 relay baton pass. The sprint relay exchanges fall into three categories and can be described in terms of what the incoming runner does with the hand and the baton at the exchange, such as

1. upsweep,
2. downsweep, and
3. push-press.

These same exchanges can also be described or referred to by what the outgoing runner does with the hand in preparing to receive the baton, in which case the exchange action would be called

1. palm down,
2. palm up, and
3. open palm.

These methods of exchanging the baton are described in the following sections.

Upsweep/Palm Down

The upsweep/palm down method is one of the oldest methods still used today. The outgoing runner, after accelerating well into the exchange zone, upon command extends the receiving hand and arm back at a diagonal angle. The incoming runner places the baton with an upward, sweeping motion into the inverted "V" formed by the receiver's hand, which is positioned palm down. (See figure 9.1.)

Advantages:
- It is easy for beginners to learn.
- Proponents feel it is a safe pass.
- Some users believe it to be more consistent.
- It may be easier to maintain baton speed through the exchange zone because proper sprint posture is maintained.

Disadvantages:
- If the pass is missed, the receiver's hand is not in a good position to grab for the baton.
- Because of the lack of arm extension and close proximity of the passer at the point of the exchange, there is a loss of free (one-meter) distance.
- Getting the short end of the stick. There is a tendency with each exchange to have less baton protruding for the next runner. There have been instances when the anchor person is presented with less than the top third of the baton. The incoming runner may have to adjust the baton in the hand prior to the exchange.
- The passer must make an effort to place the baton deep into the receiver's hand, trying to make hand-to-hand contact as the baton is delivered.

Despite the disadvantages, it should be noted that the 1990 men's French national 4×100 team set a world record using the upsweep pass. However, two U.S. teams broke the French record using the downsweep.

There is a little known variation of the upsweep technique, which we'll consider here. The Branch-out technique is named for its creator, Coach Mike Branch, formerly of Wheaton Warrenville South High School in Illinois. The key to the Branch-out pass is for the outgoing runner to extend the arm back with the hand down. But the hand should be lifted higher and further from the torso. The thumb should also be pointed out and away, with fingers back and in. The "V"

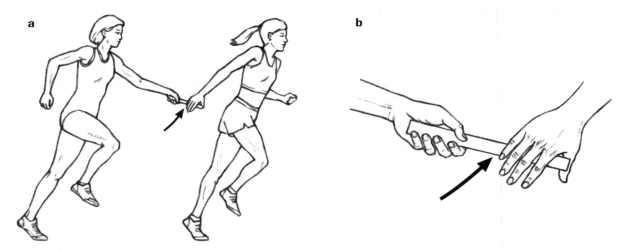

Figure 9.1 *(a)* Upsweep/palm down method of exchange. *(b)* Close-up of correct hand positions.

points back toward the incoming runner. The advantages of this upsweep/thumb out method are easy to see and measure.

Downsweep/Palm Up

The downsweep pass is popular and has been used since the 1960s. With this pass, the outgoing runner accelerates to a predetermined spot in the exchange zone or responds to a verbal command. The arm is then extended back straight. The target hand is held high (nearly parallel to the track) with the palm facing up, fingers slightly spread, and the thumb turned toward the torso. The incoming runner, while maintaining a normal sprint action, extends the baton and arm forward in a downward sweeping motion. (See figure 9.2.) This exchange may require the passer to steer the baton into the target. A little wrist action may be needed to angle the baton so that it fits the diagonal groove formed by the upwardly turned palm.

Advantages:

- The hand can be held higher and further from the body than with the upsweep method.
- The longer arm extension provides potential for greater free distance.
- This method provides a better view of the target.
- If correctly executed, the "drag time" (time spent with the arm extended behind) will be shorter and the pass can be completed in fewer strides.
- The hand-to-hand transfer is usually faster.

Disadvantages:

- The timing and placement of the baton by the passer is crucial.
- This method requires more drill and practice time, especially for beginners.
- The incoming runner must avoid doing the "wind mill"—that is, swinging the baton high and back over head prior to delivery. The passer should also avoid "freezing the stick"—that is, running with the arm and baton prematurely extended, before being close enough to make the exchange.
- There is a tendency to provide a poor target in one of the following ways.
   1. Lazy limb—The arm and/or hand is bent and not held back straight and high to provide a good target.

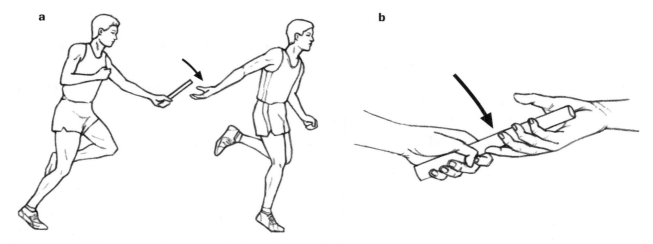

Figure 9.2 *(a)* Downsweep/palm up method of exchange. *(b)* Close-up of the exchange.

2. Pendulum swing—The target arm is prematurely straightened prior to passing the hip as it is swung rigidly backward. This action may cause a stretch reflex that forces the tight target arm down and toward the torso with each stride.

3. Bicep squeeze—Avoid trying to pin the extended arm against the body (bicep to torso) in an attempt to keep it high and steady. The action of acceleration will cause the runner's arm to move and provide an unsteady target.

The downsweep pass has been used by more U.S. high schools and colleges than any other pass. Several of the U.S. national teams have used this exchange with excellent success.

Push-Press/Open Palm

The push-press/open palm exchange method and its variations are growing exceptionally popular. This push-press method is in my opinion an advancement and a natural evolution of the best of the aforementioned exchanges. In the push-press exchange, the palm of the target hand is neither down nor up. The palm is exposed and opens out facing the incoming runner. The hand placed in this position provides a big target and can be easily seen. In this pass, the outgoing runner, upon command (verbal or nonverbal), extends the target arm rearward. This is done by driving the elbow back and high quickly. This action enables the lower arm and hand to reach out at about shoulder-level height. To achieve the desired hand position, the thumb is brushed against the side pocket area as the hand swings back past the body. The thumb is down, with fingers slightly spread and pointing away from the body.

Notice that the natural alignment of the extended arm is not straight back behind the body. If you lay a yardstick down the back of the extended arm, you will see that the nearly locked out elbow is slightly outside (not directly behind) the shoulder, and the thumb is slightly outside (not behind) the elbow. If the runners run their appropriate borders and the outgoing runner provides the target as described, the baton will travel the most direct path down the center of the lane.

The key is proper hand position; done correctly the hand creates a big target and natural fit for the baton. In fact, I often refer to relay techniques using a push-press to an open hand as a "natural exchange."

Advantages:

- The incoming runner can deliver the baton with the least amount of deviation from normal sprint arm action.
- This method provides good horizontal thrust of a near-vertical baton with long arm extension.
- This method makes it easier to steer and place the baton into the hand.
- User-friendly drills can be practiced with or without a partner.

Disadvantages:

- This method requires work with a greater number of drills.
- There is a tendency to become overconfident and careless with the method. Diligent, focused practice and/or drills should be continued three or four times per week.

The push-press pass appears to be more natural, in that it allows for normal sprint action and optimal baton speed through the exchange zone. This method and numerous variations are growing in popularity—some of the U.S. national teams and most of the elite collegiate 4 × 100 relay teams use the push-press technique.

Snatch Pass

One variation of the push-press, "natural exchange" technique that has proven effective in certain situations is the snatch pass. The snatch technique requires excellent timing and good hand dexterity. With the snatch, the outgoing runner—upon hearing a verbal cue—actively reaches back and in one quick motion snatches the properly placed baton from the incoming runner. An important key for the passer is to focus on the target hand and elbow of the receiver. If the pass is not made on the first attempt, simply try it again the very next time the elbow is swung back. The receiver's hand should be relaxed, with the fingers extended out and slightly spread. The open palm helps provide a "mitt" with which to catch and snatch the baton naturally. The snatch is risky, yes, but if done correctly, it is quick and slick.

Semi-Blind Pass

Another variation of the push-press technique is the semi-blind pass. The semi-blind pass is not usually employed in the 4 × 100 relay. However, it has proven effective in the 4 × 200, and in some cases the 4 × 400 and sprint-medley relays. With the semi-blind pass, the outgoing runner—upon cue, usually visual—turns and runs away from the passer for a few (two to three) strides, then looks back and extends the hand for a quick, but visual, exchange. The target is presented ready to receive a push-press pass. It is recommended that when running the 4 × 200, particularly indoors, each receiver face the inside of the track, taking the baton with the left hand, then switching to the right hand as soon as possible. The same principle applies when the semi-blind pass is used for the 4 × 400 exchange.

Alternating Method

In the 4 × 100 relay, passing the baton right to left, left to right, and right to left sequentially is known as the alternating method. In using the alternating method, the runner does not switch the baton from hand to hand. The runner passes the baton with the same hand in which he or she received it. The advantage of this method is that it allows the first and third runners to run as close as possible to the inside of the lane on curves. The second and fourth runners stay in the outside of their lanes so that the incoming runners can stay to the inside as the pass is made. This allows the pass to be made in a straight, forward direction and not across the body. This is a faster and more efficient exchange.

Training Drills

The following training drills, when done correctly, will help contribute to a smooth, flawless exchange. To get a feel for how the hand should be positioned, stand with your back to the wall and extend the arm so that you can touch the wall with only the tips of the fingers and thumb. The cup formed by the hand in this position provides a good mitt for a baton to fit. The fingers should be kept horizontal (parallel to the floor) with the thumb down (perpendicular to the floor). Practice swinging and extending the arm back with fingers barely touching the wall. The hand should be open, with the fingers relaxed and slightly spread. This helps provide a big (although moving) target and a natural hand position for which to receive the baton.

Bottle-It Drill

1. Place an empty two-liter plastic soda bottle on the corner of a table (a 30-inch or 76 cm stool also works well) or on a desk near a wall.
2. Position yourself with your back to the wall (as described above).
3. Standing with your back to the table, pump your arms four or five times, then quickly reach back and grab the bottle off the table.
4. Because the bottle is larger than the baton, it forces the hand into a favorable position to receive a baton.
5. Try this drill near a mirror or look back occasionally to check your technique.
6. Remember to drill with both your left and right hands.
7. When you can quickly reach back and grab the bottle on the first attempt, then you may be ready to try the snatch exchange.
8. As you become more proficient, replace the bottle with a plastic baton. To avoid cracking the baton, wrap the ends with tape.

Off-the-Wall Drill

Figure 9.3 Off-the-wall drill.

1. Stand with your back to the wall.
2. Hold a plastic baton or bottle in one hand, do a few arm pumps, and drive the elbow up high, extending the arm so that the bottle can be bounced lightly off the wall and back into your open hand. (See figure 9.3.)
3. While facing forward—away from the wall—continue doing the arm swing with the bounce-and-catch action against the wall.
4. Repeat this drill with both hands.

Press-the-Flesh Drill

1. Face the wall.
2. Hold the baton with your left hand, position your right foot forward, and flex your knees slightly.
3. Swing your arms in a natural sprint motion, then extend your left arm and baton forward in a push-press action.
4. Gently bounce the bottle or baton off the wall and back into your waiting hand.
5. Attempt to deliver the baton with a straight, horizontal motion—visualize yourself pressing the baton into the open palm (flesh) of the outgoing runner.
6. Repeat the drill with both hands (make sure to put your left foot forward when you have the baton in your right hand).

Quartet Drill

1. Line four runners up in a straight line within the lane.
2. The first runner stands with the left foot just inside the inner border. The second runner stands with the right foot just inside the outer border at the appropriate full arm's length handoff distance. The third runner stands with the left foot just inside the inner border an equal distance apart. The fourth runner stands with the right foot just inside the outer border, again at the appropriate distance from the third runner.
3. The four runners *do not* stand directly behind one another, but staggered on either side of the lane so that the baton travels down the middle of the lane. This right-left-right-left handoff allows the first and third runners to hug the inside lane and run the shortest possible distance, while the baton takes the most direct path.
4. Pass the baton forward using verbal passing cues.
5. When the fourth runner receives the baton, he or she reverses the direction of the handoff and sends the baton back through the line with the arm fully extended to the rear, the baton held perpendicular to the ground.

"About Face" is a variation of the quartet drill in which all four runners turn 180 degrees around and the fourth runner becomes the leadoff runner.

A third variation has runners switching position so that each participant receives the baton in all four positions.

Light-Touches Drill

1. Have all four runners assume the same staggered position described above.
2. All four runners must move forward with synchronized arm and leg movements.

Figure 9.4 Light-touches drill.

3. The first runner, with a baton in the right hand, lightly touches the baton in the next runner's waiting hand as it swings back in sync (figure 9.4).

4. After three light touches, the baton is passed forward.

5. This exercise is repeated between the second and third runners—three light touches and a handoff, left hand to right hand, while the motions remain in sync.

6. The third runner then performs three light touches in the fourth runner's open palm and hands off the baton right hand to left hand.

7. When the baton reaches the anchor runner, the baton is reversed and handed directly back through the line, and the exercise is repeated.

Variations on the Light-Touches Drill

The light-touches drill can have a conditioning aspect. Have the quartet (this can also be done with five or six runners) cover four laps around the track. With beginners, the first lap can be a quick walk or a slow jog.

1. On the first lap, the runners do three light touches prior to passing the baton forward.

2. The pace of the second lap is a little quicker, with only two light touches, then a grab.

3. The third lap is slightly quicker than the second, with only one light touch and then a pass.

4. The fourth and final lap is the quickest, but under control, with the baton being passed forward in sync with the receiver's arm swing and on first contact, with no touch action prior to the pass.

This drill allows the baton to be moved forward and reversed with four to six runners for up to a mile.

Mile Relay

by Karen Dennis

A relay team develops its own unique chemistry during the training process. Relay chemistry refers to the combined personalities of relay team members. Relay alchemy is the magical process of four good athletes transformed into a great relay team. The fastest four runners on your team are not necessarily the best relay combination. The best relay combination includes the fastest four runners on the team who work harmoniously together. A relay team of fast runners void of harmony is easily torn apart by dysfunction and disunity and often performs disappointingly. The coach has the challenge of selecting the perfect combination of relay components to bring about the desired result.

Team Selection

Each athlete running the mile relay, or 4×400-meter relay, has a certain role to fulfill. The coach knows the skill levels of members of the relay pool, and has observed how potential candidates perform under pressure. Selecting personnel involves matching the appropriate runner to the required role.

Lead-Off Leg

The role of the first leg is to get the team out front and to make the exchange with a lead on the rest of the field. The first runner must be aggressive enough to command a lead, yet composed under pressure as the lead runner. The lead runner must be strong and have a good sense of pace.

The lead runner remains in lane for 400 meters plus the distance equal to the 200-meter stagger to the second exchange zone (approximately 500 meters total). The first leg, running a flat-out 400-meter run, has the daunting task of setting the rhythm of the relay, and that performance will greatly determine the performance of successive legs. The first runner may be the second fastest person on the team.

Second Leg

The role of the second leg is to keep the team in the race. In dueling head to head, the second runner keeps the team in contention. The second runner must be physically strong enough to withstand possible jostling or bumping at the breakpoint and be able to run the race in traffic. If the team is not in first place, the second runner must be fearless in challenging the lead. If the team is out front, the second runner has to run a strong, flat-out 400 meters to give the third leg as much lead as possible. The second runner has to have courage, and has to be able to run the race no matter what place the team is in.

Third Leg

The role of the third runner is to put the team in position to win. The third runner is pivotal in determining the outcome of the race, as this is the final opportunity to provide a lead or to recapture the lead before the last exchange. The third runner must be physically capable of running well from behind or in front and must have confidence in his or her ability to do so. The third runner must run a flat-out 400 meters with an earnestness to set up the anchor runner to win. The third runner is often the second-best possible anchor leg on the team.

Fourth Leg

The fourth runner, or anchor leg, has the final opportunity to secure victory for the team. The role of the anchor leg is to put the relay away by running as fast as it takes to do so. The anchor, like the third leg, must be comfortable running from behind or in front. Knowing the teams' success or failure depends on this leg, the fourth runner must be self-assured and confident in his or her ability to make the impossible possible. The fourth runner is often the strongest and/or fastest leg on the relay, and is often termed the "horse."

Technique

The mechanics of baton passing is often not practiced enough to ensure exceptional exchanges, particularly in the 4 × 400-meter relay. Some people mistakenly think that time lost through a poor exchange is recovered somewhere in the next leg. The baton exchange in the 4 × 400-meter relay is as important as in the shorter sprint relays. Efficient and flawless baton exchanges result in a faster race. Furthermore, a slight lead of 5 meters in the race is lengthened to 10–15 meters with successful baton passing.

Opinions vary over the best type of exchange in the 4 × 400-meter relay. Most coaches select a visual or semi-visual exchange. In my opinion, the advantages of the visual exchange are greater than the advantages of the semi-visual exchange.

Figure 9.5   Visual exchange.

Visual Exchange

A visual exchange enables the receiver to judge the position and finishing speed of the incoming runner. The receiver takes the baton in the left hand while on the move, keeping his or her eyes on the baton. The visual pass is safe and avoids the possibility of leaving behind the incoming runner, who is greatly decelerating (figure 9.5).

Another advantage of the visual pass is that it allows the receiving runner to see his or her place between other runners in the race and the curb, and so determine opportunities to move inside to a more favorable position. Running on the inside border of the lane enables the athlete to run the shortest distance possible. In doing so, each relay member runs a more energy-efficient 400-meter race.

The receiving runner faces the inside lane stripe with the left hand extended

Figure 9.6   In the visual exchange, the receiving runner extends the left hand chest high to retrieve the baton from the incoming runner.

Figure 9.7 The incoming runner uses the right hand to pass the baton to the outgoing runner's left hand.

Figure 9.8 After receiving the baton, the outgoing runner switches the baton to the right hand, getting ready for the next exchange.

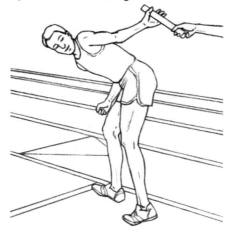

Figure 9.9 This runner's position allows for a good target of exchange for the incoming runner.

chest high to take the baton from the extended right hand of the incoming runner (figure 9.6). It is the responsibility of the receiving runner to retrieve the baton from the extended hand of the incoming runner.

Unlike in sprint relays, in which a set mark point and a blind exchange are used, mile-relay receivers must judge when to begin running against the speed of the incoming athlete. How well the exchange partners know and respond to each other in race conditions determines the amount of time lost in the exchange zone. Relay chemistry becomes an important component when the quality of the exchange depends on the receivers' ability to judge or sense the speed of the incoming runner. A perfect pass occurs when exchange partners execute in successful synergy. A measure of success is no loss of speed through the exchange zone, faster individual 400-meter splits, and optimal relay result.

Step-by-Step Formula

The first runner carries the baton throughout the race in the right hand, passing to the left hand of the outgoing runner. The incoming runner must run aggressively down the home stretch through the exchange zone and passes to the outgoing runner on the move (figure 9.7).

The second runner is positioned in his or her lane in a starting stance, with the left foot back, the right foot forward, looking over the left shoulder, and left hand extended to present a good target of exchange for the incoming runner. The exchange is usually downward with the hand facing upward. Immediately upon taking the baton, the outgoing runner changes the baton to the right hand and assumes race pace around the curve, staying in the lane until the breakpoint around the first turn (figure 9.8).

The third, and later the fourth, runner stands ready for the exchange at the common exchange line. He or she faces the infield of the track with the left hand extended as a distinct target for the incoming runner (figure 9.9). The receivers' positions on the exchange zone line depend on the place finish of the incoming runners. Receivers must judge what lane to retrieve the baton in, make room for the exchange, and check for crowded and crossover conditions.

The fourth runner takes the baton in the left hand, changes it to the right hand, and finishes the race.

Training Drills

Use the following drills to help make your relay team run like a well-oiled machine. First, remember these points:

- Practice baton exchanges at least two or three times a week.
- Practice countering the jostling that the third and fourth receivers will often experience at the exchange zone line.
- Practice countering the heavy traffic experienced at the break point on the second runner's leg.
- Curve running is more efficient with the baton carried in the right hand. Additionally, most runners prefer carrying the baton in the right hand. Energy conserved when running curves will be needed during the last 80 meters where a strong finish before the exchange is needed.
- Frequent relay practice sessions are the key in building good relay chemistry.

Michael Johnson shows off his team's relay chemistry as he takes the baton and gives his team an edge over their opponents.

Five-Man Relay

The "five-man relay" involves five athletes running 100-meter intervals over a distance of 400 meters continuously. Each runner remains at the position he or she finished the 100 m run in while the baton is carried around the track. The fifth runner takes the baton at the finish line to bring it to the first runner to repeat the drill. Each runner practices judging the pace of the incoming runner when leaving the exchange zone. The exchange partners become adept in establishing eye-hand coordination. Both relay partners must feel confident in the position of their hands when making the exchange. The coach emphasizes a steady consistent pace. The pace should start out slow and should pick up as skill levels improve. The training session is completed when the first runner has completed 16 carries of the baton, or one mile.

Rabbit Drill

The "rabbit drill" allows for a productive training session with athletes other than 400-meter runners. This drill teaches athletes to judge pace and position in the race when running from behind. Before commencing, the coach needs to know the individual 400-meter times of the training group. Consider the following example:

Athlete A = 62 seconds
Athlete B = 53 seconds

The rabbit is the slower runner. The coach sends Athlete A on a 400-meter timed run with the understanding that he or she is to keep the pursuing Athlete B from catching up before Athlete A completes the training distance. Using this example, there is nine seconds difference in speed between athletes A and B; the coach will send the pursuing Athlete B three to five seconds after the "rabbit" Athlete A begins running. The goal is to challenge the rabbit to stay ahead of the pursuing runner without panicking or tightening up. The goal of the pursuing runner is to make up the deficit while simultaneously staying within his or her own race capabilities. It is extremely important that each athlete run his or her individual race, whatever the team's position in the race.

Three-Turn Stagger Drill

The coach selects all potential relay members to participate in this drill. It is most effective with six to eight pairs of participants. Coaching objectives include the following: ensuring no loss of speed during the exchange, running aggressively around the first curve, countering jostling effects at the breakpoint, and experimenting with different relay combinations.

Divide an even number of participants into two groups: one "incoming runners," the other "outgoing runners." Arrange the runners into teams of two and assign each team a lane. Position the incoming runner of each team 40 meters beyond the 100-meter start line. The outgoing runners are in their respective lanes at the start of the mile relay. The incoming runners race to pass the baton to the outgoing runners on their team. The outgoing runners receive the baton, and at race pace challenge one another around the curve beyond the breakpoint to the 150-meter mark.

Alternate lanes after each round to give outgoing runners experience running both inside and outside lanes. After each team has run in different lanes, switch the incoming and outgoing runners and repeat the drill.

Summary

The drills and techniques presented in this chapter are designed to help give your relay team an edge, or the much sought after "relay alchemy." Relay alchemy describes four individuals with combined qualities of desire, determination, dedication, and hard work. A relay team so united and focused is capable of producing magical and memorable races.

PART III

JUMPING EVENTS

10 Long Jump

Kyle Tellez
Kathy James

In all the jumping events in track and field, there is a strong relation between the execution of the approach run and take-off and the performance of a jump. The more consistent and more technically correct the approach run and takeoff, the better the jump performance.

Most world-record performances in the jumping events in track and field have resulted from a successful approach run and takeoff. When a long jumper breaks contact with the ground, the center of gravity forms a parabolic curve. Once in the air, there is nothing that can be done to change this predetermined flight path. Therefore, the majority of coaching time in the long jump should be spent developing a technically sound approach run and takeoff.

Technique

The long jump can be broken down into four components:

1. Approach run
2. Last two strides
3. Takeoff
4. Action in the air and landing

The technical information will be explained and illustrated using a right-footed takeoff jumper who is starting the approach run with the left foot, taking an odd number of strides (19 strides), and using the hitch-kick.

Approach Run

The objective here is to develop a consistent approach run that allows for gradual acceleration, beginning with the first stride and ending with maximum controlled speed at the takeoff.

Length of the Approach

The length of the approach run should be between 12 and 19 strides (figure 10.1). The approach run should be as long as possible depending on the jumper's experience, sprinting technique, and conditioning level. The length of the approach run will determine the amount of speed that is developed.

The longer the approach run, the more difficult it is to develop a consistent stride pattern. Thus, inexperienced jumpers should begin by using a shorter approach run of 12 strides (figure 10.1a). However, as jumpers gain experience, improve sprinting technique, and get stronger through a conditioning program, the approach run can be lengthened to 14 strides and eventually 18 strides (figure 10.1b).

A successful approach run depends on the consistency of the first two or three strides. It is here that the rhythm of the run is developed. If the run is inconsistent, it is usually because of the inconsistency in the first two or three strides of the approach.

To help determine the consistency of a jumper's approach run, a check mark should be placed four strides out from the takeoff board (figure 10.1, b-c). The check mark should measure 26 to 31 feet (about 7.9 to 9.4 m) away from the takeoff board. The distance for the four-stride check mark will vary depending on the jumper's height, speed on the runway, and distance of the approach run. Experienced jumpers, who are tall, fast, and have 18 or 19 strides, should be closer to 31 feet (about 9.4 m) at the check mark. More inexperienced jumpers who are shorter, not as fast, and have 12 or 13 strides, should be closer to 26 feet (about 7.9 m) at the check mark. Thus, if during a competition, a long jumper is hitting the check mark at 27 feet (about 8.2 m) but is supposed to be hitting earlier, at 31 feet (about 9.4 m), the jumper is probably too close to the takeoff board and is fouling or shortening the last four strides to get on the board.

Keep in mind that if a jumper's takeoff foot is the same foot used to push off with at the start of the run, there will be an even (say, 18) number of strides (figure 10.1b) (e.g., start with left foot and take off with left foot). However, if the jumper's takeoff foot is not the same as the foot that starts the run, there will be an odd (say, 19) number of strides (figure 10.1c) (e.g., start with left foot and take off with right foot).

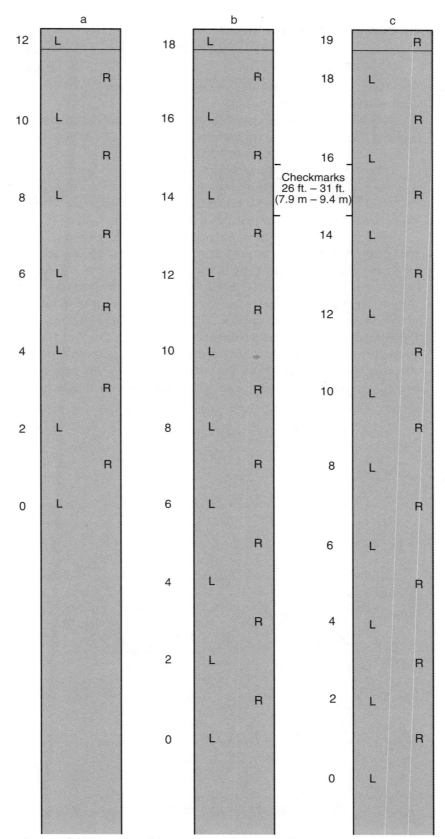

Figure 10.1 Approach runs of *(a)* 12 strides, *(b)* 18 strides, and *(c)* 19 strides.

Speed and Acceleration

The approach run should be made at the maximum speed at which the jumper can complete a successful takeoff. However, while long jumpers are trained as sprinters, raw speed is not the key to technique in the long jump—maximum controllable speed is!

Sprinting is a pushing action against the ground. Jumpers should not try to pull against the ground. The formation of the leg is ill-suited to exert a pulling force. In addition, a pulling action when sprinting is a direct cause of hamstring damage.

A consistent, fast approach run will depend on a gradual acceleration. Many inexperienced jumpers make the mistake of accelerating too fast, too soon. This causes them to decelerate toward the end of the approach run. Thus, speed is lost going into the takeoff, resulting in a poor performance.

Using a 19-stride approach run, the jumper begins the run by pushing down and back against the ground with the left foot to set the body in motion. In addition, there is a slight inclination of the whole body from the ground at the beginning of the run. As the jumper accelerates, the body gradually straightens up into an upright position by the end of the fourth or sixth stride (figure 10.2).

When establishing an approach run for beginning jumpers, it is best to work on the approach run without jumping. This way, the jumpers can isolate the approach run and develop a consistent acceleration, stride pattern, and rhythm of the run through repetition. In addition, even with experienced jumpers, it is beneficial to practice the approach run without jumping to further the consistency and rhythm of the run.

Figure 10.2 The start of the approach run: as the jumper accelerates, the body gradually straightens into an upright position.

Last Two Strides

The objective in the last two strides is to prepare, or "set up," for the takeoff while conserving as much speed as possible. Prior to these last strides, the jumper is in a full sprinting position in which the jumper continues the acceleration by pushing down against the ground (figure 10.3, a-c).

Penultimate Stride

The penultimate stride is the next to the last stride (left foot) from the takeoff, where there is a lowering of the jumper's center of gravity (figure 10.3, d-f). It is the longer of the last two strides because of the lowering of the center of gravity and the flexion of the knee and ankle of the supporting leg. There is a noticeable "gathering" of the jumper's body during the penultimate stride. In addition, the foot is placed flat on the ground.

Jumpers must feel the lowering, or "gathering," of the body during the penultimate stride. The penultimate stride is different than a normal running stride; so jumpers should not just "run" through the penultimate. It is imperative that they prepare the body during the penultimate.

Last Stride

The last stride (right foot) is shorter than the penultimate stride because of the raising of the jumper's center of gravity (figure 10.3, g-i on page 146). As the takeoff foot makes contact with the ground, the foot is placed flat and in front of the jumper's body. In addition, there is a slight flexion of the joints of the takeoff leg. During this slight flexion, the muscles of the takeoff leg are forced into an active stretching phase or eccentric contraction. Immediately following this active stretching phase, there is a shortening, or concentric contraction, of the muscles of the takeoff leg. When a concentric contraction is preceded by a phase of active stretching in the muscles of the takeoff leg, elastic energy is stored and the takeoff leg is "loaded up."

Figure 10.3 *(a-c)* sprinting position; *(d-f)* the penultimate stride; *(continued)*

The last stride is shorter in length than the penultimate stride. Therefore, jumpers should think of the last two strides as long–short. This can sometimes help them set up the takeoff more effectively. Jumpers must avoid reaching on the last stride, because placing the takeoff foot too far out into the front of the body will result in a braking or stopping effect and poor jump performance.

It is critical that jumpers stay relaxed and maintain approach speed through the last two strides. They can accomplish this by continuing to stroke their arms through the last two strides, since stopping the movement of the arms will decrease approach speed into the takeoff.

Takeoff

The objective in the takeoff is to "load up" the takeoff leg to create a vertical impulse through the jumper's center of gravity.

Contact With the Ground

As the jumper's takeoff foot makes contact with the ground and the leg is loaded up with elastic energy, a vertical impulse or lift is created through the center of gravity (figure 10.3j). This vertical impulse created from the takeoff leg projects the jumper's body up and out into the air. Coaches should encourage jumpers to think about jumping first and then running up and out off the ground. Focusing only on running up and out off the ground tends to cause the jumpers to not load up the takeoff leg and thus bypass a vertical impulse.

Foot Placement

The takeoff foot is placed flat and directly in front of the jumper's body to allow for a maximum vertical lift. If a jumper places the foot heel first, it will cause a braking or stopping effect at the takeoff. On the other hand, if the jumper places the takeoff foot high up on the toes, there will be little stabilization on impact, causing the leg to buckle or collapse. As the body moves through the takeoff and up into the air, the jumper continues to run up and out off the ground (figure 10.3, j-k).

Figure 10.3 *(continued)* *(g-i)* the last stride; *(j-k)* the takeoff;

(continued)

Body Position

The jumper's body is upright to the ground, allowing for optimal position at takeoff. Jumpers should focus their eyes up and out when leaving the ground. They should not be looking down into the sand or at the takeoff board.

To work on the technique of the last two strides and the takeoff, establish a short approach run of eight strides. Short-run jumping allows the jumpers to isolate and emphasize the proper technique. In addition, jumpers can take more jumps, since short runs reduce the fatigue during training.

Jumpers should not overemphasize jumping up high at takeoff. A high angle of takeoff usually causes jumpers to slow down considerably to achieve the height, thus losing critical speed needed at the takeoff. Jump for distance, not height.

Action in the Air and Landing

The objective for the fourth and last component is to rotate the body into an efficient landing position that maximizes jump distance.

Once contact with the ground is broken, the jumper can do nothing to alter the flight path of the center of gravity. However, the jumper moves the arms and legs about the center of gravity to counteract forward rotation and assume an optimal position for landing.

Hitch-Kick Technique

The hitch-kick technique allows the jumper to counteract the forward rotation developed at the takeoff (figure 10.3l). By cycling the legs and arms through the air, the jumper is able to maintain an upright body position and set up for an efficient landing position (figure 10.3, m-p). If the jumper did not counteract forward rotation by cycling the arms and legs, the body would continue to rotate forward into a facedown position in the sand.

Figure 10.3 *(continued) (l-p)* the action in the air;

(continued)

Other techniques for long jumpers in the air are the hang and the sail. Each of these styles accomplishes the same task as the hitch-kick by counteracting forward rotation in the air in order to achieve an efficient landing position.

In the hang technique, the jumper extends his or her body in a long, outstretched position and holds that position momentarily so that he or she appears to be hanging. Then, upon descending, the jumper snaps the legs to a forward landing position. The hang is beneficial in that the long position of the athlete as he or she rises in the air retards the tendency to tumble forward and lose extension.

Using the sail technique, the athlete immediately lifts the legs up into a toe-touching position upon rising up from the takeoff. This makes it easy for the novice to try to get into a landing position early. However, it does not counter the tendency to rotate too far forward (tumbling). This can cause the feet to lose good extension upon landing.

Landing

For an efficient landing, the jumper extends and sweeps the arms down toward the ground (figure 10.3q). This action of the arms raises the legs up toward the torso and closer to the jumper's center of gravity (figure 10.3, q-s). Thus, the action of the arms causes an equal and opposite reaction with the legs.

As the jumper makes contact with the sand, the knees bend and flex to cushion the impact. In addition, the arms are brought forward to assist the jumper's forward momentum and avoid falling back.

Remember, the best jumps come from a well-executed approach run and takeoff. Thus, if a jumper is having a problem with undesirable rotation in the air and an inefficient landing, always look to the approach run and takeoff as the source of the problem.

Have workouts and competitions videotaped so that they may be reviewed. Videotaped jumps are an important teaching tool for coaches and jumpers. In addition, watch videos of world-class jumpers and compare technique.

Figure 10.3 *(continued) (q-s)* the landing.

Training

by Kathy James

In preparing and training for the long jump, the first thing a coach and athlete must remember is to plan each practice session. Efficient workouts that are planned ahead of time produce the best results in learning and performance. Do not make up workouts as you go along; doing this creates an inconsistent training pattern during each training period. Determine the goal of each workout as you plan the training sessions. Knowing what is to be accomplished during each workout is crucial to the overall performance of the athlete. It will eliminate under- and overtraining and reduce injury. After each workout, assess the specific performance objective. Analyzing the effort and ability of the athlete to execute and complete the workout is critical in determining the feasibility and benefit of the workout.

The following components should be considered in planning workouts:

• Warm-up: Warm-up is essential to overall performance and the health of the athlete. Warm-ups proceed from general to specific, and begin slowly and gradually increase in activity level. Warm-ups prepare the muscular and cardiovascular systems for strenuous activity, reducing cramps, strains, pulls, or related injuries.

• Review: To enhance athletic performance, it is important to introduce new skills. Give a clear and simple explanation of what is to be accomplished with the skill. Be sure to review these skills during the course of the workout. It may also be helpful to demonstrate the skill to make sure it is done properly and with correct technique. Then watch the athlete execute the technique for optimum performance. Last, provide the athlete with feedback during the practice session. Give a clear and accurate reason if there is a problem in the execution of the skill. Be positive and understandable. Correct one error at a time. Feedback always motivates and encourages the athlete to execute properly and prepare for the next training sessions. It also teaches the athletes the fundamentals of the workouts they are asked to perform.

• Fitness training: It is very easy to get caught up in the technical side of long jump training and forget sprinting and strength training, especially during the season. Be sure to include this fitness training for strength and speed throughout all phases of the season.

• Cool-down: Just as it is important to warm up before practice, it is equally important to cool down at the end of a practice session. This will relax the muscular and cardiovascular systems gradually, helping to prevent injury. Walking and jogging for 5-10 minutes following the workout and concluding with stretching is a good way to cool down.

• Evaluation: Evaluate the practice by discussing the benefits of the practice session with your athletes. Keep accurate records of each training session to determine their effectiveness. Decide which goals were met and which need more attention.

The long jump incorporates speed, strength, and agility. As you plan the practice sessions, there are several essential components to consider, which are discussed in the following sections.

Strength Training

Crucial to a long jumper's success is the development of strength, specifically the development of jumping power. In developing strength elements for the long jump, concentrate on the specific qualities needed in jumping. These qualities are based on three factors:

1. Power
2. Jumping endurance
3. "Special strength"

A specific type of energy is required to execute a successful long jump. Power is the maximum available ability of the leg and back muscles during approach and takeoff. Jumping endurance is the muscular ability to withstand multiple bounding and jumping. "Special strength" is used to bridge the gap between sheer strength and explosive power. Special strength gives the jumper control over all mechanics of the back and leg muscles used in horizontal jumping. The following principles of strength training should be observed:

- Resistance is more important when training for strength.
- Strength is more important when training for power.
- Power training with weights is initiated only toward the end of the buildup training period and after lift-technique training.
- With special strength, the strength application of the legs is most effective when the athlete works on a rigid system, supported by strong back and abdominal muscles. The special strength refers to the ability to apply a large force in a very quick period of time. The "special strength" should enable the center of gravity to take a definite path. The length of time of this strength movement is directly determined by the end speed of the approach. The long jumper's speed from the approach run greatly limits the time the athlete has to apply the force at the takeoff board. Therefore, the faster the speed, the less time the athlete has to apply the force. Power exercises and special-strength training comply with the "principles of overload" to the muscles and joints and concentrate on pure maximum strength.

The most important factor in strength training for the horizontal jumps is the method used. The most productive and prominent method used by elite jumpers today is plyometrics in conjunction with weight training.

Plyometrics

Plyometrics is a type of training that combines endurance, coordination, and pure strength training, through which jumpers can produce better explosive reaction movements. However, the biggest benefit of this type of training is the development of stretch reflex in the muscles involved during takeoff and in flight.

The goal of jumping drills is to develop the neuromuscular system so that strength gains can be incorporated in speed movements. Two methods of plyometrics are used in this phase: long jumping and short jumping. Long jumping takes place during the first six weeks in order to condition the athlete and build speed endurance. These jumps can be subdivided into low-intensity long jumps and high-intensity long jumps. Both types of jumps are done over a distance greater than 30 meters but they are done at a lower amplitude or as quickly as possible, respectively. Short jumping is done over a shorter distance (less than 30 meters) very explosively. Plyometrics should be done two times per week, allowing several days rest in between. Mondays and Thursdays or Mondays and Fridays before weight training is preferable.

The following are examples of plyometric jumping exercises:

Long-Jumping Exercises

Low Intensity

High skips

Alternate bounding

Single-leg hops

Double-leg hops

RRL, LLR, RRL, LLR . . .

RR, LL, RR, LL . . .

Gallops

Bounding up a hill (or stairs)

Straight-leg jumps up a hill (or stairs)

Double-leg jumps up a hill (or stairs)

Ramps and/or hill running

Jump rope:

• single leg

• double leg

• doubles (two rope rotations/jump)

• high knees

Jumping or hopping over seven or more cones

Alternate step-ups on bench, box, or step for 30 seconds or more (figure 10.4)

Figure 10.4   Alternate step-ups.

High Intensity

Same as low-intensity exercises but performed as quickly as possible

Include a 30-meter single-leg hop for time

Short-Jumping Exercises

Any of the long-jumping exercises but performed with greater amplitude and fewer repetitions.

Standing triple jump

Standing long jump

Jumping over hurdles (about one meter apart):

• Five low hurdles

• Five hurdles of various heights

• Put two hurdles together and jump over with two legs

Jumping over boxes (12–18 inches or about 30.5–46 cm high, two to three feet or about 61 to 91.5 cm apart):

• double leg

• single leg

• alternating

• combinations

Jumping in place from half-squat

Jumping from half-squat up a hill (half the distance of long jumping but faster) or steps

Any jumps in place:

• double-leg tuck

• single-leg tuck

• pike

• split-squat

• squat jumps

• forward and backward over cone

• side to side over cone

Box/bench jumps:

• high-knee step-ups

• alternating run-ups

Timed jumps of 10–30 meters:

• single-leg hops

• standing triple jumps

• standing long jumps

Single- and double-leg bounding holding on to partner's shoulders or to railing

Table 10.1 is a great way to incorporate the above plyometric exercises into three four-week periods.

TABLE 10.1 PLYOMETRICS TRAINING SCHEDULE FOR LONG JUMP

Period 1 (4 weeks)

Week	Exercise	Reps/distance
1	Long jumping (low intensity)	4 × 100 m (choose 4 exercises)
2	Short jumping	2 × 6 reps per exercise
	Long jumping (low intensity)	3 × 50 m (1 exercise)
		3 × 50 m (1 exercise)
	Long jumping (high intensity)	2 × 30 m (1 exercise)
		2 × 30 m (1 exercise)
3	Short jumping	2 × 6 reps
	Long jumping (high intensity)	3 × 30 m
		3 × 30 m
		3 × 30 m
4	Active rest	Sprint drills

Period 2 (4 weeks)

Week	Exercise	Reps/distance
5	Short jumping	2 × 6 reps
		2 × 20 m
	Long jumping (high intensity)	2 × 30 m
6	Short jumping	2 × 6 reps
		2 × 20 m
		2 × 10 sec.
	Long jumping (high intensity)	2 × 30 m
7	Short jumping	4 exercises × 3 sets of 6 reps
8	Sprint drills	2 × 25 m

Period 3 (4 weeks)

Week	Exercise	Reps/distance
9	Short jumping	3 × 2 × 6 reps or
		3 × 2 × 30 m
10	Short jumping	4 × 4 × 6 reps or
		4 × 4 × 30 m
11	Short jumping	5 × 4 × 6 reps or
		5 × 4 × 30 m
12	Short jumping	2 × 6 reps

Free-Weight Exercises

The following free-weight exercises will help develop a long jumper's explosive strength, or power.

Squat Movements

Back squat
- full
- half-jump
- static dynamic

Front squat
- full
- static dynamic

Pull Movements

Cleans
- midthigh pull
- below-knee pull
- full pull
- clean from midthigh
- clean from below the knee
- full clean

Snatches
- midthigh pull
- below-knee pull
- full pull
- snatch from midthigh
- snatch from below the knee
- full snatch

Press Movements

Bench

Incline

Behind-the-neck-press
- seated
- push

Jerk
- split
- power

Medicine Ball Exercises

Using a medicine ball can also be an effective way to develop the upper and lower body.

Upper Body

Week one, do 10 repetitions of the following exercises. Week two, do 15 repetitions. Week three, do 20 repetitions. Week four, do 15 repetitions.

Chest pass

Overhead pass

Underhand pass

Seated rotations

Kneeling pass

Seated roll back-and-up pass (Athlete holds the medicine ball overhead, rolls back with feet coming up, rolls back up to a sitting position, then tosses the ball.)

Seated cross-body scoop

Side-overhead-extension pass

Bend-over between-legs pass

Lower Body

Thigh bounces

Foot passes

Heel passes

Leg-raise rollover—put back

Seated quad lifts

Lying hamstring lifts

"Fire" balls

Ninety-degree "drives"

Types of Workouts

The following are different types of workouts that should be incorporated into your athletes' training regimen. Each workout is designed to improve a different aspect of the long jumper's performance.

SPEED ENDURANCE

High oxygen debt and lactic acid buildup with close to full recovery between each run. These workouts' emphasis should be on quality.

Reps × m	Rest
5 × 100	5-10 min.
3 × 150	5-10 min.
2 × 200	10 min.
1 × 400	10 min.

TEMPO ENDURANCE

This aerobic workout will increase oxygen intake, which will shorten recovery time. Tempo workouts are done at a slower pace, which will help the runner learn rhythm. The emphasis should be on quantity, not quality, with rest kept short.

Reps × m	Rest
6 × 200	2 min.
4 × 300	2 min.
50-100-150-200-250-300	Walk the same distance for rest

STRENGTH ENDURANCE

Activities in strength-endurance workouts typically last longer than10 seconds. They include uphill running and resistance type running. The emphasis is on sprint musculature.

> 6 × 100 m hill
>
> 6 × 15-20 sec. resistance running
>
> 2 × (4 × 15-20 sec.) jump rope

POWER SPEED

Power speed workouts emphasize speed of muscle contractions. They are usually done with fewer than 10 repetitions, and no more than 10 seconds per repetition.

> 6-8 × short hill runs 50-60 m
>
> 6-8 × 30 m assistance running
>
> 6-8 × 10 sec. fast rope jumps

ENDURANCE RUNNING

This totally aerobic running workout consists of 15 to 45 minutes of running at a steady pace. Base training.

Developing a Training Program

Keeping these types of workouts in mind, table 10.2 presents a sample training program for long jumpers. The emphasis of each type of workout changes as the season progresses. You can tailor the workouts to meet the needs of your athletes while still maintaining the basic premise.

TABLE 10.2   SAMPLE WORKOUTS

Technique, Speed, and Strength: Weeks 1-4

Day	Workout
Monday	3 × 300 m with 200 m of walk or jog recovery Drills: 3-6 × 60 m of A-skip* and B-skip** 3-6 × 60 m of high knees Event-specific drills Weights
Tuesday	Tempo runs: (+) = 50 m of jog; (−) = 100 m of walk between sets 100 + 100 + 100 − 100 + 200 − 100 + 100 + 200 − 100 + 200 − 100 + 100 + 100 −
Wednesday	Power speed (progresses to power technique): 6 × 20 m of A-skip into 20 m sprint 6 × 20 m of B-skip into 20 m sprint 3 × 60 m of running bounds 6-10 × 50 m Event-specific drills Weights
Thursday	6-8 × 200 m, with 200 m of walk or jog Drills: same as Mon.
Friday	8-10 × 150 m, with 150 m of walk recovery Weights

Speed, Strength, and Endurance: Weeks 5-12

Day	Workout
Monday	2 × 300 m; 1 × 200 m, with 10 m recovery Technique drills/weights
Tuesday	8 × 100 m at 85-90% speed Light technique drills

Wednesday	Jog and stretch/weights
	Event technique
Thursday	3 × 200 m
	Light technique drills
Friday	5 × 150 m at race pace, with full recovery
	Weights
Competitive Phase	
Monday	2 × 200 m fast, with full recovery
	Light technique drills
Tuesday	Full technique drills
	Weights
	6 × 60 m at 60-70%, with full recovery
Wednesday	Jog and stretch
Thursday	3 × 150 m fast
	Technique drills
	Weights
Friday	Rest
Saturday	Competition

* A-skip—skipping in which the free leg swings up until the thigh is parallel to the ground and the heel of the free leg meets the hips then extends down to meet the ground.

** B-skip—same as the A-skip, except that the free leg extends straight forward (as in a Goose Step) before landing.

Summary

As mentioned earlier, it is best to devote the majority of training time for the long jump to developing a technically correct approach and takeoff. This is because of the strong relation between correct technique or execution of the approach run and takeoff and performance of the jump. The various drills and workouts presented in this chapter are meant to enhance one's performance by developing power, speed, and endurance. As we all know, once you're in the air, there's no changing your course. Therefore, you must train hard to develop the consistency necessary to be successful in competition.

Dean Hayes

11 Triple Jump

The triple jump is a unique event requiring a combination of speed, strength, and balance. It is composed of three distinct phases that must flow into one another. They are the hop (taking off and landing on the same foot), the step (landing on the opposite foot), and the jump (performed similar to the long jump). The hop and jump are relatively easy to master, but the step is a difficult skill. The triple jump was formerly called the hop-step-jump, but the name was changed to emphasize the equal importance of each phase.

Triple jumpers must possess above-average ability in sprinting and jumping, and at the same time possess powerful muscles and good motor skills. The program discussed in this chapter is for both the beginning and advanced jumper.

Technique

Proper technique is essential. It is something that triple jumpers will call on time and time again to give themselves an edge in competition. Teaching and reinforcing technical precision early on will make it second nature in competition.

Approach

The triple jump approach should be long enough to allow the jumper to accelerate to nearly full speed. At the same time, the approach must be relaxed so that the jumper is under control. If the approach is too slow, the jumper will lose momentum in the later phases of the event. If it is too fast, the jumper will be unable to control the legs and keep them from collapsing. The length of the run should be 100 to 130 feet (about 30.5 to 39.6 m). The beginning jumper's approach should be about 100 feet (about 30.5 m). As the jumper gains experience and maturity, the approach can be lengthened. Beginning jumpers may wish to use a check mark along the latter part of the approach. As jumpers gain experience, they may prefer using only the beginning mark. The jumper should practice the approach until it is consistent. Approach steps should be worked on just before the competitive season begins.

Hop

The first phase of the triple jump is the hop, and the first part of the hop is the takeoff. The objective in the hop is to go forward and up (not up and forward as in the long jump). This is accomplished by keeping the body upright and rotating the heel of the hop leg high up under the buttocks and then extending it as far forward as possible (see figure 11.1a-c). The idea is for the athlete to feel that he or she is "running off the board." Remind the jumper to stay upright and not look down or lean forward, as the leaning makes it difficult to bring the leg up for the next phase.

There are three methods of arm action:

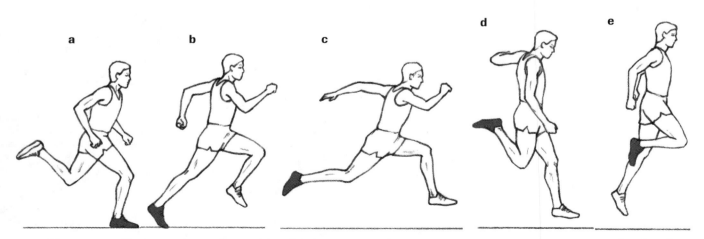

Figure 11.1 The hop and step phases of the triple jump.

(continued)

1. Single-arm action
2. Double-arm action
3. Combination

The combination usually is a single-arm hop and double-arm step and jump. The double arm begins in the last step before the board as the jumper begins the action to get the arms in place for the takeoff. The athlete stops the arm that is going back. He or she stops it at the hip on the takeoff, and then lets it go forward with the other arm so that both arms go forward as the leg rotates under the buttocks. The athlete's hands should not go higher than the chin. If the arms are driven too high, the foot will come down too hard and too fast. A great number of jumpers draw both arms behind the back about one and a half steps before the takeoff board. This is acceptable for beginners, but after some experience it is better if the jumper can change to the previously discussed method. Pulling both arms back tends to slow down the approach just before the board, and the loss of speed at this point hinders the flow of the other phases.

The single-arm method is simply a running motion off the board, as if the jumper is taking one more step, only the "running step" is a hop (figure 11.1).

Select the method of arm action based on the speed of the athlete. As a rough guide, the fast athlete can best use the double-arm method, the jumper of average speed can use whichever method is most comfortable, and the slower athlete usually benefits from single-arm action. The coach and athlete should experiment and use the method best suited to that athlete.

In the hop, the leg should be pulled through for extension; and as the foot is about to land, it should be flattened so that the jumper can "roll" over the foot into the next phase (figure 11.1c). Landing on the toes interrupts speed and flow; landing on the heel can cause heel bruises. Also, a "heel landing" makes it more difficult to control the forward movement. The landing should be very slightly on the heel, followed by a "rolling" action of the foot.

Due to the nature of triple jumping, athletes should wear light, durable shoes with heel cups inserted in them. Constant pounding and landing on the heels necessitates using heel cups to avoid bruises and injuries.

Figure 11.1 *(continued)*

Step

Just before the hop is finished, the arms are pulled back again in preparation for the step—the second phase of the triple jump. The step is accomplished by bringing the other leg (opposite of the hop leg) forward (figure 11.1d-f, pages 160-161). The jumper should strive to get the upper leg perpendicular to the body (hip area) or parallel to the ground. The arms come forward if double-arm action is utilized. If the single-arm method is used, the opposite arm goes forward as in running. Again, the arm(s) should not go higher than the chin.

There are two methods of executing the step. One method is to keep the body upright and the upper body basically perpendicular to the ground. The upper leg is parallel to the ground, and the lower leg is positioned so that the toes are just ahead of the knee. This is done so the jumper can "ride" the leg, or hold it up. At the last instant, the jumper extends the leg and reaches out as far as possible. This extension is aided by pulling the arms back to prepare for double-arm action in the jump phase. Again, the foot should hit the ground almost flat-footed. The heel "barely" leads the action.

The other method for "stepping" is to let the lower leg extend ahead of the knee during the step. This requires the upper chest and head to be stooped slightly forward in an effort to hold the foot up (figure 11.1f-g, page 161). As the foot is extended, or held forward, the arms are drawn behind the back to prepare for the jump phase (figure 11.1h-i, page 161).

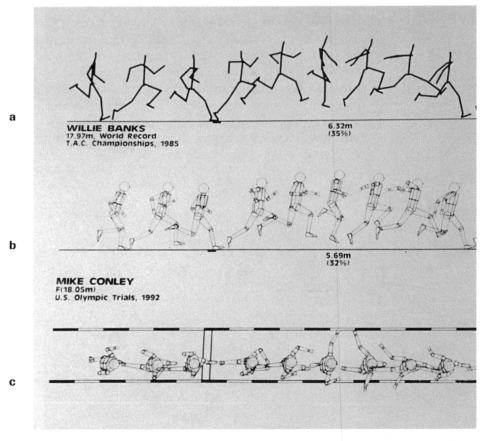

a

WILLIE BANKS
17.97m, World Record
T.A.C. Championships, 1985

6.32m
(35%)

b

5.69m
(32%)

MIKE CONLEY
F(18.05m)
U.S. Olympic Trials, 1992

c

Figure 11.2   Triple jump technique for *(a)* Willie Banks and *(b)* Mike Conley. Part *(c)* shows an overhead view of the triple jump.

Jump

As the jump phase is initiated, the arms are interchanged if the single-arm method is used. If the double-arm method is used, the arms are pulled through with a punch, and the athlete executes a jump similar to that of the long jumper. Generally, a hang style of jump is used because there is not enough time for a hitch-kick.

The jumper should try to get as high as possible, with the arms (both are used in the hang style) reaching up and then extending forward. The feet are extended so that the heels lead the way into the pit.

Figure 11.2 shows the jumps of two of the leading triple jumpers in U.S. history, Willie Banks and Mike Conley:

- Note their single-arm action off the board to maintain speed.
- Note that in the hop and step landing, they land "barely" heel first in an effort to roll into the next phase.
- Note how erect their body is at some early point in the hop and step, the lead with the knee in the step, and the rotation of the hop leg up under the buttocks.
- Note the double-arm action in the step and jump phases.
- Note Conley's lower hop angle to maintain speed. Each phase gets higher.

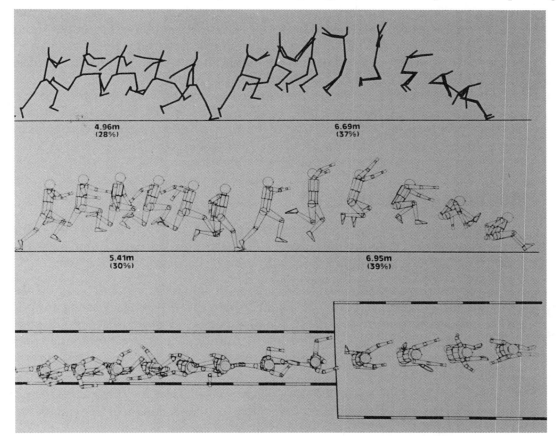

Figure 11.2 *(continued)*

- Note the double-arm hang style in the jump phase.
- Note the effort to lead with the heels into the pit.
- Note the two contrasting (but correct) styles with the arms in the jump phase. In one, the arms drive up high (Conley); and in the other, the hands go in front of the body and back around high over the head (Banks).

Teaching Progression

The triple jump is an unnatural event and should be introduced to prospective jumpers by having them watch films to get a quick preview of the event. Film study should be followed by a brief demonstration of a standing triple jump—emphasizing the leg movements only. Instruct the prospective jumper to do a few standing triple jumps. Jumps should be done with each leg to decide which is most comfortable. Emphasize an even distance for each phase; do not allow the athlete to go for distance. Instead, stress learning the leg movements of each of the three phases. Although a beginner will probably have problems with the flow of the triple jump, it will begin to come after a few attempts. "Flow" is the bounce or rhythm that is so important to good triple jumping. It gives the jumper the exhilarating feeling of flying through the air.

If jumpers do not try to extend their reach too far, they can keep the jump under control and feel encouraged about their progress. Also, this will keep them from leaning too far forward during the jump and give them time to have an active "phase leg." The phase leg should be developed next, by having the jumper stand on one leg and jump up, making the standing leg rotate under the buttocks and reach out in front before landing. The athlete should alternate legs for this drill so that coordination is developed in both legs.

Of the three triple jump phases, the step is the most difficult to master. The hop is relatively easy to perform, but the recovery is difficult. The athlete usually will not have problems learning the basics of the jump phase. The greatest progress in triple jump training will come from improving the step. However, one must remember that each phase is dependent on the others.

Bounding Exercises

The next stage of development comes through bounding exercises. In the beginning, these should be done for control rather than for strength. Later, strength (endurance) can be included. Three main exercises are used in this stage:

1. Hopping exercise. This should be done with both legs (R-R-R-R . . . or L-L-L-L . . .). In the beginning, it is done for about 25 meters with each leg. As the jumper grows stronger and more confident, the distance is increased. Check to be sure that the jumper's body is upright throughout the hopping. It is recommended that beginners do two sets of 25 meters of hopping on Monday, Wednesday, and Friday (three days a week).

2. Step exercise. This is R-L-R-L-R. . . . Again, emphasize the upright body and "bounce" in the legs. The beginner just reaches out as far as he or she can, being careful not to lead with the toes. The landing is flat-footed, with a "pawing" action just before the foot strikes the ground.

3. Hop-to-step exercise. This exercise helps the jumper in changing from the hop to the step. The drill is R-R-L-L-R-R. . . . The coach should watch the jumper perform these exercises. Also, it is beneficial if two or more jumpers work together, as the competition tends to make the jumpers run faster and stretch farther. The triple jumper works on the jump phase by doing pop-ups, just like the long jumper. The pop-up should be done from a short approach and using the hang style, since the time in the air is too short for a good hitch-kick.

Running and Jumping Exercises

The next step in developing the triple jumper is to incorporate a short run with the jump. Two exercises are helpful here:

1. The first drill is running over low hurdles. This is done at least twice a week. The hurdles should be spaced at high-hurdle distance and "three-stepped."

2. In the second exercise, the athlete should attempt to jump low hurdles spaced apart to allow an even distribution, or the hop, the step, and the jump. The athlete should use a three- or five-step approach. This gives some speed but not enough to cause a total breakdown of the step phase. Emphasize a "level flight" during each phase, keeping the body upright. If the jumper gets too high in a phase, the landing leg will break down, which curtails momentum for the next phase.

Arm Action

The next step in developing a triple jumper is deciding what type of arm action should be used. Some jumpers use single-arm action in the hop to maintain speed, and use a double-arm action in the step and jump.

At this stage, the athlete should be ready to attempt the complete triple jump. Start with a seven-step approach (under control) and stress the hop phase, with an easy step and jump included. The hop should be relatively short so it does not cause the jumper to break down. Also, the jumper should avoid getting too much height, because this causes a jarring effect and can lead to a breakdown, too. The head should be level, with the eyes focused straight ahead. The athlete should attempt to go through the complete triple jump to learn extension in each of the three phases.

The final phase of instruction is to lengthen the approach. A distance of about 120 feet (about 36.6 m) should be adequate. Use a controlled run to begin with, and increase the speed as the athlete is able to use it.

Training

The training program used is the most important factor in the success of a triple jumper. The program that follows should be used in its entirety. Leaving out one segment will hinder the effectiveness of the program. A good conditioning base is important, and development of the leg and arm skills is necessary. The drills must be done over and over until they become automatic. The triple jumper must develop "thinking feet." Make a special effort to develop the parts of the program where the jumper is weakest. Triple jumpers must train regularly and aggressively in order to compete successfully. However, a well-trained jumper does not leave his or her best jumps on the practice field.

Drills

The following drills may be used as part of your overall training program.

Standing Triple Jump

The athlete faces the long jump/triple jump pit and places a mark 20–25 feet (about 6.1–7.6 m) from the pit. From the mark, the jumper does a standing triple jump and lands in the pit. Next, mark off the hop distance, the step distance, and the jump distance. Concentrate on knee drive for the hop and step, and arm action (both arms driving) for the jump. The distance should be 8–10 feet (about 2.4–3 m) for the hop, 11–13 feet (about 3.4–4 m) for the step, and 12–15 feet (about 3.7–4.6 m) for the jump. Anything between 30 and 38 feet (about 9.1–11.6 m) is a good distance for beginners for men. Women's distance should be proportional.

Hurdle Hopping

Four to eight low or intermediate hurdles are placed five to six feet (about 1.5–1.8 m) apart. The jumper, with the aid of the double-arm upswing, leaps over the hurdles with both legs together and with the knees brought up to the chest in order to clear the hurdle. As strength increases, the height and the number of hurdles can be increased. Adjust hurdle height and the distance between the hurdles for individual jumpers. Beginners will likely have difficulty with intermediate hurdles.

Split-Squat

This is a squat jump in which the legs are alternated. Disregard arm action because this is not a triple jump action. Bring front knee up close to about a 90-degree angle, with a slight bend in the back leg. Then alternate legs.

Double-Leg Jump

Drive off both legs with the use of the knees and ankles. As soon as the jumper is off the ground, the left knee is driven up as high as possible, beyond parallel. Land on both feet. Settle down and drive right back up this time, lifting the right knee as high as possible. Keep the foot under the knee while using arms vigorously.

Hopping Drill

Stay on the same leg, with a single-arm action (unless double-arm action is normally used). As the jumper lifts off the jumping leg, he or she brings the thigh to parallel and, as that leg returns to the ground, the opposite knee comes from the behind (split) position and forward as it would in the step phase.

The following three drills are the core of the triple jump training program. These drills help the jumper to learn to perform each phase of the triple jump correctly. At the same time, the drills give the jumper the thrill of competing. The drills emphasize each phase and the movement from one phase to the next.

Bench Drill #1

The benches are 12 inches (about 30.5 cm) wide so that good foot placement can be taught. They are 18 inches (about 46 cm) high. The jumper "bounces up" on to the bench and then drives off. The sequence of this drill is hop-step-hop-step-hop-jump (figure 11.3). Alternate the starting leg so that both legs are developed equally.

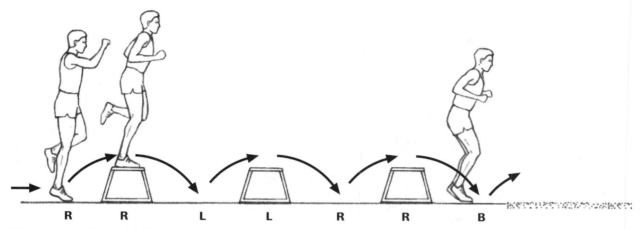

Figure 11.3 Bench drill #1.

Bench Drill #2

The second drill develops the step phase and encourages a "bounce" action. This drill has the jumper stepping over the benches with another alternate step between the benches. (See figure 11.4.) The step between benches is a real "jump step." The legs can be reversed in this drill, too.

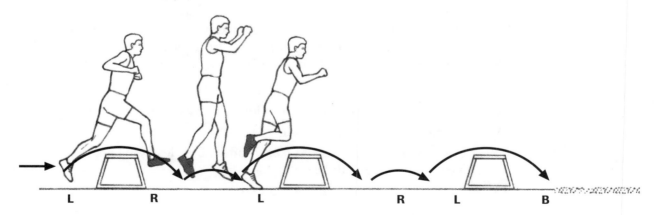

Figure 11.4 Bench drill #2.

Bench Drill #3

The third drill is a pop-up drill (figure 11.5). The athlete runs to and then jumps off of the bench into the pit. It requires only a short run and therefore does not fatigue the jumper. In fact, a five-step approach can be used for *all* the drills.

Each of the drills ends with the jump phase into the landing pit. The heels lead the jumper into the pit.

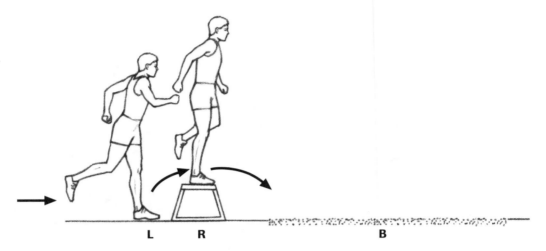

Figure 11.5   Bench drill #3.

Weight Training

Weight training is a major portion of the triple jumper's training routine. Proper lifting techniques should be followed. The athlete should begin with a very light weight and increase the weight gradually. Weights should be lifted regularly—at least three times a week. As training progresses, workouts should be more intense. Athletes should be tired after weight training, but they should not be totally exhausted. If the weight workout is too difficult, the athlete's jumping workouts will be adversely affected.

Table 11.1 is a weight routine recommended for triple jumpers. The following guidelines should be followed in the weight-lifting program for jumpers:

- Lift every other day.
- Alternately work the upper body and lower body during workouts.
- Wear a weight belt for heavy lifting.
- Lift in a group. Athletes must help each other. Besides being safer, this adds incentive to "lift more with less effort."
- Do not increase the poundage too quickly.
- Periodically schedule a testing session in which maximum lifts are used to test increases in strength.
- It is best to use free weights in training because balance is learned and stress is put on the athlete through a greater range of motion. Weight machines are recommended for younger athletes or large groups since poundages can be easily changed.
- Jumpers must stretch and loosen up before the weight workout.

TABLE 11.1 WEIGHT-TRAINING WORKOUTS FOR JUMPERS

Exercise	Sets × Reps
Knee extensions	3 × 10
Leg curls	3 × 10
Incline sit-ups	3 × 15
Leg presses	4 × 10, 7, 4, 2
Toe raises	3 × 20 [using a two-inch by four-inch (about 5 cm by 10 cm) board under the toes]
Half-squats	3 × 8 (use one-half of body weight)
Split-squats	2 × 10 (use one-fourth of body weight)
Knee raises	3 × 15
Step-ups	3 × 10 (with heavy weight)

Half-squats and split-squats are coordinated in two-week periods. Squats are done M-W-F, and split-squats are done W-M-F.

Developing a Training Program

As in all other track and field events, the type of exercises, the number of reps, and the level of intensity differs during each part of the season. The key is to develop a program that allows athletes to peak during top competitions. Table 11.2 presents a sample training program for triple jumpers. The early season workouts emphasize volume running and physical conditioning, while the in-season workouts prepare the body for key competitions.

TABLE 11.2 SAMPLE WORKOUTS FOR TRIPLE JUMPERS

Early Season (Fall)	
	In the early season, utilize lots of volume running, such as 8 × 300 meters, 10 × 200 meters, or 6 × 400 meters. Use a long grass run of 5 miles at least once per week. Do an abundance of hill running and stretching. The jumper must be in good physical condition before the beginning of the regular training program. The triple jump is a very physically demanding event.
Monday	Grass run (3-5 miles)
	100-200-300-400-200-100/jog same
	Weights
Tuesday	10 × 200 m, with 200 interval
	Run stadium steps with weight jacket
	Do easy takeoff drills (just to get the arm technique)

(continued)

(continued)

Early Season (Fall)		
Wednesday		8 × 300 m, with 300 interval
		6 × 75 m easy
		Weights
Thursday		Grass run
		Run stadium steps
		Takeoff drill
Friday		Grass run
		Weights
In Season		
		Here is the workout schedule for the remainder of the year. This routine can be varied according to faults or weaknesses found in the jumper's technique. Skip one weight training session before a big meet, such as the conference or state meet. The same is true for bench workouts.
Monday		Bounding: 3 × 25-100 m of hopping. Use the regular hopping leg twice and the other leg once. If an athlete is having trouble making the transition from one phase to the other, he or she should use 3 × 50 m of R-R-L-L-R-R, as this incorporates the bounding and adds practice of changing from the hop to the step. Also, this drill helps to improve the capabilities of each leg.
		Running: 2 × 300 m for endurance; 6 × 75 m for speed.
		Weight lifting
Tuesday		This is a "drill" day:
		Bench work—do 6 good drills of each of the 3 exercises.
		Run 10 × 3 low hurdles set at high-hurdle spacing (10 yards between). This is for rhythm and evenness of steps on the runway. It also teaches aggressiveness.
		Run 6 × 100 m or work on the actual approach. Run stadium steps. Our athletes use a weight jacket and run stadium steps 5 times. If steps are not available, use a hill. This is a good day to practice the actual triple jump takeoff. This is done at a reduced speed, but correct techniques are stressed—especially the correct arm action.
Wednesday		Use the same basic workout as Monday, but use running of 5 × 25 m, 5 × 35 m, and 5 × 50 m.
Thursday		The same workout as on Tuesday.
Friday		Same as Monday, except much more relaxed and easy.

Competition

The season itself is just a means of testing the progress of the jumper. If the jumper also long jumps, it is probably best to take only three long jumps and three triple jumps if both are on the same day. If one achieves a big personal best, it is usually better to skip the next jump to collect oneself. Also, train as regularly as possible, easing up in training only in the two to four practice sessions preceding the peak event of the year. Finally, remember that your jumpers' aim is to do their best, not worry about their place in the competition.

Summary

With solid practice habits, triple jumpers should feel confident in their ability. Let your athletes know that their goal is to do their best in a certain meet, not achieve a certain distance. Remember to work on the parts of the jump that give the athlete the most trouble. Repeating the things the athletes can do well doesn't give them the help they need. Practice hard so you know your jumpers are ready.

12 High Jump

Sue Humphrey
Doug Nordquist

The high jump was revolutionized in the late 1960s by Dick Fosbury when he "backed" over the bar to an Olympic gold medal in Mexico City. A bit later, on the female side, Canadian Debbie Brill was experimenting with the "Brill bend," a backover style similar to Fosbury's. The uniqueness of these styles adds to the beauty of the high jump for the spectators. Speed and power are required of the jumper as heights are over eight feet for the men and pushing toward seven feet for the women.

Twenty-eight years after Fosbury's Olympic gold medal, Americans were treated to another one in Atlanta when Charles Austin won and set a new Olympic record of 7 feet, 10 inches. Bulgarian Stefka Kostadinova added the gold medal to her world-record performances as she dominated the women's competition during the 1990s.

As biomechanical studies provide ongoing statistical data to coaches and jumpers, athletes continue to push themselves to greater heights through better training both on and off the field. The ceiling on this event is continually being raised!

Technique

With the advent of the foam landing pit, the high jump was changed forever. The soft and safe landing surface allowed Dick Fosbury to develop his revolutionary back-layout technique. Since its successful use in the 1968 Olympics, the "Fosbury flop" has dominated the world high jump scene. The reasons for this are many: it enables the jumper to utilize the speed that can be generated in the approach run-up; the rotations developed in the takeoff are used to the advantage of the jumper; it enables the jumper to clear the bar in an easy and efficient manner; and the basic technique can be mastered with relative ease for early success.

The technical aspects of the jump can be broken down into three basic phases:

1. Approach
2. Takeoff
3. Bar clearance

Approach

The approach is probably the most neglected portion of the high jump, and probably the easiest aspect to isolate and improve. Many, many high jumpers, from young to world class, have major problems with the approach. These athletes spend more workout time with the takeoff phase and the bar clearance phase because they believe them to be most important. This is an inefficient use of time and effort. To understand why, think backward from bar clearance. Bar clearance is affected by the height of the center of mass in the parabolic arc, as well as by the resultant rotations over the bar. Both of these are influenced by the takeoff, which is the result of the body position at touchdown. The body position at touchdown is influenced by the approach. This is why the approach is so important. If the athlete cannot arrive at a consistent takeoff point with an optimum amount of speed, developed through a consistent step-by-step acceleration, the approach is not being used effectively. Thus, the jumper is not going to achieve the maximum amount of vertical lift at the takeoff, or the proper amount of resultant rotations.

Length of the Approach

The approach should be long enough to develop a nice rhythm and generate adequate speed for the takeoff. The approach length is usually 8 to 12 running strides (during this chapter we will refer to a 10-step approach as the norm). The path of the curve should be a modified J, which allows the body to get into the proper position (lean) at the takeoff (figure 12.1). Although a 10-step approach is probably the average, the approach can be as short as 7 steps, with a run-in, or as long as 12 steps from a standing start. Phase one of the approach starts with the first three to four steps in a straight line, followed by a three-to-four-step transition to the last four steps, which curve gradually toward the near standard. The touchdown (sometimes called the plant) should be at the near standard to provide a solid, visible, and consistent landmark for the placement of the touchdown foot.

Layout

The layout of the path of the modified J approach is important. The athlete needs to have a "straight-ahead" mark to focus on during the initial portion of the run-up.

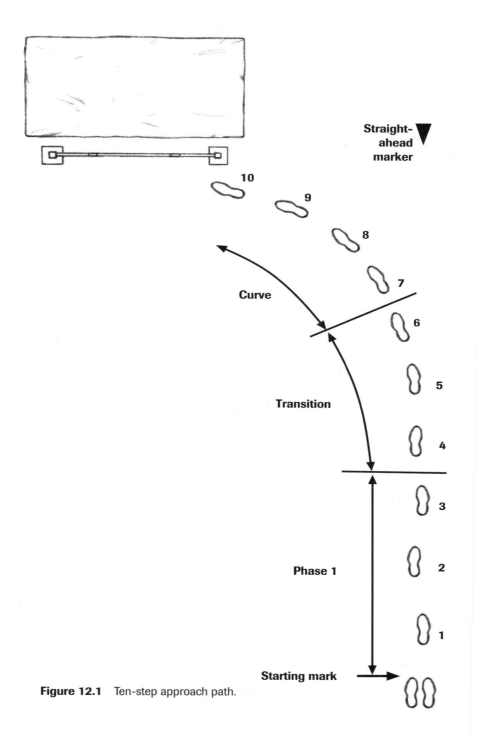

Figure 12.1 Ten-step approach path.

An initial mark can be established by having the athlete measure out from the near standard, and parallel to the bar, 15 of his or her own feet, in a heel-to-toe manner (figure 12.2 on page 176). The marker that is then placed will be 10–16 feet (about 3–4.9 m) from the near standard, on an imaginary continuation of the line of the bar. This distance will vary from athlete to athlete; the taller, stronger, faster athletes will be using a wider radius, and so the straight-ahead mark will be farther away from the near standard than the mark for a shorter, younger athlete.

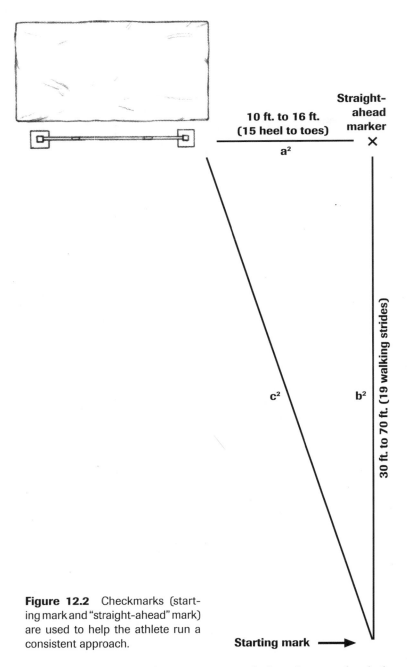

10 ft. to 16 ft. (15 heel to toes)

Straight-ahead marker

a^2

$\times$

c^2

b^2

30 ft. to 70 ft. (19 walking strides)

Starting mark ⟶

Figure 12.2 Checkmarks (starting mark and "straight-ahead" mark) are used to help the athlete run a consistent approach.

The athlete should then walk out 19 walking strides perpendicular (90-degree angle) to the imaginary line continuing straight out from the bar (figure 12.2). This starting mark will be anywhere between 40 and 70 feet (about 12.2–21.3 m) from the straight-ahead marker, depending, again, on the athlete. This will give the athlete an approximate starting mark for a 10-step approach. Standing at this starting mark and facing the straight-ahead marker, the jumper will start running at the straight-ahead marker by pushing off with his or her takeoff foot. The athlete will continue to run for three or four steps at the straight-ahead marker, then gradually curve toward the near standard and past the bar (figure 12.3). If the takeoff foot's touchdown is well inside the standard, move the starting position back; if the takeoff foot's touchdown is well outside of the standard, move the starting point up. This "trial and error" method is the only way to fine-tune the approach. If necessary, use check marks in the approach to help the athlete to run a consistent and proper-shaped approach. Remove the marks as soon as possible so that the athlete will be able to focus attention on other aspects of the approach.

Once a consistent starting position is developed, which may take several workout sessions, measure the starting point with a tape measure. Use the Pythagorean theorem ($a^2 + b^2 = c^2$) to triangulate the approach viewpoints: one corner being the standard, the second corner being the straight-ahead mark, and the third being the starting point. This will allow the approach to be the same at each venue at which the athlete will compete. Don't be afraid to make slight adjustments, up or back, based on facility conditions, athlete freshness/fatigue, or weather conditions. As the season progresses, the approach length will increase as the athlete's strength and speed increase and as his or her comfort and confidence in the approach grows.

Consistency

One of the most important aspects of the approach is consistency. Consistency in running mechanics, stride length and frequency, the line (shape) of the curve, and

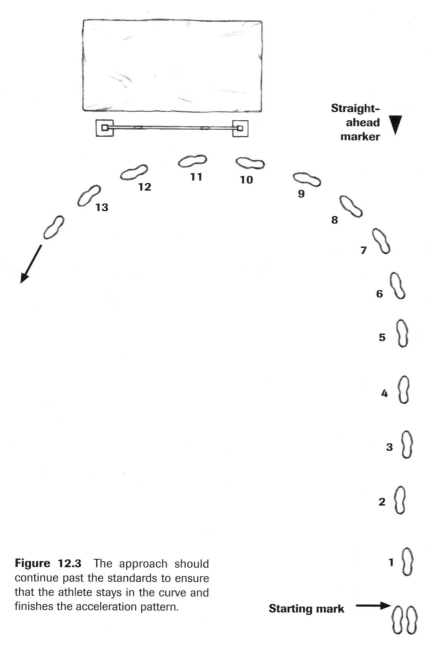

Straight-ahead marker ▼

Starting mark →

Figure 12.3 The approach should continue past the standards to ensure that the athlete stays in the curve and finishes the acceleration pattern.

the acceleration pattern are all necessary for a consistent approach. The jumper wants to have the touchdown foot in the same place in relationship to the near standard every time. This is developed through repetitive running of the approach without jumping.

One way to check consistency is by timing the athlete's approach. Start as the first step leaves the ground and stop at the touchdown. Keep a log of each jump, with approach times and the result and quality of each effort. This gives immediate feedback to the coach and athlete by allowing comparison between good and bad jumps. In a meet situation, this will allow the coach to identify if the athlete's approach speed is too fast or slow and advise the athlete accordingly.

Good running mechanics are necessary to a consistent approach. The approach stride is similar to that of a quarter-miler, relaxed but powerful, running with an upright posture. These good running mechanics must be developed away from the high jump apron through the use of interval training on the track and must be constantly reinforced in drills as well as on the high jump apron.

Beginning Approach

For the approach to be consistent, step one needs to be consistent. If the first step is only two inches off, by the tenth step that could be magnified to over a foot and a half in either direction! Many approach problems can be rectified with a consistent first step. Whether the athlete starts from a standing position or is moving into the starting mark, step one needs to be a solid, deliberate, upright, and powerful running stride. This will set up a dynamic pattern of stretch reflexes in the muscles, which allows for more powerful contractions, thus a stronger takeoff. Consistency is developed by eliminating variables.

Steps two, three, and four are in a straight line toward the marker. The arm and knee actions are exaggerated. The athlete is running in an upright manner. The eyes are focused on the straight-ahead marker. The acceleration rhythm is started here. Be sure each of these steps is slightly faster than the previous one.

A common problem with jumpers is that they will either cut in or swing the approach path out wide instead of running straight at the straight-ahead marker. This can be seen by the coach from directly behind the athlete (figure 12.4). Both changes in the line of the approach adversely affect the radius of the curve. You can rectify this problem by reinforcing that the eyes are to focus on the straight-ahead marker.

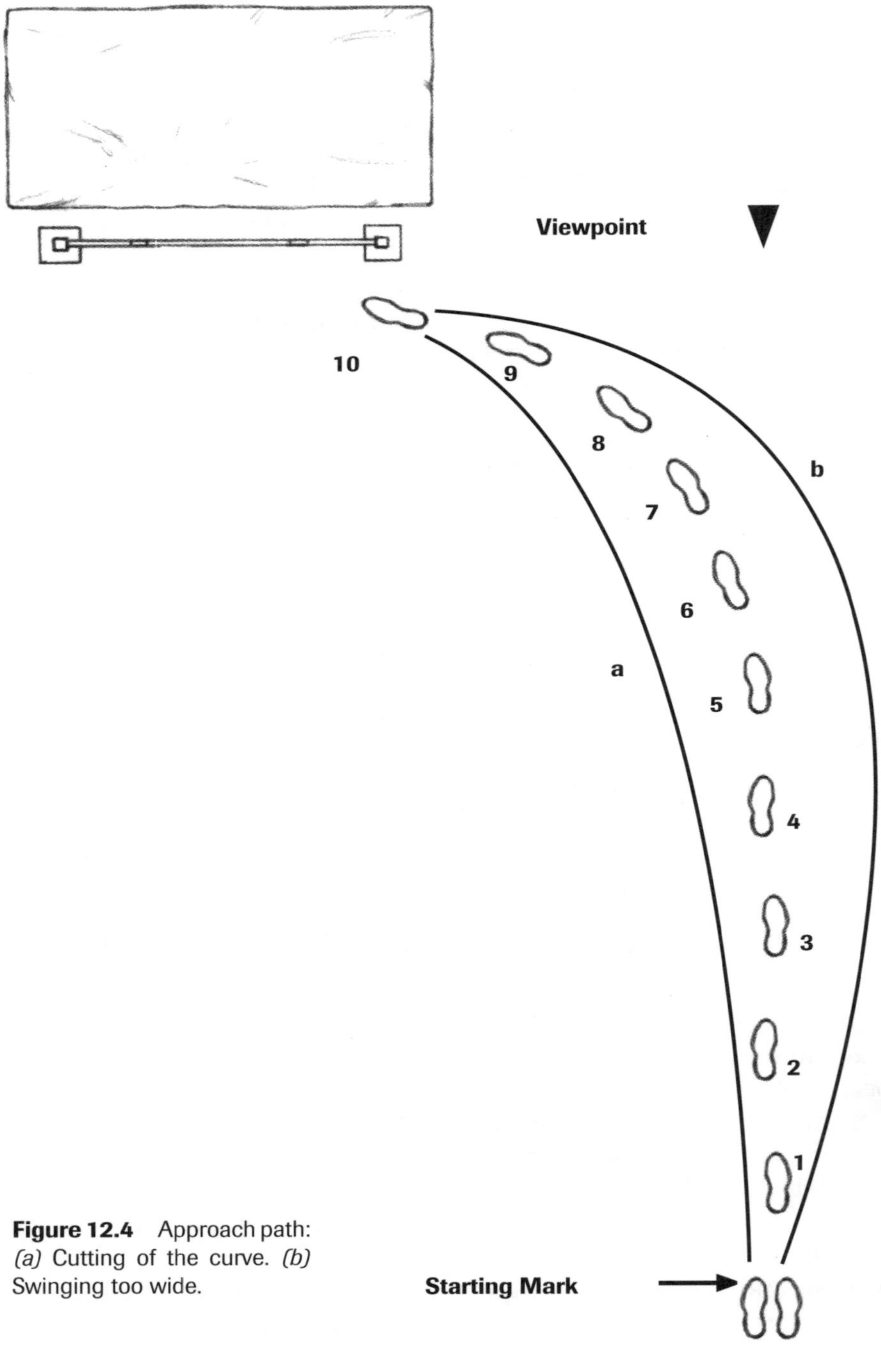

Figure 12.4 Approach path: (a) Cutting of the curve. (b) Swinging too wide.

Transition

Another key aspect of the approach is called the *transition*. Transition will occur in three steps when the jumper moves from the straight-line segment of the approach to the curved segment of the approach. This transition happens over steps four, five, and six (in the 10-step approach). There should be no visual point where the jumper starts the curve. On step four the athlete should gradually shift his or her eye focus toward the near standard. This will start the displacement of the center of mass slightly into the center of the developing curve. Step five, being the outside foot, should cross over the centerline just slightly. The eye focus should now be on the near standard. Step six should continue around the curve with an even more pronounced lean. The eye focus will then move to the far standard. The lean becomes more visible as the center of mass is displaced further inside the curving line of the feet until the point of takeoff. Remember, this lean comes from the ankle and not the waist. The athlete should maintain an erect running posture.

More important than the foot on which the curve is initiated is that it be a smooth transition. A common mistake here is to make step five a "cut" toward the bar (like a post pattern in football). This must be avoided because it will take away the lean at the takeoff (the importance of this will be discussed in the takeoff section), since the jumper will be running straight at the bar without a curve to the touchdown. This problem is easily viewed from behind the athlete in the approach or when standing at the straight-ahead marker looking toward the starting marker. Teaching the athlete to cross over with step five will keep him or her from stepping out of the curve with the outside foot (step five on a 10-step approach), and so keep him or her from making a "cut" to the bar.

Curve

The last four steps in the approach are on a curve. This is one of the hardest aspects of the approach to execute. A properly run curve enables several things. Primarily, the curved approach is what generates the rotations through the jumper's body, allowing the proper bar clearance. Second, it allows the jumper to jump vertically (straight up) and still land safely in the pit. Third, it will increase the force that the athlete applies on the ground. Finally, the curve helps the athlete to lower the body's center of mass prior to the jump. Be sure that the athlete is leaning in to the center of the curve from the ankles and not the hip.

Eyes are focused on the junction between the bar and the far standard. Do not allow the jumper to focus on the middle of the bar because it will take him or her out of the curve. Also, do not allow the jumper to look down at the takeoff point, since that will cause him or her to lean forward.

As the athlete is running the approach, have him or her run the curve past both of the standards and not into the pit. This will keep the athlete in the curve through the touchdown, reinforcing the proper body lean at touchdown. It will also build the habit of not going under the bar, which may save a jump in a meet. A good drill for staying in the curve is to run in circles (12–15 feet in radius) while focusing on running mechanics and posture. Do this as part of the warm-up process. Start slowly, and gradually increase the running speed as long as the mechanics don't change.

Practicing the Approach

After the approach has become comfortable, start to increase the approach speed. The approach should start deliberately, and then the speed should gradually increase all the way to the takeoff. This gradual acceleration is important, since the ability of the athlete to convert the horizontal velocity (speed) to vertical velocity (lift) is the single biggest advantage of the flop style of high jumping. The approach speed needs to be at its peak at the takeoff, so deceleration during the last few steps is detrimental to the jump. Be careful not to allow the athlete to shorten the strides while picking up the tempo of the approach run. Listen to the rhythm of the feet during the approach; each step should be slightly faster than the previous steps, while keeping the stride length the same. The acceleration can be compared to a ball rolling down a ramp, gradually increasing its speed over the length of the ramp.

The approach needs to be run over and over again. There is no other way to develop a consistent approach. Start training the approach without jumping in the early season and continue through to the week of the "big meet." The time constraints for the training of school-aged jumpers does not change the facts—repetition here is the only way! Patience will pay off later in the season. The good jumpers have consistent, gradually accelerating approaches that were developed through a great deal of approach-work repetition. Practicing the approach without jumping will help your jumpers to develop the consistency needed to jump high.

Remember to work the acceleration; listen to the rhythm of the feet. If the athlete is slowing down over the last three steps, have him or her start the approach more slowly to facilitate the pattern of acceleration. Once the pattern is set, have the athlete start a little faster, but be sure that the acceleration pattern remains. Also, have the athlete try not to break the plane of the bar after the last step. This will help to maintain the lean all the way to the touchdown. Not decelerating until the far standard is passed will help maintain the acceleration to the touchdown. To develop a consistent approach, run the approach, run the approach, and then run it again!

If the athlete is having a hard time maintaining the approach fundamentals when jumping, do not be afraid to lower the bar—even as low as three or four feet. This will allow the jumper to focus on the approach phase and not the height of the bar.

The Last Few Steps

As we discussed earlier, the rhythm over the last three steps must happen fast! But it must also put the athlete in the proper takeoff position. Step eight should be a normal running stride. As the athlete moves to step nine, the *penultimate step,* he or she prepares for the touchdown. At step nine, the jump foot is already moving forward in a sweeping motion to the touchdown point.

The rhythm is quite important. The rhythm of steps eight, nine, and ten should have the same rhythm as in speaking the words "day, today," or the rhythm of a skipping motion (L LR RL LR etc.). This rhythm is implemented as you run through step nine to quicken step ten.

Now remember, the important thing is to start slow. Start by jogging through the rhythm of the last three steps slowly in a straight line. It will feel awkward and mechanical at first, but with time and practice it will become more natural. (I used to practice the last three steps walking between classes in high school; it looked weird, but it worked). Once you feel comfortable with the last three steps, speed up the jog. Work for fluidity in movement while exaggerating each movement. When this is consistent, move the tempo up to a slow run in a straight line. Again, make it look smooth, with exaggerated movements while maintaining the rhythm. Now, run the drill in a curve. Remember that the last step is fast. The touchdown foot should "sweep" quickly into position, not cycle near the buttocks. As you progress with this drill, try to jump straight up and land in the same place from which you took off.

Now it's time to add the last aspect of the jump to the drill—lowering the center of mass. In order to jump up, the athlete must lower the center of mass prior to leaving the ground. This must happen gradually in the high jump. The lowering of the center of mass is from the hips and not the shoulders. It will be a gradual lowering over the last four to five steps and not an immediate drop on step ten. This lowering is only about an inch total over the last four steps. If the athlete's leg feels as if it is going to buckle, the last step is too short or the athlete has lowered too much. On the last step, the more obtuse, or straighter, the angle of the knee, the stronger the leg will be. Work on placing the foot softly with a sweeping motion of this fast, soft, last step. The normal progression for developing this aspect of the jump is anywhere from two to three months to maybe a year.

Now, when the first jumps are taken, *don't change anything!* Keep the bar low and concentrate on executing the run. Once the approach is solid, then, and only then, move the bar up. Each jump session should start with several approaches to pattern the rhythm and acceleration. This is a never-ending process of developing and refining. Be patient and don't shortchange this aspect of the total high jump. This is where the average athlete has an advantage over those jumpers that have great "hops" but nothing else. And if that athlete has a great hop—look out!

Takeoff

In the last section on the approach phase, we mentioned the importance of a consistent proper foot placement at the touchdown in preparation for the takeoff. Remember, once the jumper has left the ground, the maximum height of the center of mass has been determined. That is why the isolation of the touchdown position is quite important.

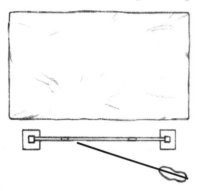

Figure 12.5 The foot should be pointing inside the far standard at takeoff.

Foot Placement

Foot placement is quite important for the safety of the athlete. The foot should touch down about three feet (about .9 m) outside the near standard at an angle that points toward the far standard (figure 12.5). This foot placement angle is a result of the direction of the last step. The foot should never be pointed outside the far standard, this puts too much stress on the ankle and can cause serious ankle injuries. This foot placement position also uses the standard as a solid visual reference, allowing the jumper to see where the foot is to be placed.

Using this point for the takeoff also has several benefits after the jumper has left the ground. It allows the jumper to use all of the pit for safety. And it allows the athlete to pass over the bar in the middle, the lowest point as well as the most forgiving if hit.

Body Lean

For the athlete to jump off the ground, force needs to be applied to the ground. The greater the force, the higher the jump. The takeoff phase of the high jump allows the jumper to transfer the speed (horizontal velocity) generated in the approach to lift (vertical velocity). If the jumper is in the proper body position at touchdown, he or she will be able to efficiently transfer this horizontal velocity to vertical velocity. This speed conversion is where the flop style of high jump has the advantage over the other styles. Basically, the faster a flop high jumper can run and transfer that speed, the higher he or she will jump. This reinforces the importance of acceleration in the approach, referred to in the previous section: the faster the speed at which the athlete completes the acceleration of the approach, the higher he or she will jump.

How does a high jumper manage to jump up while accelerating to the touchdown for the takeoff? Well, this may sound difficult, but it can be done. Remember that one of the big advantages of the flop style of jumping is the conversion of the approach speed to lift. A good "flopper" will convert his or her horizontal velocity (approach speed) to vertical velocity (lift) through applied force to the ground. If we remember our basics, the greater the vertical velocity, the higher the center of mass will travel, thus the higher the jump. How does the jumper change or convert the horizontal velocity to vertical velocity? Body lean!

There are actually two angular components to the proper "lean" at touchdown: backward lean and inward lean (figure 12.6). Lean creates the three rotational forces at the takeoff, which move the body around its center of mass once the jumper has left the ground. The first rotation is a result of the backward lean (as in the long jump), and the second rotation is a result of the inward lean (into the center of the curve and away from the bar). With just about all jumpers, the backward lean component happens naturally. This creates a *forward somersaulting rotation*. This is the rotation that the long jumpers fight with the hitch-kick to prevent them from landing on their face. This is useful as well as desirable in the Fosbury flop. The second component of the lean, the inward lean, is the result of running the proper curve. This component is much more difficult and often

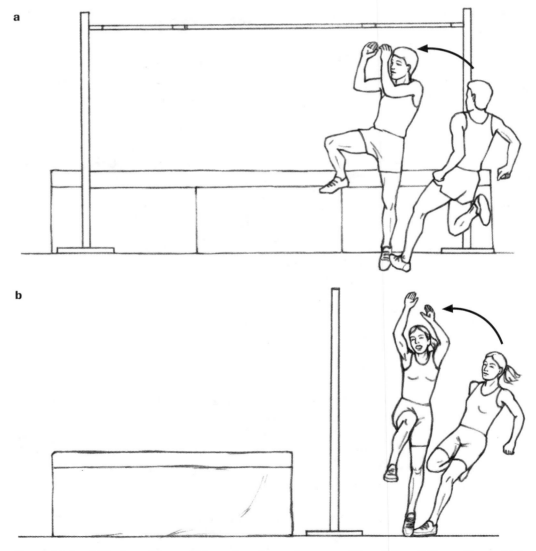

Figure 12.6 *(a)* Backward lean, which creates a forward somersaulting rotation. *(b)* Inward lean, which results in a lateral somersaulting rotation.

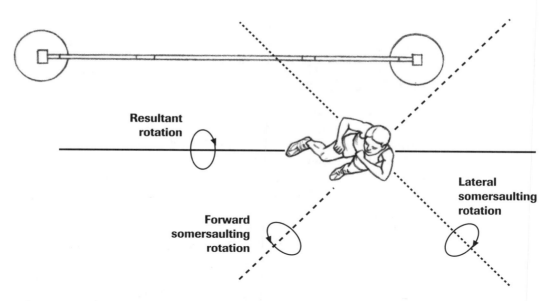

Figure 12.7 The rotations created at takeoff (including forward and lateral somersaulting) dictate the body's movement over the bar, or the *resultant rotation.*

lacking in some jumpers. It creates a *lateral somersaulting rotation,* like a cartwheel. This inward lean allows the athlete to jump straight up and not into the bar, as well as brings about the forces that allow the body to rotate over the bar. The third rotation is the *transverse rotation,* which is like the ballerina's pirouette. This is how the jumper is able to get his or her back to the bar. This rotation is a result of the knee's blocking action. When these three rotations—forward somersaulting, lateral somersaulting, and transverse—are combined, the result is what we see happening to the jumper over the bar, called the *resultant rotation* (figure 12.7). Further discussion of the rotation will have to wait until discussion of the bar clearance phase.

In order to jump *vertically,* the center of mass needs to be directly over the touchdown foot at the point of takeoff. So, at the start of the takeoff phase, the center of mass should be behind and inside the approach circle. This allows the center of mass to continue to travel directly over the foot to the point of takeoff, allowing the jumper to jump vertically. This is sometimes called the "hinge" moment. Without the lean, the center of mass would pass by the vertical takeoff position (the center of mass over the takeoff foot), causing the jumper to jump into the bar. The leaning position at takeoff creates an eccentric thrust, which can develop some rotational forces, but at the cost of vertical velocity. Jumping straight up at the takeoff is important in the *high* jump. If a photograph is taken just before the moment the foot leaves the ground, the jumper should be completely vertical.

If the curve in the approach is executed correctly, the athlete does not need to think about jumping into the landing pit. The jumper's center of mass will continue on a straight-line path, tangential to the curve, into the landing pit—just as when a yo-yo swung above your head and let go travels in a line tangent to the curved path away from the center of the arc. The jumper that stays in the curve and "hits the vertical" at takeoff will get the maximum height over the bar, and still land safely in the pit. Most young jumpers do not execute this phase correctly and jump into the bar, thinking that's necessary to make it to the landing pit. A jumper can get away with this only as long as the bar height is below his or her standing height. So, it is important to teach the correct lean from the beginning, to quell this habit early in the jumper's development.

Blocking Action

The use of the arms and free leg are another important aspect of the takeoff phase of the high jump. These three limbs combine for what is called "blocking," a stopping of one or more body parts to accelerate another. The more efficient and aggressive the block, the more force is applied and the higher the jump. First let's address the free, or "drive," leg. The free leg should move through as fast and as high as possible; the toe should not drag on the ground. The thigh should be at least parallel to the ground, if not higher. The thigh should also finish parallel to the bar. The knee *should not* be driven across the body to rotate the back to the bar (transverse rotation); although, if the curve is run properly, this may seem to be happening. Remember, if the jumper is running the curve to the touchdown properly, the free leg will have to start behind and inside the touchdown foot and move in a circular path around the touchdown leg. This will create enough transverse rotation to get the back to the bar. If the last portion of the curve is flat, or straight, the jumper will then need to manufacture this transverse rotation by driving the knee across the body. *This action will disrupt the vertical line of forces in the body, moving the arm into the bar and knee away from the bar and causing a break at the hip and loss of precious height over the bar.*

The arms, too, are part of the blocking action. Actually two types of arm blocking actions can be used, single-arm or double-arm blocks. There are advantages and disadvantages to each. Both will be discussed.

In the double-arm block, at the touchdown both arms are as far back as possible and move through together and stop abruptly, with the forearm at shoulder level and the hands high. Getting the arms back with a minimum amount of effort and disruption to the run-up is important. There are two effective methods of achieving this. The least disruptive way of getting both arms back is to keep the inside arm (the left arm for the left-footed jumper) moving normally throughout the approach and hold the outside arm (the right arm for the left-footed jumper) back on the penultimate step. This action should be walked through slowly many times to pattern the correct movements. The advantage of this method is that there is a minimal amount of disruption to approach-running mechanics, so that it is easier to maintain the acceleration pattern all the way through the takeoff. The disadvantage is that it is not as powerful as the "swim."

The "swim" method of getting both arms back for the double-arm blocking motion is to have the arms together in front of the body on the penultimate step, then pulling them both back together in preparation for takeoff; it looks like the breaststroke. This method has the advantage of being more dynamic and results in a more powerful blocking motion. The disadvantage is that it is a greater disruption of approach-running mechanics; so the athlete is more apt to slow to the takeoff.

The single-arm block is also used by many successful jumpers. The arms do not stop moving throughout the approach. On the penultimate step, the inside arm is forward, and stays forward and reaches high as the outside arm continues forward through the takeoff. The advantage of this method is that there is no change in the approach-running mechanics; so it is easier to maintain the approach acceleration through the takeoff. It also allows the center of mass to be higher at the point of takeoff. But the disadvantage is that the inside arm is usually reached out toward the bar, causing the athlete to miss the vertical takeoff position and to jump into the bar. This is a big problem for the young jumper as the bar goes higher.

The last thing to discuss on the subject of arm blocking is the shoulder angle to the bar during the takeoff. The shoulders should be at least perpendicular (at a right angle) to the bar but better turned slightly away, showing the back to the bar slightly. This will help the jumper attain vertical position at the takeoff. It also aids in the rotation over the bar. This change in the shoulder angle should be done at the touchdown and not before.

Bar Clearance

As we have discussed, once the jumper leaves the ground, the flight path of the center of mass has already been determined. The body will rotate around the center of mass in its predetermined parabolic path. The athlete can only speed up or slow down these rotations by moving his or her limbs. Again, this is why most attention to technique must be on the aspects preceding takeoff. The conservation of momentum will allow the jumper to speed up the rotation by shortening the levers—that is, by moving the arms and legs closer to the center of mass. Conversely, the rotations can be slowed down by lengthening the levers—that is, by moving the arms and legs away from the center of mass.

Head and Shoulders

As the body (center of mass) rises, the rotations created at takeoff will dictate the body's movement around the bar. As the jumper leaves the ground, the takeoff leg is kept low, and the blocking knee stays up. The head is balanced on the shoulders, not at all tilted into the bar. If the head is looking at the bar, the shoulder and hip on that side will drop.

The head and back should pass the bar first, with the back flat to the bar and the shoulders approaching parallel to the bar. Again, the head should be balanced on the shoulders, looking up.

Hips

As soon as the shoulders pass the bar, they should be lowered (some say "head back"), causing the hips and buttocks to rise as they approach the bar. This is the "arch" over the bar. This is where the rotation needs to be the fastest, so the feet should be as close to the buttocks as possible and the arms at the athlete's side. This combination of the short-lever, tight-body position (arch) and the rotation generated through the takeoff phase will allow the jumper's hips to rise sufficiently to clear the bar (figure 12.8).

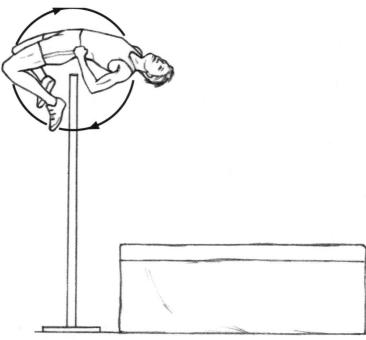

Figure 12.8   Rotation over the bar.

One misconception is that if the jumper hits the bar with the buttocks at the "un-arch" phase or drags the bar off with the calves, he or she needs to "hold the arch longer" or "kick the feet harder." This is commonly bad advice, since both problems are usually caused by a lack of rotation at the point of takeoff. Telling a jumper to hold the arch longer is almost like telling him or her to hang in the air longer—it can't be done, because of the forces acting upon the body. If the athlete has the proper rotation, the hips will continue to rise as the athlete clears the bar. But a lack of rotation will cause the jumper to appear to be "shot" in midair and drop "dead" on the bar.

Legs and Feet

As the hips clear the bar, the hamstrings need to be raised. This is done by lowering the hips. The athlete should bring the chin to the chest, lowering the hips and so raising the hamstrings. This will simultaneously raise the knees, putting them in the proper position to clear the feet. With the knees up, straightening the legs will clear the feet. As the athlete continues to descend toward the pit, the rotation needs to be slowed; so the athlete will keep the legs straight and extend the arms out away from the body. The jumper should land in the pit on the upper back, not the neck, to ensure a safe landing.

Training

The high jump is an explosive, powerful event that calls for primarily anaerobic training. Even though a broad conditioning base is needed, the event is based upon speed, power, and a quick conversion from horizontal speed to vertical lift.

Warm-Up

Traditional warm-ups begin with a walk/jog ranging from 400 meters to a mile, followed by a variety of stretches and four to six 100-meter accelerations.

More active warm-ups are becoming common today. The warm-up begins with a jog of 400 to 800 meters, followed by both static and dynamic flexibility work. Next are sprint drills consisting of 3–4 sets over 30 to 50 meters of high knees, skips, butt kicks, carioca, and backward runs.

Dynamic flexibility work of total body circles, scissors, leg swings, side bends, hurdle seat exchanges, lunges, and inverted bicycles is repeated for two to three sets of 10 reps. Hurdle mobility drills should be added in two to three times a week. The number of hurdles used and the height of the barriers depend on the training age of the jumper.

Circuit Training

General strength exercises to work the entire body should be done at least twice a week. These circuits would include push-ups, sit-ups, squat jumps, lunges, back extensions, toe touches, and other similar exercises. The main goal of these drills is to develop and strengthen the body/pillar, which will provide a good founda-tion for continued training and an injury-free condition.

Multiple throwing drills with a medicine ball and/or shot put should also be done twice a week. Again, the weight of the implement depends on the training age of the athlete. Coaches can create a variety of exercises that the athlete can do by himself or herself or with a partner. Again, the goal is to develop the total body and provide a good base for training. Proper technique in these drills is vital for maximum exercise benefit and to prevent injuries.

Multiple jumping circuits, primarily using body weight, are also done twice a week. Exercises include hops, standing long jumps, standing triple jumps, rocket jumps, lunge jumps, tuck jumps, butt kicks, bounding, and depth jumps. Some of these can be done over hurdles to add variety and different training effects.

General strength conditioning, multiple throws, and multiple jumps are done twice a week, but not all on the same day. Two of the series can be scheduled on the same day, if needed. The number of repetitions will depend on the training age of the athlete and the time of season. For example, an experienced athlete might do three sets of 12 repetitions in preseason, two sets of 15 repetitions in early season, and one set of 8 to 10 repetitions in the competitive season. A novice should cut these numbers at least in half. It is very important that coaches monitor athletes and their recovery from workout to workout. Adjust the number of repetitions accordingly. It is better to do less work volume than too much!

Weight Training

Lifting phases are divided the same way training seasons are. A coach/athlete must also plan out the jumper's seasonal goals and priority times for strength training. Workouts should include total body development throughout all phases.

Conditioning Phase (Preseason)

The first phase, when the athlete is returning to training, should focus on a good overall conditioning base. In a year-round program, this phase lasts from six to eight weeks, with progressive loading occurring. High school athletes should use a four- to five-week conditioning phase. At first, circuits can be used to develop overall fitness, and then a specific number of sets and repetitions can be established. The volume at this time is 50–65% of the jumper's tested maximum.

Maximum Strength Phase (Early Season)

Lifting for maximum strength becomes a focus during the preseason and early season. The workout program should include three to five sets of 10 to 15 repetitions at 50–85% of the lifter's maximum, three times a week. This phase lasts six to eight weeks for the year-round athlete and four to five weeks for the high school athlete.

Power Phase (Competitive Season)

When the jumper transfers from maximum strength to power during the competitive training phase, the workout changes to three to five sets of five to eight repetitions at 65–90% of the lifter's maximum, two to three days a week. This phase lasts four to six weeks for the year-round athlete and three to four weeks for the high school athlete.

Peaking Phase (Late Season)

Late-season lifting involves a power phase to stay sharp and explosive. The program consists of one to three sets of one to four repetitions at 75–100% of the lifter's maximum, once or twice a week. Typically, this phase lasts two to three weeks for a year-round athlete and two weeks for the high school athlete.

Commonly Used Lifts

These lifts will be used throughout all of the training phases. It is not the exercise but the number of repetitions and weight load that determine the type of training per phase. Not all exercises are done each workout.

- snatch
- cleans (various starting positions)
- squats (various degrees)
- one-legged squats
- step-ups
- lunge jumps
- hamstring curls (single and double leg, standing/seated position, if possible)
- heel raises
- shin stretches/strengthening
- upper-body lifts (bench, incline, lat pulls, rowing, triceps press)
- abdominal work
- lower-back work (dead lift, good mornings, back hyperextensions)
- mid-upper back (bent-over rowing, pull-ups, chin-ups, one-arm dumbbell rows, reverse flys, lat pull-downs)

A good indicator for developing a lifting program is based upon a one- or five-repetition maximum lift. Since many lifters/coaches are worried about maxing a high weight because of the injury risk, some coaches have used a percentage breakdown to project a five-rep max. After deciding what goal weight a lifter should lift for a single max, the coach would then take 90 percent of that number to project a five-rep max. For example, if the single-rep max goal would be 200 pounds, a five-rep max would be 180 pounds. If the goal single-rep max would be 250 pounds, take 90 percent of the 250 pounds, which would be 225 pounds, for the five-rep max.

Creating a training program is one of the most challenging and exciting duties a coach has. Since each athlete is different and reacts differently to various training stimuli, it is vital that a coach continually monitor how an athlete is reacting to each training session. Coaches should not be afraid to make changes in the plan, as needed. There is not one specific training plan that will make each jumper an Olympic champion. Writing effective training plans is an ongoing project for coaches and a very important one in the overall development of an athlete's success.

Plyometrics

Jumpers must develop a solid training base first before attempting to add plyometrics to their plan. At least two to four weeks of conditioning work should be done to prepare the athlete for this type of power training. Plyometrics are done to create and maintain power and explosiveness, which are vital to any jumper.

Athletes should start with short drill distances of 10 to 30 meters with four to eight repetitions, and then progress to 40 to 50 meters with three to four repetitions of each exercise.

It's a good idea to start backing off the plyometrics around 14 days before "big meets" to refresh the legs.

Samples of low-intensity plyometrics are:

high skips

bounding

single-leg hops

double-leg hops

RRL, LLR, RRL, LLR . . .

RR, LL, RR, LL . . .

jump rope

gallops

double-leg jumps

ramps

hills

hopping and jumping over cones

step-ups

stair running

walking lunges

standing long jump

standing triple jump

hurdle jumps

jumps in place:
- double-leg tuck
- single-leg tuck
- pike
- split-squat
- forward/backward/ side-to-side over cones
- squat jumps

These drills become higher intensity if done quickly and/or over a longer distance. The drills above can be used for height and/or for distance. Coaches can create different purposes for these drills in their workouts. High jumpers do "high" jump plyometrics to be event specific. Yet, "long" jump plyometrics provide needed power and explosive training. Table 12.1 on page 190 is a sample plyometrics workout plan for the preseason, midseason, and late season.

Training Drills

The following drills, when incorporated into your athletes' complete training program, are meant to improve technique and create a consistent approach and execution.

Event-Specific Drills

curve runs of 20–40 meters in the direction of the approach curve

S runs up and down a field

J runs of 40–50 meters in direction of approach

walking approaches

scissors jumps from a short approach

short approaches of three to five strides with some type of takeoff

technique jumps

full approaches with takeoff

full jumps

box jumps from a short approach

backovers from the ground and/or a box

back arches on the ground

TABLE 12.1 SAMPLE PLYOMETRICS WORKOUTS FOR HIGH JUMP

These workouts should be done twice a week during the preseason, midseason, and late season.

	Week	Number of jumps per session
Preseason	1	300*
	2	350
	3	400
	4	250
Midseason	5	150**
	6	200
	7	250
	8	150
Late season	9	100***
	10	150
	11	200
	12	150

About two weeks before the peak date(s) of major meets, start tapering off these exercises.

Power circuits should also be created. Coaches can put together a combination of hops, skips, hurdle hops, box jumps, lunges, and short sprints to vary the power training.

Sample Circuit　　10 hurdle hops

3 × 30 m of high skips

3 × 30 m of bounds

3 × 10 hops on right foot and then on left foot

3 × 3 lunges

5 split-squat jumps

sprint 30 m

* Jumps in place using only body weight for resistance

** Add in movement to jumps, boxes, cones, etc. for extra resistance

***Power movements done quickly over a short distance or in place

Technique Drills

There are three approaches to doing technique drills:

1. "Quality" days are when the bar is four to six inches (about 10 to 15 cm) below the jumper's best mark and about 15 jumps are taken. Enough rest is allowed between each effort so that quality is key. The coach/jumper can vary the bar height as the workout continues.

2. "Endurance" days are when the bar is started eight inches (about 20 cm) below the jumper's best. The purpose of this workout is to take 25–30 jumps at a variety of heights. The jumper takes three clearances at the first height, then moves the bar up two inches and clears it three times. The bar continues to be raised until the jumper has two misses, and then it is lowered an inch.

Once the jumper misses a height twice, the bar is lowered until the jumper gets three clearances in a row; then the bar goes back up. The bar continues to be raised or lowered, with a jumper never having three misses in a row.

Although plenty of rest is taken, the jumper must be in good shape to continue good technique throughout the workout. If the jumper gets technically sloppy, the coach should stop the workout so that bad habits aren't reinforced.

3. "PR (personal record) jumping" is when the bar is set within two to three inches of the jumper's best. Approximately 12–14 jumps are taken, working on good technique at a high height. Bar clearance isn't as important as learning to look at the bar at a greater height, staying relaxed, and using the distance in front of the bar effectively.

A short stable box (approximately four inches or 10 cm high) could also be used from a short approach (4–5 strides). This drill gives a jumper extra height and allows greater heights to be attempted/cleared in practice settings.

Workout Reminders

Keep in mind some of the following ideas when structuring a practice session:

- Speed or technique activities come before strength work.
- Power work isn't done with intensive endurance.
- Games and speed endurance can be used after power training.
- Throwing events come after power training.
- Leave some time between power training and technique work.
- Always use proper technique.

Training Seasons

The entire season can be divided into one or two peaks, depending on the training age and goals of the athlete. Each part of a training season can be divided into the general categories of preseason, early season, competitive season, and a peak.

Preseason

For an athlete training year round, training during the fall preseason keys on conditioning and "getting into shape." Overall, one wants more volume and lower intensity in this phase. (See table 12.2.) The motto for this phase might be "training to train." A five-day training week could be divided into two to three days of conditioning runs of two to three miles, or longer intervals of 500–700 meters on grass; two days of shorter intervals of 150–350 meters, preferably on grass/soft surfaces; and two to three days of strength training. This phase would last six to eight weeks for a year-round training plan, but only four to five weeks for a high school athlete.

High school athletes who have a short preseason phase before meets begin should have some type of conditioning phase for two weeks before preseason work. If the athlete has been active in another sport, he or she should possibly take a few days of mental and physical rest before beginning training. Any aches and pains from the previous sport should be allowed to heal before adding additional stresses from training.

Early Season

As the athlete enters the early season, two days of event-specific work should be added. Weight training is still keyed toward building strength. A philosophy during this phase would be of "training to compete." The intensity increases while the volume is lowered (table 12.3). This period also will last four to six weeks for a year-round program and three to four weeks for the high school season. Since more

TABLE 12.2 PRESEASON WORKOUTS FOR HIGH JUMP

Early Preseason Phase

Monday	3-4 × 600 m on the grass, weights
Tuesday	6 × 350 m
Wednesday	15 min. run on the roads, weights
Thursday	10 × 200 m
Friday	8-10 × 50-80 m hill runs, weights

After four to six weeks of general conditioning, one of the conditioning days can be changed to include more event-specific work, and plyometrics should be added to the strength/power training.

Late Preseason Phase

Monday	4-5 × 500 m, weights
Tuesday	Plyometrics, event-specific work (sprints, approach drills)
Wednesday	5-6 × 300-400 m, weights
Thursday	Plyometrics, 8-12 × 150-200 m
Friday	8-10 × 50-80 m hill runs, weights

TABLE 12.3	EARLY SEASON WORKOUTS FOR HIGH JUMP
Monday	8-10 × 200-400 m, weights
Tuesday	Plyometrics, event-specific work (HJ drills)
Wednesday	8-12 × 50-90 m (speed work), weights
Thursday	Plyometrics, event-specific work (HJ drills)
Friday	Speed work, weights

TABLE 12.4	COMPETITIVE SEASON WORKOUTS FOR HIGH JUMP
Monday	Speed (30-60 m sprints), plyometrics
Tuesday	Event drills and actual jumping, weights
Wednesday	Conditioning (250-300 m repeats)
Thursday	Event drills and actual jumping, speed, weights
Friday	Speed
Saturday	Competition

technique work is added, this is a difficult training time. Athletes will be tired!

Competitive Season

During the competitive season, athletes should do two days of event-specific work, including approach and event drills; two to three days of weights with more power work; one to two days of plyometrics; two to three days of speed work; and one conditioning day of 200–300-meter runs. This period should last four to six weeks in a year-round program and three to four weeks in a high school season. See table 12.4.

Peaking Phase

As the athlete prepares for the year's major competition, the volume of work lessens as the intensity stays high. Workouts should be adjusted to one conditioning day of 150–200-meter repeats, two to three days of speed work, one to two days of weights/power, and one to two days of event-specific work. See table 12.5 on page 194. This is the shortest phase of the season, when the athlete is ready to perform at his or her best! For a year-round program, peaking should cover three weeks; in a high school plan, it would last two weeks.

When an athlete has a double-peak plan, a return to a brief conditioning phase is needed after the first peak. The human body can hold a high level of training for only a short period before it needs to be recharged for the next level of training.

Coaches should adjust the time in each phase to the overall season length. One way of planning a season is to select the main performance date and count the weeks backward. This will ensure that the athlete is rested and ready for "the meet."

TABLE 12.5	PEAKING PHASE WORKOUTS FOR HIGH JUMP
Monday	Speed, weights
Tuesday	Event specific, speed
Wednesday	Conditioning
Thursday	Event specific, weights
Friday	Speed or active rest
Saturday	Competition

Competition

Once all the "on the track" training is completed, the jumper faces the ultimate challenge of competing. Some athletes have "the eye of the tiger" and do their best when the meet arrives. Others practice like champions, but lose their confidence when they put on their uniforms. Coaches and athletes must recognize the psychological part of each event and train for it, too. As the saying goes, "High jumping is 80% mental." Yet, do we work on this part for 80% of total practice time? Very few athletes and/or coaches could answer yes! Psychological preparation is definitely a neglected area in sports today.

Goal Setting

To develop a psychological plan, an athlete must know what he or she plans to achieve through training and competition. All those involved must think about and determine their goals. This goal setting should be directed by a coach or more experienced mentor. It is vital that the athlete create a plan of action that specifies the expected end result of training and competing. For example, some athletes have the goal of being the best in their school, or their state, or their country, or even in the world! If the athlete dreams of becoming the best at the state championship while the coach believes the athlete can make the team but has little chance of scoring, there is a great gap in the expectation level of the two people most directly involved with the athlete's development.

Therefore, one of the first things an athlete should establish is what level of competition he or she would like to achieve and what level of talent he or she realistically has. Once those things are established, the athlete plans the steps for achieving what can be realistically achieved. These short-term, intermediate goals enable the athlete and coach to keep track of progress and make adjustments as needed. It helps if the athlete writes the goals down and posts them in a place where they will easily be seen daily. This constant reminder of the expected final result helps "train" the mind on what the body wants to achieve.

Mental Preparation

Throughout an athlete's career, several factors will influence what final performance level is reached. The athlete can control some of these factors; many he or she cannot. Actually, the only thing the athlete can control is how he or she reacts and responds to different incidents! For example, if the weather is bad during the biggest meet of the year, the athlete can't change that fact. However, the athlete can control how he or she mentally prepares and reacts on that day.

Therefore, each athlete and coach must develop an individual training plan that includes every possible warm-up and competing situation. This can be done by practicing in all types of weather conditions and having confidence and a positive mental outlook about competition in such conditions. Sometimes, team goals can affect which athletes a coach uses for a "big meet." These situations need to be discussed with the athletes involved. Even though not all parties might agree with the coach's decisions, those decisions prevail.

Over time, each athlete should research and practice using different types of mental preparation tactics to discover which one(s) work best for him or her. Once the strategies are narrowed down to the most effective ones for the specific athlete, a self-plan should be created and followed. Adjustments will need to be made as the athlete grows and develops different practice and competitive strategies. Coaches should realize that each individual has his or her own needs and should create his or her own specific goal plan. It is hoped that coaches and parents will be supportive as an athlete works toward achieving both short- and long-term goals.

Mental Imagery

Some of the mental preparation techniques commonly used by jumpers are mental imagery, affirmations, relaxation training, and coping strategies. With mental imagery, the athlete visualizes the "perfect" performance over and over in his or her mind without even jumping. Once the athlete has the proper technical mechanics in mind, mental practice can be used, with the jumper putting his or her body into a mental color video that shows the athlete completing the "perfect" jump. It is important that this imagery be as real as possible, including color, crowd noises and scenes, sounds, and a picture of the athlete clearing the bar successfully! The athlete should start the "video" at the back of the approach, continue through takeoff and actual bar clearance, and even include getting off the pit to waving at the cheering crowd.

The athlete should repeat this picture in his or her mind often, both at the high jump apron and away from the track, to reinforce the kinesthetic patterns expected. All mental practice must be of successful attempts and techniques. The athlete should feel in charge of the situation and feel good about the progress being made.

Affirmations

Affirmations can also contribute to positive performances. These are short, strong statements about the athlete or performance. They are phrased in the first-person "I" and tie into the athlete's goals. For a high jumper, possible affirmations are "I'm fast," "I'm strong," "Stay quick," and "Jump high." Affirmations can be written on cards and carried throughout the day and/or posted in lockers and at home. Again, all thoughts must be positive. Negative thoughts are not allowed!

Relaxation

Athletes usually perform their best when they are relaxed. When most elite athletes are asked about their record performances, they comment that it seemed so easy and nothing special. The athlete was so relaxed and confident, that he or she wasn't "making" it happen; he or she was just "letting" it happen. This type of relaxation is what the athlete wants to feel when competing.

Many articles written by sport psychologists give routines for practicing relaxation techniques. One key is to practice the routines on a regular basis, in various training sessions and then in low-key competitive situations.

These skills work for many athletes, but not all. If after repeatedly practicing relaxation techniques, the athlete isn't finding positive results, he or she should use another strategy.

Common Fears

Some athletes have a fear of failure and become overly anxious about what others will think of them based on how they perform. Such athletes will need to focus on the personal sources of the fear of failure and work with a coach or parent to reduce or eliminate these fears. It is very important for an athlete to honestly evaluate his or her personal feelings and how they might affect a performance.

Athletes must realize that competitive careers are just one part of their lives and not base their entire identity on athletics.

Some athletes have a fear of success and never reach their projected potential because of this fear. These athletes aren't comfortable with the responsibilities of being number one. Coaches and parents might see these athletes backing off in a meet when an improvement seemed possible, or the athletes seem happy to stay at the level they are currently at and don't try to move up to the next level. This fear has kept some very good athletes from reaching their full potential. The mind is so powerful. If there is fear about being number one, an athlete's perspective of himself or herself must be broadened.

On the other hand is the athlete who thrives in competitive situations and actually improves as the level of competition rises. Such athletes have a positive self-esteem, which includes seeing themselves as winners. These athletes also must be challenged and expect to better themselves. What seems to challenge this type of athlete is winning. They are competitors. But if the level of competition is low, they will win without being challenged enough to fulfill their potential. Coaches still need to work with this type of performer and keep him or her focused on the goal and the preparation needed to achieve the goal.

Balancing the mental needs of an athlete can be as delicate as coordinating the physical demands of an athlete at the elite level. Unfortunately, there is no one way of doing this training; it is an ongoing adventure for both athlete and coach. But, when they do reach this type of preparation, the results are fantastic. It should be every coach's ultimate goal to experiment and work with an athlete so as to prepare him or her not only physically but mentally. If two athletes are close in physical traits, the athlete who is mentally toughest will be the victor! As coaches, we must address this vital component of preparation.

Summary

If the techniques in this chapter are implemented, the athlete will be successful. Remember to move slowly and thoroughly through each technical element. Keep the focus on only one or two technical elements at a time. Allow the athlete to master one technical element before moving to the next. Be patient with the work on the approach; the dividends paid out later will be enormous. If the technical aspects of the approach are solid, almost everything else will "jump" into place.

But in the end, all that matters is what my coach Jim Kiefer would tell me when I got caught up in too many technical thoughts: "Doug, jump high and don't knock the bar off!" Good luck!

Likewise, Sue's final encouragement to her jumper, Charles Austin, before he went into the Olympic final was to "have fun and take care of business." Have a great season!

13 Pole Vault

Jim Bemiller

The pole vault may be the most exciting and challenging of all track and field events. An accomplished vaulter clearing a crossbar at record height is one of the most dramatic events in all of sport. The vaulter usually possesses all-around athletic ability. To be successful, the vaulter must develop the skills of a sprinter, long jumper, and gymnast, as well as the specific conditioning to take part in competitions that may last over three hours. Finally, a vaulter usually possesses an inquisitive and fearless attitude. World-class vaulters, such as world-record holder Sergei Bubka, exemplify this type of bold, explosive athlete. As coaches we should endeavor to prepare our athletes by helping them to master the basic elements of vaulting technique as they develop their all-around physical conditioning.

The coach should keep in mind that the pole vault has many inherent variables to consider: the athlete's speed, how high the athlete grips on the pole, selecting the proper pole size, bar height, standard placement, wind conditions, differing facilities, and so on. One of the keys to successful coaching is the ability to synthesize these variables so that the athlete can concentrate on mastering the basics of technique. The coach should emphasize safe and aggressive execution of fundamentals.

Characteristics of the Pole Vaulter

Good vaulters come in all shapes and sizes; but when scouting for potential vaulters, the coach should keep in mind the following general characteristics: speed, gymnastics ability (body control), gripping ability, eagerness to learn, and an aggressiveness that is combined with communication, teamwork, and analytical ability. Speed allows the athlete to create pole speed (the speed at which the pole rotates about its base in the planting box). Gymnastics ability gives body control and strength. Gripping ability allows the vaulter to grip as high as possible on the pole, while allowing the pole to move to a vertical position as the athlete swings around the top handhold. An eagerness to learn is necessary given the technical demands of the event. Aggressiveness is necessary for the explosive energy required.

Speed

Speed is the most important characteristic of a successful vaulter because ultimately the speed of the athlete at takeoff directly correlates with the ability to hold higher on the pole and ultimately clear higher heights. Coaches should not overlook promising hurdlers and relay-team members when searching for potential vaulters.

Gymnastics Ability

Successful vaulters must develop gymnastics ability, so that they have a kinesthetic awareness of body position in relation to the moving pole. Gymnastics ability also enables the vaulter to have body control during movements in the air. Gymnastic strength is more desirable than simple weight-lifting ability, because the latter does not necessarily provide vaulters with the ability to manipulate their own body weight in a coordinated and aggressive fashion. Beginning coaches often overlook the development of general gymnastics ability. This is an area where many young athletes have potential but need to develop their abilities.

Gripping Ability

The athlete's ability to grip as high as possible on the vaulting pole while creating sufficient pole speed to successfully complete the vaulting action is dictated by the athlete's height and extended reach, combined with speed of approach. Ultimately, the higher the vaulter is able to hold on the pole while still moving the pole to vertical, the greater the maximum height obtainable.

Eagerness to Learn

The coach should look for athletes who are willing to learn, because the process of developing their technique will take several seasons. The vaulter must be "coachable" and be able to improve. The athlete must become a student of the event, striving to develop his or her technique and eager to analyze errors and work to correct them.

Aggressiveness

Most vaulters are aggressive risk-takers, which is natural considering the event. But successful vaulters also are able to communicate with the coach and other vaulters about technique and training. Vaulters should be able to work with their teammates in practice and competition. The pole vault is a team sport in many respects; there is always equipment to be moved, steps and poles to be caught, and the need for immediate feedback and consultation. A very successful coach once told me, "There are two types of vaulters. The wild and crazy daredevil, and the analytical chess player type who is always looking forward to the next move." Whether coaching "daredevils" or "thinkers," the coach should mold the group into a cooperative training unit to be as efficient as possible.

Technique

The athlete and the pole must work together to form a system that allows the athlete to hold as high as possible on the pole while using proper technique. The athlete's horizontal speed in the approach is transferred to vertical rise during takeoff, drive swing, and extension phases. Vaulting technique begins with the first steps of the run and continues sequentially with the lowering and planting of the pole, takeoff, the drive swing, extension, clearance, and landing. The following are descriptions and analyses of these various phases of the vault. As stated, the vault is a sequential event, and the coach should teach proper technique from the first steps of the approach forward. Whatever the time constraints, the athlete should become proficient in carrying and running with the pole before moving on to the later phases of the takeoff and airborne movements. Faulty technique in the beginning phases of the approach and takeoff will only make later phases more difficult to complete successfully.

The following descriptions and accompanying figures apply to the left-handed vaulter.

Grip and Pole Carry

The key in the grip and carry is for the vaulter to run efficiently during the approach and perform an efficient, aggressive planting of the pole as he or she prepares for the takeoff. While carrying the pole, the vaulter's top hand should be positioned near the top of the left hip. The vaulter's left hand should hook the top of the pole with the thumb in a closed, comfortable position. The vaulter's bottom arm should be positioned approximately 4–6 inches (about 10–15 cm) from the center of the chest or left side. The bottom (right) arm should maintain the elbow below the right hand and maintain a straight or cocked back right wrist. The right wrist should never droop down or bend toward the athlete's palm. The distance between the hands varies with the individual, ranging from 18 to 24 inches (about 46 to 61 cm). The width of the grip should be such that if the athlete were to assume a handgrip on a horizontal gymnastics bar equivalent to the grip on the pole, he or she could hang and swing up and over the bar efficiently. This grip width allows the vaulter to perform later phases in technique efficiently and aggressively.

The vaulter should begin the pole carry by raising the end of the pole almost to vertical along his or her side, which allows a more effective run. The high pole carry enables the vaulter to control posture from the beginning of the approach because the pole will be easier to carry and the weight of the pole will be exclusively on the left hand. The left hand should remain close to the athlete's left hip during the pole carry. The left hand should not drift behind the vaulter's hip during the approach, because this will cause poor posture during the approach and problems during the planting phase.

Approach

The length of the approach in competition varies with the individual, but ranges from 100 to 150 feet (about 30.5 to 45.7 m, or 7 to 10 right footstrikes), depending on the ability and the experience of the athlete. The approach should be long enough to allow a relaxed start and gradual increase in rhythm and acceleration to reach a maximum controllable speed during the plant and takeoff phases.

The athlete should begin with a longer, more powerful stride in the approach and finish with a fast rhythm. The vaulter begins by placing the right foot on the starting check mark. This starting position produces a balanced body position as the vaulter holds the pole on his or her left side. The vaulter begins the approach by rocking back onto the left foot so as to push forward in a powerful manner to develop a consistent posture and rhythm as soon as possible.

The crescendo of the approach should be based on the athlete gradually increasing speed throughout the length of the run-up while maintaining proper sprinting posture. While performing the approach, the vaulter's chest should be square with the runway, and the vaulter should drop the pole gradually in readying for the plant. The coach should consider the vaulter and pole as a single system, and the lowering of the pole should be synchronized with the vaulter's speed in the approach. The coach and athlete should strive to develop a consistent approach pattern that allows the vaulter to reach and control maximum speed while developing an efficient planting action in preparation for an aggressive jump and takeoff. The vaulter's approach and lowering of the pole should be synchronized so as to increase the vaulter's ability to perform a quick, aggressive plant and takeoff.

Proper sprinting mechanics should be observed. The body lean of the athlete should originate from the ankles as the vaulter pushes out at the beginning of the approach with "long and strong" strides. Do not allow the athlete to bend forward from the hips as the run progresses. The running posture should remain tall as the athlete approaches the takeoff and maintains efficient sprinting technique. As the pole drops, the athlete's strides should accelerate. Correct timing of the pole drop will help accelerate the athlete as he or she approaches the takeoff. The stride rate of the athlete should increase as the plant is initiated. The coach should emphasize that the approach and lowering of the pole is a continuous movement, synchronized to allow for a quick, aggressive takeoff action.

Generally, the coach uses three check marks for the approach run. The beginning mark is the starting point of the approach. This is the only mark the athlete should be aware of during the approach. The second check mark, or coach's mark, should be placed six strides (three right footstrikes) back from the takeoff point to help the coach monitor the consistency of the vaulter's approach. The third check mark is the takeoff point, which should be directly underneath the vaulter's top hand when the pole contacts the back of the planting box.

The coach generally will observe three scenarios during the athlete's approach:

1. If the athlete is consistently inside (closer to the box) the coach's mark and is taking off from inside the optimal takeoff point, the coach should consider moving the athlete's starting point "farther out," away from the box.

2. If the athlete is consistently outside the coach's mark but is still planting "under" (inside the optimal takeoff point), the coach should consider shortening the athlete's starting check mark, to reduce the tendency of the athlete to overstride into the takeoff.

3. The third general possibility is that the athlete is too far out at takeoff and that the corresponding coach's mark is also too far out. The coach corrects this by moving the athlete's starting point forward.

The vaulter must count each time the right foot strikes the runway. As stated above, most vaulters take between 7 and 10 strides (right footstrikes) in the approach, depending on their ability and conditioning. Counting the strides allows the athlete to be certain of when to initiate the planting and jumping action of the takeoff. Failure to count causes the athlete to "feel" or "eye in" the plant and takeoff, which leads to indecision and false perceptions of the proper sequence of the planting and takeoff action. Work on approach techniques on the track, away from the runway.

Pole Plant and Takeoff

The plant and takeoff are critical to execute for a successful attempt. Developing solid fundamentals in the efficient planting of the vaulting pole is essential. The last four strides should be executed in a fast, rhythmic manner, and the plant is initiated three to three and a half steps before takeoff. If the vaulter has a nine-stride approach (18 steps), the planting action should begin as the eighth stride (eighth right foot) contacts the track, if not slightly before. The vaulter's pole carry should coordinate the start of the planting action, with the pole passing through a horizontal position as the vaulter begins the planting phase on the next-to-last right stride. As that penultimate right foot strikes the track, the vaulter moves the pole forward and upward so that the left hand is close to the left shoulder and both arms are aggressively punching the pole forward and upward. When the penultimate stride, or last left foot, touches the ground, the left arm should be moving past the athlete's head as both arms continue to punch forward and upward. As the left arm moves upward, the upper body of the vaulter will rotate slightly to the left and then return to a square position to allow the pole to remain close to the left shoulder as the athlete punches the plant upward.

The right hand should be a fulcrum about which the top arm rises as the pole tip is directed into the planting box. As the left arm passes the fulcrum, both arms are directed aggressively upward. The right hand should not be allowed to drop or be extended down toward the planting box. Both hands continue to actively push the pole overhead as the takeoff foot strikes the track. Both arms are straightened at the completion of the plant, giving the body an extended "tight" position in all joints except the lead leg, which is driven, like a long jumper's, at right angles to the trunk. As the athlete drives off the takeoff, similar to the takeoff for the long jump, it is imperative that the wrist, elbow, and shoulder of the left arm are in an extended, "strong" position.

At takeoff, the vaulter's eyes, head, and chest should be directed upward and outward, similar to a long jumper. The athlete's focus should be on driving off the takeoff foot and up through the extended arms as he or she attempts to move the pole as high and forward as fast as possible. In the correct takeoff position, the pole is directly over the takeoff foot and the left arm is as high as possible (figure 13.1a). During the planting phase, the pole should be moved forward and upward close to the athlete's body, so as to not upset his or her balance during the plant and takeoff. The athlete should perform the plant and takeoff phase with hips and shoulders square to the runway, with a slight opening of the upper body as he or she curls and punches the left arm overhead. (The left arm curls as the vaulter pushes the pole toward the box, then it comes upward to raise the grip above the head.) The plant should be performed actively and aggressively, but the vaulter must have a smooth transition onto support of the pole. The sensation should be that of driving the pole upward and forward as a result of an early, aggressive, high plant.

As the plant phase is completed and the pole is supported against the back wall of the box, the athlete's takeoff leg is extended as the top arm is fully straightened and pressed upward. As in the long jump, the vaulter's lead leg performs a strong drive off the ground such that the thigh is parallel to the pole when the takeoff action is completed (figure 13.1b). The takeoff action should move forward and upward, leading with the upper body, not with the hips. The top arm remains stretched and strong, while the lower arm produces active resistance against the pole. Because of the width of the grip and the active takeoff, the lower arm will bend, but should not be allowed to get too close to the pole. The plant and takeoff should be performed in a balanced, yet active and aggressive, fashion. As stated, the optimal takeoff spot is vertically under the top hand, since the vaulter can raise the pole to a maximum above the track only by taking off from the vertical position beneath the grip. A fully extended, aggressive takeoff position is the key to the proper execution of the swing and extension phases on the pole.

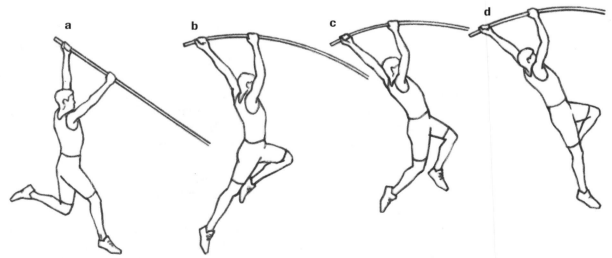

Figure 13.1 *(a-d)* Pole vault progression.

Drive Swing

The drive swing phase begins shortly after the takeoff, as the athlete moves forward and upward in a strong, stretched position. The drive swing should be performed as quickly and powerfully as possible to utilize the momentum the athlete has generated in the approach and takeoff phases. As the stretched takeoff leg catches up with the lead leg (figure 13.1c-d) and both legs begin a fast upward movement, the vaulter shifts the pole forward with the shoulders and fixed arms, as if rowing a canoe paddle. The athlete should make this a continuous movement of driving the lead leg and swinging the trail leg as aggressively as possible, to promote a position where he or she can project the hips as a gymnast would on the rings if attempting to swing from a hanging position to an upside-down position. Imagine that gymnast—hanging motionless from a set of rings and asked to project the hips as high as possible over the head. He or she will not try to pull the feet and knees up and curl the body upside down, but will instead begin to swing and whip kick the legs, using the shoulders to rotate and create a swinging motion to project the hips as high as possible. Similarly, the vaulter uses the shoulders and fixed arms in a rowing motion as he or she rotates through the shoulders and simultaneously swings the feet and hips upward in an aggressive building of momentum (figure 13.1e-g).

The term "drive swing" is used because the athlete should continue to move the pole to a vertical position during the swing. The upward and forward movement of the top of the pole should not be restricted, resulting in a momentum-building swing that allows the vaulter to penetrate and land safely in the pit. The athlete should refrain from throwing the head back in an attempt to raise the hips. The head should remain in line with the body during the swing and should also not focus on the crossbar during the movement. Both throwing the head back and focusing on the crossbar restrict the raising of the athlete's center of gravity (hip and torso area) during the swing.

The swing up should be accomplished by simultaneously shifting the body parts: legs and hips up and shoulders down. Correct gymnastic-specific drills are important to create a fast, momentum-building swing as the pole continues to move forward and upward. It is particularly important to maintain the

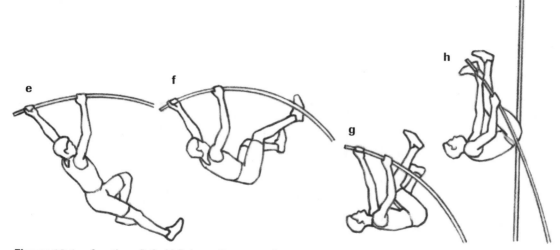

Figure 13.1 *(continued) (e-h)* Pole vault progression.

(continued)

rotation through the shoulders when the athlete has covered the bent pole with hips and legs. If during this phase the athlete incorrectly attempts to pull with the arms or bends the left arm, or bends excessively at the knees or hips, the pole will begin straightening faster and will throw the vaulter away from the pole, not allowing the vaulter to obtain as high a trajectory as can be obtained by moving the shoulders downward while the hips rise close to the straightening pole. As the hips swing upward, the right elbow will break and move to the left side of the pole to allow the vaulter to continue the swing as close as possible to the unbending pole.

Extension, Turn, and Clearance

As the pole straightens, the athlete should begin an aggressive vertical straightening of the body, including the torso, hips, knees, and feet. The athlete should be moving parallel to the pole and as close as possible to the pole as it unbends (figure 13.1h on page 205). As the athlete extends upward along the unbending pole, he or she initiates a body turn around the pole. The turning movement begins when the right shoulder has reached the height of the right hand (figure 13.1i). The movement is assisted by the turning of the legs and arms. Both legs should remain close together, and the trunk and legs are to be kept as rigid as possible to avoid any loss of vertical velocity. A good key for the vaulter is to attempt to turn the left

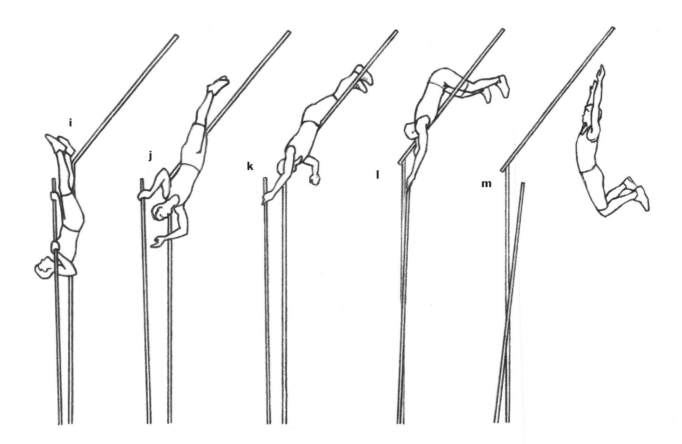

Figure 13.1 *(continued)* *(i-m)* Pole vault progression.

hip as close as possible into the top hand as the body turns and extends. The athlete has now extended and turned as a unit, and the vaulter's stomach is now facing the crossbar (figure 13.1j-k). The entire extension-and-turn phase is an explosive culmination of the takeoff and swing phases and should be seen as a quickly executed straightening of the athlete's body, analogous to an upside-down power clean. The right arm reaches its full extension and releases the pole; then the left arm is released (figure 13.1l-m). The arms are quickly lifted away from the crossbar as the thumbs rotate down and inward, causing the elbows to rotate away from the crossbar. During the clearance phase, the athlete's chin must remain tucked close to the chest until it crosses the crossbar. If the athlete prematurely lifts the head, the chest will be thrown into the bar.

The proper execution of the preceding technique makes it possible to perform a safe landing in the landing pit. To avoid ankle sprains, the athlete should never land on the feet. All safety padding should be in place and maintained properly to avoid injury.

While it is important for the coach to understand the preceding technical aspects of the event, the athlete will not be able to focus on so many details while performing. The vaulter should develop the athletic skills needed for the vault through physical activities and specific training drills prior to actual vaulting. During vault sessions, only one aspect of a technique and a quick rhythm should be emphasized. For example, "tall plant and fast swing" could be the focus of a vault session. The coach should also continue to emphasize the aggressive rhythm of the vault. The athlete should always aim for active, powerful execution of the correct technique rather than simply "hanging on" the pole during the vault or segmenting the phases during execution. Coaches should keep the focus on executing the basics aggressively; otherwise the old problem of "paralysis by analysis" is likely to occur. The complete vault, from takeoff to landing, lasts slightly over one second; so the athlete does not have time to analyze during execution. Coaches must keep it simple and attack the basics.

Teaching Progression

A novice vaulter should be introduced to the event by being allowed to watch more experienced vaulters train and compete, if possible. This gives the beginner a perception of the correct techniques and effort required to vault safely and effectively. If live demonstrations are not available, make available videotapes of correct technique.

Step One: Away From the Runway

Begin by teaching the novice vaulter the proper grip and hand spread on the pole, as described earlier. Away from the runway, teach the vaulter to run correctly, with good posture and relaxed rhythm and with a slight forward lean. The vaulter should run on the balls of the feet, like a sprinter or long jumper, and be relaxed enough to develop a smooth rhythm during the pole carry.

From the outset, have the vaulter develop the technique of counting the right footstrikes (if he or she is a left-handed vaulter) and practice making the transition from the run to the planting position with a quick and aggressive three-step pole plant. The vaulter should progress to an approach run of 50–75% effort while maintaining a good rhythm during the run, and show a quick planting and tall jumping position off the ground.

Step Two: Long Jump Runway

After the vaulter has demonstrated proficiency on the track by making consistent approaches of five to seven strides and finishing with a rhythmic plant, he or she can move to the long jump runway. Remove the butt plug of the pole and have the athlete grip 8–12 inches (about 20–30.5 cm) in excess of his or her extended reach on a pole placed vertically. Instruct the athlete to reproduce the run and plant action done on the track and have him or her plant into the sand and vault with a straight pole into the long jump pit for depth. The coach should monitor the athlete during this drill to be sure that he or she has established a sound rhythm of running and planting the pole with a fully extended plant-and-takeoff position. Do not be concerned with the pole bending; rather, emphasize the extended top arm and strong jump and takeoff into the sand pit. The athlete should land on the feet and continue to jog out the back of the pit. The emphasis should be on a tall, "tight," aggressive takeoff, and on the athlete moving the pole forward and upward with the arms and chest to achieve as much depth as possible into the pit. Because of the low grip, the pole will remain ridged and the pressure of the bottom arm will not be a factor.

Step Three: Pole Vault Runway

When the athlete shows a consistent approach and tall, aggressive plant position and takeoff, he or she may progress to the pole vault runway. Recreate the drill described above on the pole vault runway, having the athlete use the same five footstrike approach to jog, plant the pole, and swing into the pit. Emphasize the correct planting and takeoff positions and establish the correct takeoff point below the athlete's top hand when the pole is placed at the back of the box. The athlete should be encouraged to develop a rhythmic run and planting cadence, leading to an aggressive takeoff that allows him or her to plant the pole and swing into the back of the pit safely on the athlete's back. Gradually add more strides, more speed, and a higher handhold as long as the athlete continues to vault with proper takeoff positions. This should lead to efficient pole speed to land safely in the middle or back portions of the landing pit.

Step Four: Seven-Stride Approach

Once the athlete establishes the rhythm of an aggressive plant, takeoff, and swing, he or she will continue to progress toward a seven-stride approach. Do not be concerned with the athlete bending the pole during these initial drills. A pole that bends too easily from a short approach causes bad habits to be ingrained by the vaulter, such as being able to pull down on the pole at takeoff, sinking rather than jumping properly into the pit, or pulling in with both arms instead of pushing the pole forward while jumping.

Step Five: Short-Approach Vaulting

When the athlete is proficient from a seven-stride approach on the track, and can show proficiency in the short approach and plant sequence, he or she can move to the runway for short-approach vaulting. The coach should make sure that the pole being used is sufficient for vaulter's weight and handhold, to allow him or her to safely enter the pit. From this approach distance, the athlete should be able to safely begin bending the pole and landing in the middle to back portion of the landing pit.

Step Six: Vaulting With a Crossbar

When the athlete has mastered short-approach vaulting and exhibits a quick and proper plant and takeoff that results in a safe landing in the pit, he or she may progress to vaulting with a crossbar. The coach should require that the athlete vault while keeping the crossbar at maximum settings behind the vertical plane of the vault box.

At this point, the athlete may begin to continue the swing around the top hand and allow the hips to rise and turn as he or she attempts to cross the bar while presenting the stomach and chest to the crossbar.

When teaching beginning vaulters who are using a short approach of seven strides or less, a grip height of 12 feet (about 3.7 m) or less is recommended.

The coach should always stress the importance of an aggressive and proper plant and takeoff.

Coaches should explain to novice vaulters that all vaulting poles have a definite bend when they are made. By rotating the pole you can locate the "bow." The bow should face the pit as the vaulter leaves the ground. Therefore, the bow will face toward the runway during the carry and approach run.

Step Seven: Short-Run Vaulting

The athlete is now ready to start short-run vaulting at low heights. The athlete should begin by using a pole rated at his or her own weight, with a low handhold. As the athlete's proficiency and confidence increases, he or she and the coach can begin to focus on the various phases of the run, plant, takeoff, swing, and extension.

Training

The overriding training philosophy should be one of maintaining a balance between all of the components of training. As we develop a workout schedule, we must keep in mind the example of former Polish national coach Andrzej Krzesinski, who has produced many world-class vaulters. Coach Krzesinski believes that training should be like charging a battery. The process should be done over a long period of time, with the athlete gradually developing fitness and technique. Overemphasis of any component will result in a deficiency in another training component. For example, overemphasis in weight training before a technique session the following day will cause the technique session to suffer. (See table 13.2 on page 212 for a sample workout structure.)

Each training situation is unique in regard to equipment, time constraints, and of course the characteristics of the athletes themselves. So a coach should structure workouts by considering these parameters. The following are general considerations.

General Fitness

The athlete should complete a general conditioning program of approximately three to four weeks. Longer cross-country runs of 15–20 minutes should be structured two to three times a week to develop a cardiovascular base. General weight-lifting conditioning should also be done two to three times a week. Gymnastics training, or swing drills on a rope or high bar, should be done at least twice weekly during this base conditioning phase. General technique sessions should be conducted two to three times a week to develop the athlete's skills of running with the pole and proper planting and jumping techniques. Walking or jogging plant drills should be performed daily. The athletes should not be allowed to do any actual pole vaulting during the general conditioning phase. After the athlete has developed general fitness and can demonstrate proper running and planting techniques away from the runway, vaulting sessions can be added to the workout schedule.

After achieving general physical and technical conditioning, the athlete should follow a workout schedule that favors a balance between all facets of his or her training. As mentioned above, each training situation is unique; therefore, the coach must adapt these general training parameters to the individual athlete. Following are the basic components of the vaulter's training cycle, which must be adapted to each individual training situation.

Running

Two to three times a week the athlete should run intervals of varying distances not to exceed 300 meters. In the early season, a typical running workout would consist of 4 × 300 meters at less than maximum speed, but hard enough to have to work to maintain speed (perhaps @ 90-95% of maximum), followed by 4 × 100-meter easy accelerations to warm down. As the season progresses, athletes will progress to shorter distances such as 6 × 150 meters or 10 × 100 meters. Schedule interval sessions for after vaulting sessions, if the athletes can handle this workload.

Technique Session

Technique sessions should be held two to three times a week. Technique sessions may include actual vaulting (table 13.1) as well as the other drills described. Each technique session should focus on two or three of the drills, with a primary focus in mind. For example, one technique session per week may be focused on running with the pole, proper running posture with the pole, and rhythm of approach runs on the track. A second day of technique might concentrate on the planting and jumping action, using pop-ups, takeoff drills, or straight-pole/sand-pit jumping. Always practice some sort of plant drills to establish proper rhythm.

Gymnastics Training

Gymnastics training should be scheduled two to three times per week. Participation in a beginning gymnastics class or training at a gymnastics facility with an experienced gymnastics coach is preferable. The emphasis should be on drills involving swinging from the rings or horizontal bar. Conditioning of the shoulders and torso should be a priority.

Weight Training

Weight training should be scheduled two to three times a week and tapered during the competitive season. Beginning athletes should concentrate on general weight training; but as their experience and physical maturity increases, they should focus on more explosive Olympic-style lifting.

TABLE 13.1	**SAMPLE VAULTING TECHNIQUE SESSION**
WARM-UP	
	We begin by jogging at least three-quarters of a mile to one mile and performing stretching and flexibility drills for 15 minutes. The athletes do 2 × 70-meter and 2 × 80-meter accelerations to warm up.
	All athletes then measure their approach runs and begin by choosing three warm-up drills to develop the areas they wish to focus on in practice. For example, the athletes may do five to eight repetitions of swing-ups, takeoff drills, or low-grip straight-pole vaults. These drills are followed by four to six approach runs done on the track to complete the warm-up and to check the vaulters' approaches before they begin vaulting.
VAULTING SESSION	
	If the vaulter is jumping from a short approach (7 lefts or rights), he or she may be able to complete 15-20 vaults per session. If the athlete is jumping from a longer approach (9 or 10 lefts or rights), he or she may complete 10-15 vaults per session.
	Each session should focus on one aspect of the vault that the athlete is attempting to improve. For example, the aspect might be early plant; aggressive, relaxed and consistent approaches; or accelerating through the drive and swing phases.
	The training groups should always work together. After the athlete takes a practice vault, he or she receives feedback from the coach and then catches the next vaulter's takeoff step and pole. The athlete proceeds back the runway to catch (identify) the next vaulter's coach's mark, and finally moves back in the rotation for the next attempt. This rotation creates a good system of feedback for all athletes as they train. Vaulting workouts should be done when the athletes are in relatively fresh condition and can aggressively complete their attempts. Always begin on smaller poles with lower grips, and move to heavier poles and higher grips if needed or desirable during the workouts. All practices are conducted with the standards placed at maximum settings (80 centimeters) to promote safety and aggressive and powerful takeoffs and swing rhythms.
COOL-DOWN	
	As a cool-down, the athlete should always jog easily for approximately 10 minutes and stretch out for another 10 minutes before moving on to the next component of the training.

Rest and Recovery

At least one session per week should involve active recovery by the athlete. These activities include easy jogging, stretching, swimming, underwater vaulting, and so on. Pole vaulting sessions require the athlete to be relatively fresh and able to complete jumps with an aggressive run and plant. Therefore, the coach should

TABLE 13.2 ‖ SAMPLE WEEKLY WORKOUT FOR VAULTING

Because each coach's situation is unique, a coach must develop a weekly cycle that works best for him or her. A typical early season workout schedule could be constructed as follows:

Monday	Vaulting technique session followed by interval training or hurdle drills.
Tuesday	Gymnastics training followed by light jogging and weight training.
Wednesday	Vaulting technique session followed by pole runs and long jump drills.
Thursday	Gymnastics training and weight lifting.
Friday	Pole vault plant drills and light jogging and stretching prior to a competition. If no competition on Sat., approach runs and interval training, such as 6 × 150 m.
Saturday	Competition. If no competition, pole vault drills and weight lifting.
Sunday	Active rest.

The following is a typical weekly training schedule we have used at the University of Tennessee:

Monday	10 × 100 m accelerations, followed by light plyometrics or hurdle drills and hurdle running.
Tuesday	Gymnastics training, followed by weight lifting.
Wednesday	Vaulting and technique session, followed by film review.
Thursday	Gymnastics and weight training.
Friday	Technique drill session, followed by intervals—for example, 6 × 150 m.
Saturday	Active rest—for example: swimming, underwater vault drills, and stretching.
Sunday	Vaulting session, followed by weight training and film review.

Again, balance is the key. The coach must be sensitive to each athlete's ability to accept different workloads. Also, different athletes may not be able to perform similar workouts. Some may need more or less work in each area. For example, vaulting three times a week may not be possible for some athletes, and their workouts should be limited accordingly.

make sure that sessions on vaulting technique are preceded by easy or medium-effort days. During early season competitions, a day of rest and recovery with easy activity prior to competition is beneficial. Prior to late season competitions, two days of rest and recovery are preferable. Rest and recovery periods are not synonymous with inactivity. Athletes should always jog, stretch, or do other light activity during these resting components.

Integration

Because vaulting has various training components, vaulters should be integrated into other workout groups if possible. Too often the vaulters are left on their own when not actually vaulting. The coach can maximize efficiency and develop team spirit by having the vaulters run with the sprinters, perform drill sessions with the hurdlers and long jumpers, and lift with the throwers. At the collegiate level, decathletes and vaulters are natural workout partners.

Table 13.2 on page 212 illustrates a weekly workout structure showing the types of training that should be added to the athletes' weekly workouts.

Correcting Common Faults

Some of the more common faults that athletes and coaches may encounter include these:

- Decelerating at takeoff
- Taking off from an inside, or "under," position
- Keeping the head and eyes focused on the bar, killing swing/inversion
- Failing to extend both arms at takeoff, resulting in coming down on the bar
- Inconsistent approach run

The following drills should be used to correct these common faults:

Stiff Pole Vaulting

The vaulter uses a low handhold and a six-step run with a ridged pole. The emphasis should be on a tall and tight takeoff and fully extended top arm. If the athlete does not reach the vertical, the grip should be lowered; but if the athlete does reach the vertical and passes quickly into the pit, the handhold may continue to be gradually increased until the athlete makes a vertical position in the direction of the landing area.

Approach Runs

The athlete's run should be marked on the track, away from the box or landing area, by measuring his or her steps from a towel or small sand tube representing the box. All athlete and coach marks should be included. The vaulter simulates his or her approach plant and aggressive takeoff. This drill will encourage consistency and confidence in the approach and plant. Remember to always run through the takeoff and simulate a strong jump. The athlete is to run *through* the takeoff, not *to* the takeoff.

Pop-Ups

The vaulter jogs from a short approach with a low handhold and practices planting the pole in the box, then simulates a quick, rhythmic plant and swing, landing on his or her back in the pit.

Takeoff Towel Drill

To correct the habit of chronically taking off too far under the top hand, the coach places a towel six inches in front of the vaulter's ideal takeoff point. Instruct the vaulter to run, plant, and take off from behind the towel. The vaulter will be aware of the towel without focusing on it. The innate fear of stepping on the towel is generally strong enough to break the chain of ingrained movement patterns.

Counting

Teach your vaulter to count every time the left foot (for a right-handed vaulter) contacts the track during the approach. The athlete will now be able to anticipate the beginning of the plant on the correct count. (*Note:* Some vaulters prefer to count backward, as for a rocket launch; I suggest experimenting.) This drill will help vaulters who feel the plant action sneaks up on them and catches them unprepared to begin to plant and take off.

Push

Coaches can increase their vaulter's takeoff velocity and resulting penetration by actually pushing on the athlete's back at takeoff. The coach should stand on the left side of the runway (for right-handed vaulter) and push the vaulter between the shoulder blades using the right hand. Spotting the athlete helps the vaulter become more confident and thus more aggressive. The push is especially useful in helping a vaulter raise the grip or when switching to a larger pole.

Short-Run Vault

The vault is performed with a shorter run (seven strides). Have the athlete concentrate on one phase that needs improving. The short approach allows more vaults to be completed during a practice session, and allows vaulters to focus on technique using smaller poles with which they feel confident.

Takeoff Drill

Beginning from a four-step approach, the athlete walks and performs the planting and takeoff motions and extends into a tall, tight takeoff position. The coach spots the athlete from behind by firmly grasping the back and lat area as the vaulter rises from the ground and returns to the runway. This drill will show the athlete that the arms must be fully extended and rigid and that the drive leg and chest must also remain rigid as he or she leaves the ground. For a right-handed vaulter, this drill can also be performed with the coach spotting the athlete from the left side of the runway. The athlete jogs or walks a four- to five-step approach; during takeoff the coach spots the vaulter with the right hand in the center of the athlete's back between the shoulder blades and the left hand on the athlete's left thigh. The athlete must remain "tight," with a firm grip on the pole. The coach stabilizes the athlete as he or she jumps off the ground and assists the return to the runway. The athlete must lead with the chest and drive knee and hold this position throughout the drill. To finish the drill, the athlete returns to land on the takeoff foot and takes several jogging steps backward. If the athlete aborts the drill, the coach must spot the athlete by wrapping his or her arms around the athlete's torso and gently lowering the athlete to the ground.

Gymnastics Apparatus

The athlete may simulate phases of the vault on gymnastics rings, parallel bars, rope, or other gymnastics devices. The gymnastics apparatus is very beneficial in teaching the athlete to swing aggressively and control the body so that the hips rise while the shoulders lower. It is also valuable for teaching the athlete to swing and rotate through the shoulders rather than pull and curl upside down. A beginning gymnastics course can help teach spacial awareness and body control.

Vaulting for Height

Set the bar at the vaulter's personal best or at one or two feet above that. This encourages the vaulter to extend aggressively and to refrain from looking at the bar, which causes the athlete to flag out instead of continuing upward.

Videotaping and Imagery

Videotape technique practices as much as possible so that athletes can observe their technique. The vaulter's internal imagery may be quite different than what he or she sees on the video replay. The vaulter should also use visualization to mentally rehearse performing the correct techniques.

Adjustments for Weather

It is important to practice vaulting in less than ideal conditions. Vaulters should practice into a head wind or shifting wind on a regular basis so that they learn to make adjustments by shortening their run, using a softer pole, and lowering the handhold. Vaulters should practice making these same adjustments for vaulting in wet conditions so that they will make the proper decisions during competition. If there is a tail wind, vaulters must make similar adjustments to take advantage of good conditions. In good conditions with favorable winds, vaulters may be able to raise their handhold and increase the length of the run. In better conditions, vaulters will also be able to use stiffer poles. The coach should monitor all practices and be especially vigilant if poor conditions arise. The athletes are eager to compete and are aggressive in nature; so the coach must decide if inclement weather should prohibit them from vaulting. As a good rule of thumb: If the athlete is "in the air," the coach should be there supervising.

Competition

Vaulters should abide by the motto of "Be Prepared." Vaulting competitions will generally last several hours; so athletes should prepare themselves with proper clothing and equipment such as extra towels, umbrellas, tape measure, and chalk or tape to ensure a good grip. Vaulters must also keep properly hydrated during the competition. During longer competition the athletes may consume small amounts of fruit or light snacks to maintain their energy levels.

After a proper warm-up, including pole runs and technique drills, the athlete should take from three to five full-approach jumps with a small pole. The opening height should be approximately one and one-half feet below personal best or the goal height he or she has set for that competition. The coach and athlete should gauge the wind and weather conditions for adjustments in these general parameters. If there is an unfavorable wind, or cold or rainy weather, the athlete may start with a smaller pole and a lower opening height, or may even run from a shorter (seven left or right footstrikes) approach run. I recommend that the vaulter jump every height in the competition after starting, to develop confidence and rhythm in his or her vault. Passing heights is only for the most experienced athletes. If the vaulter needs to switch to a stiffer pole because he or she is getting too much depth, or the pole is moving to vertical faster than the athlete can swing upside down, I recommend switching poles on the first attempt at a new height, if possible. Vaulters should stick to their game plan and focus on their approach and takeoff during competitions. Don't let other competitors affect your decisions.

It is very important that teammates work together during the competition to help with steps, poles, and standards, because in all probability, the coach may not be allowed into the meet area or may have been called away to coach other events. Teammates working together is a big advantage during competition.

Summary

Successful vaulting requires consistent proper technique by the athlete, coupled with aggressive execution. To vault safely, the athlete can never go "half-speed" on the runway. By developing proper technique through planting drills and approach runs, the athlete will develop the confidence and consistency to vault effectively and have fun.

PART IV

THROWING EVENTS

14 Shot Put

Bill Godina
Ron Backes

Most coaches believe that technical proficiency is more easily achieved by initially teaching all putters the glide technique. Later, at the high school or college level, the coach or athlete will determine the best technical path to take (glide or spin). Coaches should keep in mind that many of our world-class spinners, such as John Godina, were 60-foot gliders in high school. The glide provided them a solid understanding of the power position and release movement. Traditionally, this group was very sound in the glide before switching to the rotation. Once the transition to the spin technique is made, some athletes see dramatic improvements in their performances. It is often characteristics like strength, flexibility, and speed that dictate which technique is best for a particular athlete. With a little experimentation, the athlete and coach can determine which technique will result in the best performances.

Glide Technique

When Parry O'Brien, a young University of Southern California athlete, turned the starting position of the shot-put movement 90 degrees, a historical breakthrough in technique occurred in the event. And O'Brien became the first man to break the 60-foot barrier. He competed on four Olympic teams, won two gold medals and one silver medal, and, from 1952 to 1956, had 116 consecutive victories, a record that still stands thirty years later. O'Brien's distance records were progressively broken, climaxing in 1965 when another American, Randy Matson, shattered the 70-foot barrier. "Gliders" continued to push back shot-put distances, culminating with Ulf Timmermann's world record of 75 feet, 8 inches (about 23.06 m) in 1988. Although the spin technique has grown in popularity in recent years, many world-class throwers continue to use the glide.

Since the world record for the men's shot, 75 feet, 10-1/4 inches (about 23.12 m) , was achieved by a spinner, why do world-class athletes continue to use the glide? The answer lies in two dimensions—simplicity and consistency. The fact is, the glide movement is linear and simple, unlike the rotational style of the spin, which is highly complex. The glide can be used with more consistency because it has three phases that are readily achieved; the rotational movement has more opportunities for error.

Phases of the Glide

In the glide technique, three principles are essential to putting the shot far. These are angle of release, height of release, and velocity of release. The optimum angle of release in the glide is 40 to 42 degrees. The higher the release from horizontal, the more distance is achieved. Finally, the velocity of release (how fast the shot leaves the hand) is the primary determiner of distance achieved. One of these factors, the height of release, is determined by the height of the athlete and cannot be influenced by coaching or training. However, the other two factors can be influenced by strength/power training and technique development.

Sometimes described as the linear style, the shot-put glide has the least complex technique of the four throwing events. What is forgotten by many is that the glide is a rhythmic activity that must be sequentially executed to achieve optimum results. The physiological differences in athletes necessitates variations of the technique described in this chapter. Our focus will be the critical path of certain events that must occur regardless of individual variation.

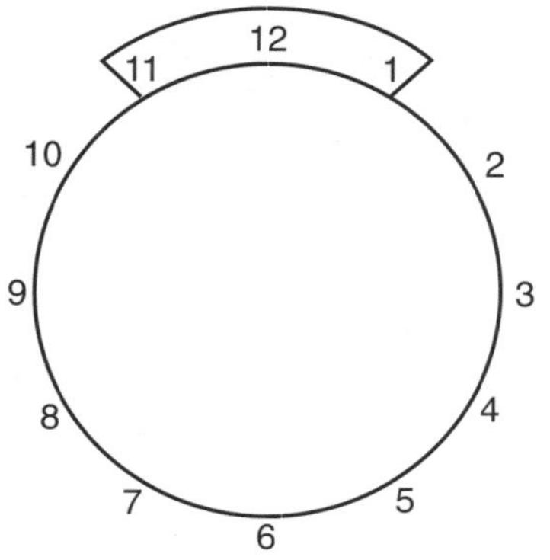

Figure 14.1 Directional focus of circle, with 12 o'clock as the direction of the throw.

Starting Position

The athlete faces 6 o'clock in the ring (figure 14.1). The weight/center of gravity is over the right foot. (Our example will use the right-handed shot-putter.) The shot is held on the center fingers and tucked against the neck with the thumb down (figure 14.2a). The angle between the torso and upper arm is 90 degrees. The head is square, with the eyes focused on a point outside the ring—for quick reference, select a distance equal to the diameter of the circle (about seven feet). The torso can be in either an upright starting position for a dynamic start or a lower, more traditional position. Regardless of the starting position, the back and neck must be in a straight plane.

Movement is initiated by pushing off the support leg and thrusting the nonsupport leg toward the front of the ring (figure 14.2b). The hips begin to settle toward the center of the ring. The right heel departs the rear of the circle last. Throughout the initial movement, the upper body remains facing the six o'clock position, while the lower begins to turn and face 3 o'clock on the circle (figure 14.2c-d). The feet land with the left toe between the right instep and heel. This relationship of upper and lower body is commonly called "separation." The center of gravity is over the right leg. The shot is behind the right hip ready to follow the body through to release. This is the "power position," which will generate torque and permit application of force throughout the throw.

Proponents of the vertical start position believe that the "dynamic start" increases the shot velocity along the path of travel and requires less strength. On the other hand, those beginning lower, in the "T position," believe this creates a more precise power position for more efficient application of force. The T position requires more strength to propel the athlete toward the front of the circle.

Figure 14.2 *(a-d)* Shot put technique, starting from the "T position."   *(continued)*

Glide

The two main approaches to achieving the power position are the long/short glide and the short/long glide. The model long/short glider was Al Feuerbach. His technique consisted of a very dynamic start, which drove his right foot 8 to 12 inches (about 20 to 30.5 cm) beyond the center of the ring while achieving the power position (figure 14.2e). The short/long glide was highly influenced by German coaches, who produced the prototype in Ulf Timmermann. The initial movement, though dynamic, is shorter, with the right foot at or behind the center of the ring. The proponents of the short/long glide believe that the shot is more easily driven through a single plane with greater velocity and that the force is less likely to be split. When matching the technique to the athlete, one should consider speed, [strength, agility, and height. Historically, the smaller [5 feet, 11 inches to 6 feet, 1 inch (about 180 cm to 185 cm)], more athletic individual appears to be more successful with the long/short technique.

The throw is initiated from the power position. The hips begin to turn around the center of gravity, which passes through the ball of the right foot, which never stops turning (figure 14.2f). The upper torso trails the hips as torque is applied from the legs. At 2 o'clock the upper body and shot accelerate and catch the lower torso.

Delivery

The delivery phase begins with initiation of the arm strike and the shot being pushed from the neck. The lead leg straightens and begins a blocking action, which halts left-side movement and accelerates the right side and the shot (figure 14.2g). At release, the arm is fully extended: the thumb is pointed down and the shot is flicked away with the fingers. The head is up and the eyes are focused on the trajectory.

There are two primary methods to finish the throw. The first is the reverse. In the reverse, linear momentum from the block is dissipated by exchanging the positions of the left and right feet (figure 14.2h). The right arm is extended and the left arm is parallel to the ground. The putter lands flat-footed on the right foot and faces 9 o'clock. The second method, used by many European throwers, is the nonreverse throw. In the nonreverse, the feet remain essentially in the power position at release. The right foot moves forward four to eight inches (about 10 to 20 cm) following release. Current biomechanical research indicates that the nonreverse technique is more efficient since it permits application of force over a longer path during delivery.

e   f   g   h

Figure 14.2 *(continued) (e-h)* The glide and delivery.

Teaching Progression

Technique is most successfully taught and coached from the front of the circle to the rear of the circle (from 12 o'clock to 6 o'clock).

Grip

The first step is to grip the shot in a manner that facilitates the application of force during the delivery phase. The shot is placed on the pads of the center three fingers in the palm of the hand. The thumb and fifth finger stabilize the shot in that position.

Carrying Position

Once a comfortable grip is achieved, the coach and athlete must determine the correct carrying position for each thrower. The shot is positioned on the neck to permit release with the thumb pointing down and the fingers fully extended. A starting point is on the neck under the right jaw. Through experimentation, the optimum position is determined and is programmed into the athlete's muscle memory. Keep in mind that the position points for the indoor and outdoor shot will differ and must be determined by experimentation.

Control

Control and kinesthetic awareness of the legs and right side of the body in the power position is critical. The power position is established with the heel of the right foot aligned with the toe of the left foot. The feet are approximately shoulder-width apart. This position permits maximum generation of torque and application of force by the largest muscle group in the body, the legs.

To progressively train the athlete, drills at the front of the ring are critical.

Double-Pivot Drill

The first drill, the double-pivot drill, is the beginning of harnessing the legs and hips in the put. The feet are positioned in the correct heel-to-toe relationship, with the shot correctly positioned on the neck. The athlete squats down on the balls of both feet, facing 3 o'clock. From that position, the thrower raises to the vertical position while pivoting simultaneously on the balls of both feet. The pivot is 90 degrees, with the center of gravity over the right foot. The arms are extended and the shot is released. The head is back, with the eyes overhead. Both feet finish in the 12 o'clock position.

Nonreverse Throw

Drill number two focuses the ballistic qualities of the thrower. This is a nonreverse throw in which the body extension beyond the toe board is emphasized. Transfer of momentum from the right side of the body to the left side culminates in a hard block. This simulates the shot acceleration experienced in the full throw. The athlete begins facing 3 o'clock. The left leg is slightly bent, with weight on the right side. The right foot pivots violently 90 degrees, turning the right leg into the bent left leg. The left leg locks and initiates the block, which results in acceleration of the shot. The lift creates a stretch reflex, which contributes to an increase of shot velocity. Both feet finish pointed in the 12 o'clock position.

Full-Reverse Stand Throw

Drill three is the full-reverse stand throw. The athlete assumes the power position. The lower body faces 3 o'clock, and the upper body is in the 6 o'clock position. Many publications describe this upper to lower body relationship as "separation." The legs drive violently with a rotational lift. The left leg locks to establish the blocking force. The right foot replaces the left foot, landing on the bottom of the entire foot parallel to the toe board. The thrower's upper and lower body is facing 9 o'clock. The right arm is up and extended. The left arm is extended back and parallel to the surface of the ring for balance.

Before teaching movement from the back of the ring, make sure the thrower has mastered drills one through three. The thrower must feel the right side and understand the importance of legs in acceleration and ballistic delivery of the shot in the block. Finally, the controlled reverse enables the thrower to remain in the ring, resulting in a fair throw.

Rhythm and Speed

The final phase of the teaching progression deals with initiation of the glide from the back of the ring. The athlete faces 6 o'clock, glides to the center of the ring, pauses, and releases the shot using the double-pivot, nonreverse, and full-reverse stand throw drills. Once the thrower has achieved consistency of foot placement, the pause is eliminated. The focus becomes rhythm and speed in transition to one of the three throwing drills.

The glide remains the foundation for shot-putting. For a successful glide, the grip, implement position, singular line of power, and active right side must maximize velocity from the rear of the ring to the middle. The block by the left side cannot be neglected if shot acceleration is to occur and maximum velocity achieved. The glide is taught in segments, but the coach must tie the pieces together through the development of rhythm and consistency. Remember, each athlete is biomechanically different, but the principles described must be achieved by all if they are to succeed.

Spin Technique

by Ron Backes

The spin technique was a major reason why I was able to compete in the 1992 Olympic Games in Barcelona, Spain. In high school, using the glide technique, my best mark in the shot put was 50 feet, 5 inches (about 15.4 m). However, I did manage to throw the discus 181 feet, 9 inches (about 55.4 m). This discrepancy in performances led my first college coach at Hamline University, Dick Mulkern, to suggest I take the spinning action used in the discus and apply it to the shot put. Thus, I started using the spin technique. I quickly took to the spin and saw dramatic improvements in my performance and my enjoyment of the event. Under the guidance of my coach from the University of Minnesota, Steve Forseth, I achieved a career best 68 feet, 11-3/4 inches (about 21 m) with the spin technique. Even when I was throwing the 16-pound (about 7.3 kg) shot put 68 feet (about 20.7 m) with the spin, I could only muster 61 or 62 feet (about 18.6 m to 18.9 m) with the glide. I am not opposed to using the glide technique; however, some athletes, like me, might benefit from using the spin.

The following are some of my personal insights and experiences over the past 17 years of performing and coaching the spin technique. It is my hope that these will aid you in your coaching of the spin.

Philosophy

My philosophy regarding the spin technique has always been *simplicity*. When done correctly, the spin technique should appear efficient and effortless. The athlete may even say, "That felt easy" or "I hardly felt that one." This is a sign that the athlete has finally mastered a smooth and efficient throw. It is important for athletes to focus on "big picture" concepts like balance, rhythm, and the feeling of different positions of the throw. As a coach, it is important to use common vocabulary and simple analogies to help athletes master these concepts. By doing this, small technical problems will often take care of themselves.

Developing a Common Vocabulary

A key factor in mastering the spin technique is the development of a common vocabulary between the coach and athlete. Common terms will enhance the communication process, reduce chances for misunderstanding, and help in competitive situations. I suggest coaches develop a handbook that outlines the training plan, describes the program philosophy, and lists terms and definitions to give to his or her athletes. This will improve coaching effectiveness and build confidence and trust with the athlete. Some examples of common terms that relate to body position include:

Power position—for the right-handed thrower, this is the position in which the athlete's left leg touches down in the front of the circle while the right leg is near the center of the ring. The shoulders face the 6 o'clock position while hips are facing 3 o'clock.

Wrap—the relationship of the left arm to the right leg in the power position. It refers to the left arm position, which appears to be across the body at the moment the athlete reaches the power position. This helps keep the shoulders from opening too soon.

Cowboy—the bowlegged starting position in the back of the circle.

Separation—the relationship between the upper and lower body during the spin movement. The lower body is always moving ahead of the upper body so as to drag the upper body along.

Torque—the muscular tension between the abdominal oblique muscles and the trunk, which is a result of separation.

Explaining Complex Concepts

Another aspect of coaching that helps the athletes is the coach's ability to communicate complex concepts using simple terms, "key" or "cue" words, and simple analogies. This is especially important when coaching the spin technique as it will help simplify what some deem a more complex set of steps than that of the glide. Simple terms help both experienced throwers and rookies learn or correct technique. Key words or cues are short phrases that help the athlete focus on a specific aspect of the technique. They are extremely useful in competition when the athlete needs to limit the number of things to think about and when direct coaching contact is limited.

Because of the shot put's technical nature, there will be a lot of frustration. The coach and athlete must be patient. Improvement will not always be steady. It usually comes in spurts, between long bouts of frustration and angst. Humor is also a necessary element if a coach wishes to have a long career!

Phases of the Spin

All technical descriptions in the following sections will be for the right-handed thrower.

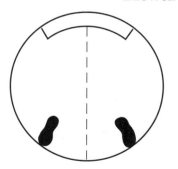

Figure 14.3 Starting or "cowboy" position of the spin technique.

Starting Position

Start by straddling the centerline with the feet just slightly wider than shoulder-width apart and the toes pointed out about 20 degrees (Figure 14.3). The athlete's legs should be in a bowed position and that distance between the knees should be maintained as they start their turn. My coach, Steve Forseth, termed this, "the cowboy position." The knees are slightly bent (1/2 squat depth) in a classic upright athletic position. The athlete's hips should be positioned on top of them not leaning too far forward or sitting too far back.

Wind and Entry

About 60 percent of the weight is then shifted to the left leg and kept on the left leg during the pre-turn wind-up. I suggest keeping the right foot flat and grounded during the wind-up. The left arm, left knee, and foot turn together inward during the wind and then outward during the entry to initiate the throw. (The entry is the beginning of the spin move. The wind is a preliminary move in the opposite direction to create separation at the beginning of the move into the spin.) At the point where the athlete completes the wind-up and starts to move into the throw, the right foot needs to immediately come off the ground. If the right foot is late in getting off the ground it will be difficult to get on balance over the left leg, and the left leg will have a tendency to drag behind on the entire throw.

The athlete often will try to use the upper body to create momentum to start the throw. The movement in the back of the circle needs to be initiated with the lower body.

360-Degree Drill

A drill that I use to practice the start is called the "360-degree" drill. The athlete gets into the starting position and attempts to pivot on the left leg, completing a full 360-degree turn landing in the same exact position they started in. The emphasis in this drill is to go slow while keeping the right leg low and wide. Just as in the actual throw the left arm should not move ahead of the left leg. This is a great drill for working on balance, and it can also be used in the discus. I recommend using it in the warm-up, performing three sets of ten repetitions.

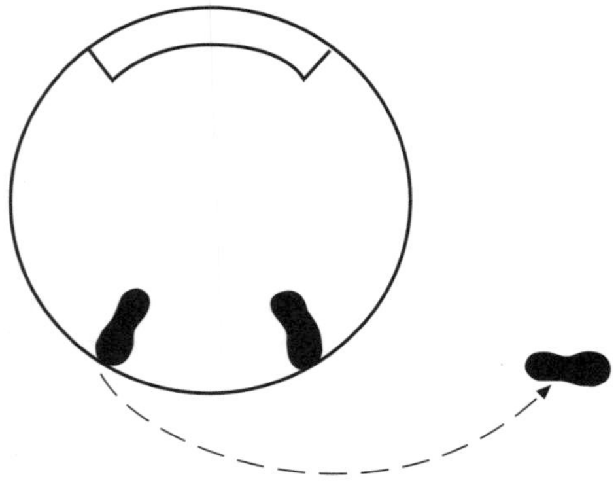

The right foot is swept wide and low as the athlete makes the first 180 degrees of

Figure 14.4 In the 360-degree drill, the right foot is swept wide and low to make the first 180 degrees of the initial turn.

the initial turn (figure 14.4). The left arm should never get ahead of the left thigh and knee. The movement is like that of a door. The left side is the hinge and the athlete, like a door, moves around the left side.

After the first 180 degrees of the turn comes the drive into the middle of the circle. I feel this is the critical point in the throw. It is where the athlete will establish torque and separation for the release of the shot. As in the release of the shot where the athlete "blocks" the left side in order to accelerate the right side, the same principle applies as the athlete comes out of the back of the ring. When the athlete is facing the throwing sector, the left foot should stop rotating and be pointing down the right hand sector line or at least to right of center (between 1 and 2 o'clock, as shown in figure 14.5). The left arm is pointed to the center of the sector and held as the athlete drives the right hip ahead of the shoulder into the middle of the circle. A good key here is to have the athlete try to feel the right leg passing underneath the outstretched left arm.

The right foot is carried in a wide sweeping motion with the toe pointed out as if the athlete is kicking a soccer ball at the 180-degree point of the initial turn. As the athlete turns the right hip into the middle of the circle, the left arm is brought back across the body in a wrapping motion. I call this the "wrap." It helps keep the upper body back when the athlete lands in the power position (figure 14.6). The athlete focuses on keeping the weight over the right leg as the left leg is moved quickly to the front of the circle. Once the right foot makes contact with the circle, it should continue to turn as the left leg wheels to the front and the athlete completes the throw.

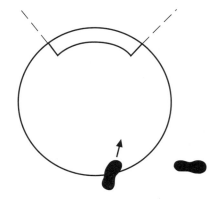

Figure 14.5 During the drive into the middle of the circle, when the athlete faces the throwing sector, the left foot stops rotating and points between 1 and 2 o'clock.

Figure 14.6 The "wrap," where the right hip turns into the middle of the circle and the left arm comes across the body.

Because of the tremendous force created by the right leg sweep, the spin technique may produce a slightly narrower stance at the front of the circle than the glide technique would. This is typical and does not negatively affect the throw in any way. The key is that the right foot continue to turn in the middle of the circle.

Another advantage of stopping the left foot rotation when it is pointing down the right sector, besides an acceleration of the right side, is that the thighs will come together and the wheel of the left leg will be tight and quick. The block, or holding of the left side out of the back, also helps prevent an athlete from overrotating and the left leg from swinging wide and slow to the front and landing in an open position.

The rhythm of the throw through these two phases, given that the technique is performed as prescribed, is another important factor and is key to long throws. The first 180 degrees of the turn is done in a smooth and controlled manner. Compared to the rest of the throw, it is the slowest movement. When the left side is blocked, the right leg and hip will accelerate into the middle of the circle. The left foot should be picked up off the circle as soon as possible so that it may be wheeled to the toe board as quick as possible. Both feet should land almost simultaneously. Good technique can be heard as well as seen. In my mind I hear the rhythm played out in a series of sounds: "Voom—boom/boom". The "voom" is a long drawn-out sound I associate with the wide sweep of the right leg. The "boom/boom" sound represents a quick placement of the right and left feet at the front of the circle. Individuals may use other sound descriptions to describe this movement. Using "voom—boom/boom" helped me focus on a single concept that involved many parts of the technique.

Delivery

The position of the body when the left leg first touches down at the front of the circle indicates whether or not the athlete has performed the technique correctly up to this point. It will also tell you if the athlete will have a chance for a good throw. The athlete's weight should be predominately over the right leg. The shoulders will be facing the back of the circle. The left arm will be pulled across the body making an "X" across the right thigh. Again, I refer to this as the "wrap." The right foot should be pointing to somewhere between 3 and 6 o'clock (see figure 14.7 on page 228).

The movement in the front of the circle is a continuation of what has been established coming out of the back of the circle. The hips and right foot should continue to turn as the shot is kept back and behind the right hip. The left arm should be extended and brought up and over at the release. The left arm is then bent and brought down to the side. I tell my athletes to try and imagine they are squeezing an orange underneath their armpit. The hips accelerate up and on to a strong block.

Figure 14.7 The spin technique from start to finish.

The block at the point of release can be thought of in terms of the whole left side. The athlete's left leg should be aggressively straightened; there should be no bend in the left leg. There should be no bending back or break of the left hip. The overall concept here is that the athlete be tall on the left side when releasing the shot. The higher the release point, the longer the distance. The release point should be out in front of the toe board. The hip turns through the release and continues to turn after the release of the shot. It is similar to the concept of a sprinter not stopping at the finish line but instead running through the finish line, maintaining maximum speed. In the same way, the thrower focuses on the right hip turning all the way through even after the shot is released. I like to tell the athlete to "finish the throw." The thrower should finish with a high right shoulder. The finish should resemble that of a gymnast who sticks the landing. In the same way, the thrower should stick the finish. The athlete will end up facing the back of the circle or rotating all the way around after the release of the shot. This is a good indication that the athlete is balanced and has completely followed through on the finish.

Figure 14.7 illustrates each phase of the spin technique.

Troubleshooting

The following are a few troubleshooting tips that will help keep your athlete moving in a positive direction.

Testing Balance

The overriding factor in the spin technique is balance. The coach should easily be able to recognize an athlete who is not balanced. The athlete may have trouble staying in the circle; throws may go out of the sector; the athlete's shoulders may be tilted or they may appear to be falling into the middle of the circle (figure 14.8); they could have trouble completing a full turn on a 360-degree drill. The athlete should be in control of the body during the entire throw and follow-through. A good way to test balance is to ask athletes to stop in different phases of the throw. If they can stop and hold a proper position, it is a good indication that they are balanced.

Checking the Position of the Shot During the Throw

Figure 14.8 Tilted shoulders or a forward falling motion are signs that the athlete is off-balance.

Another important concept in the spin is the position of the shot relative to the right hip during the throw. When the athletes set up in the back of the circle, the shot is positioned behind the right hip. As they perform the technique, as a full throw or from the power position, the shot needs to stay behind the right hip until the very point of release. In the spin, this relationship of the shot and right hip is established during the initial turn and the leading of the hip into the middle of the circle. It is important to maintain the relationship during the drive to the middle of the circle, the wheel, and the release. If the shot moves ahead of the right hip during the initial turn and drive into the middle, the athlete will land with the shot ahead of the hip and will not be able to regain a proper relationship for the release.

Videotaping the Athlete

Videotaping competitions and practices will help the coach help the athletes master the spin technique. If athletes do not have a coach to observe them, videotaping will allow them to, in essence, coach themselves or send the tape to a coach and receive long-distance coaching. If a coach is present, then this allows both to view areas of improvement and determine what needs to be emphasized in practice. It also gives the athlete an opportunity to voice opinions and demonstrate his or her comprehension of specific concepts.

The spin technique is a viable option for athletes and coaches at all levels. Coaches who have not had exposure to the spin should not shy away from teaching it to their athletes. Almost all of the concepts for the discus are the same for the shot-put spin. Keep it simple; focus on big concepts; and put in a little time to study the technique. Be a student of the sport. Balance is the key in all aspects of throwing the shot put. The athlete must be balanced throughout the entire throw. Remember also to design a balanced training program as described in the next section. It is my hope that all of these principles, combined with an intense desire to compete, will bring you much success.

Training

While throwing technique is, of course, vital, the development of strength and power cannot be neglected. Both are essential elements of shot-putting. The coach and athlete must understand and develop a strength-training program. An effective program includes weight training, plyometrics, and the use of variable weight implements. The strength lifts are squats and the bench press. The power lifts are cleans and snatches. During early phases of training, the volume (number of repetitions) is high and intensity (weight) is low. As the season progresses toward the culminating event (state, regional, or NCAA championships), the volume is reduced and the intensity increased. For developmental athletes, each core lift is performed once a week. For advanced and elite throwers, the core lifts may be executed twice a week, with a rest day inserted in the middle of the program.

As with weight training, plyometrics begin with high volume and low intensity twice a week. In the middle of the season, the volume drops to weekly, and the final quarter of the season has no plyometrics exercises. For the novice throwers, floor exercises and boxes, no taller than 18 inches (about 46 cm), are recommended. For advanced athletes, a 24- to 30-inch (about 61 to 76 cm) box is satisfactory. The boxes are spaced three to five feet (about 91 to 152 cm) apart. The athlete does a series of hops on and off each box. This exercise can be done taking off from both feet, alternating feet, or hopping on one foot only.

Another box drill is to place a box next to, but outside of, the throwing circle at 6 o'clock. The athlete starts on top of the box then spins to the power position into the circle by hopping down. This enhances the athlete's strength and power.

Finally, variable weight implements can be used to develop both strength and power. Overweight implement training during the beginning and middle of the season builds strength, and using underweight implements during the final quarter builds hand speed. The use of variable weighted shots should be structured like a lifting workout, identifying the number of sets and number of throws per workout. The implements should conform to the "10% rule"—that is, the weight is ±10% of the standard implement. (See table 14.1.)

Table 14.2 presents a comprehensive sample training plan for shot putters that follows the progression from high volume, low intensity during the early training phase to low volume, high intensity as the season progresses. It can be altered based on the needs of the athletes at a particular phase of the season.

TABLE 14.1 VARIABLE WEIGHT IMPLEMENTS FOR SHOT PUT

Standard	Overweight	Underweight
4 kg.	10 lb.	8 lb.
12 lb.	13 lb.	10 lb.
16 lb.	18 lb.	14 lb.

TABLE 14.2 SAMPLE TRAINING PLAN FOR SHOT PUT

All weight training sessions should include several sets of abdominal and abdominal rotation exercises.

Pre-preparation Phase (2 weeks)	
Throwing	Volume—Complete 10-20 throws, twice a week, using competition weighted implements. Focus—Start with the basics, introducing the event to new throwers and re-teaching the veteran athletes on the team. Focus on the big concepts like proper throwing positions and using the legs to throw the implement.
Lifting	Circuit training. Pick 10 exercises encompassing the whole body. Perform each exercise for 30 sec., rest 15 sec., and perform the next exercise in the circuit. Use 30-50% of max. weight or 1/3 of body weight. Record the number of reps for future reference and goal setting.
Running	Run 2-3 days a week. Alternate among long, short, and hill days. Long sprint—5 × 200 m, walk 200 m for recovery. Short sprint—8 × 100 m, walk 100 m for recovery. Hills—6 × 150 m, walk back for recovery.
Plyometrics	One day per week. Multiple sets of 10 and 5 reps, 60 total contacts, double leg variations, boxes or hurdles no higher than 18 in. (about 46 cm).
Medicine ball	Two days a week. Pick 3-6 exercises performing them from each side of the body. Do 2-3 sets of 10 reps per exercise. Exercises could include: overhead backward,

underneath forward, back to back partner exchange, side rotation throws (power position), overhead stepping forward, overhead from sit-up position, hip throw (hold ball on hip performing a power position movement) or any event-specific movement.

Preparation Phase (10-12 weeks)	
Throwing	Volume—Complete 20-30 throws, 2-3 days a week, using regulation and heavier implements (1-2 lb. or .45–.9 kg over regulation).
	Focus—Identify and prioritize technical aspects for each individual. Start to set technical goals in each practice. An example might be for athletes to learn the grip and once they have that down, move on to mastering a starting position.
Lifting	3 or 4 days per week
	Examples: 4-day program
	Mon. Pulls (cleans, snatch, or high pull) and squat
	Tues. 1 or 2 pushes (bench, military, incline) + supplementary
	Thurs. Pull and squat (light)
	Fri. Push and supplementary lift
	3-day program
	Week 1
	Mon. Bench and press (upper body)
	Wed. Pull and squat
	Fri. Incline and upper body
	Week 2
	Mon. Pull and squat
	Wed. Bench and press (upper body)
	Fri. Pull and front squat
	Sets and reps: Initial exercises should be preceded by a sufficient number of warm-up sets using a lighter weight. Each set should progress in weight. The focus is on increasing the weight used on the last set compared to the last time performing the lift. Pulls—3 or 4 sets of 5-6 reps Presses—3 or 4 sets of 8-10 reps Supplementary—3 sets of 8-10 reps
Running	Run 2-3 days a week. Alternate among long, short, and hill days. Long sprint—6 × 150 m, walk 150 m for recovery. Short sprint—8 × 80 m, walk 80 m for recovery. Hills—6 × 100 m, walk back for recovery.
Plyometrics	One to two days a week. Multiple sets of 10 and 5 reps, 60 total contacts per session, double leg variations, boxes or hurdles no higher than 18 in. (about 46 cm).
Medicine ball	Same as in conditioning phase.
Precompetition Phase (10-12 weeks)	
Throwing	Volume—Complete 20–30 throws, 2-3 days per week, using regulation weighted implements.
	Focus—Start to design and practice a competition routine to use when the season

(continued)

(continued)

Precompetition Phase (10–12 weeks)	
	starts. Once basic technique is mastered, start to work on the rhythm of the throw, slow and relaxed to quick and explosive.
Lifting	Pulls—3 or 4 sets of 3–4 reps Presses—3 or 4 sets of 5 reps Supplementary—3 sets of 6-8 reps
Running	Run 2–3 days a week. Alternate among long, short, and hill days. Long sprint—8 × 100 m, walk 100 m for recovery. Short sprint—8 × 40 m, full recovery. Hills—5 × 60 m, full recovery
Plyometrics	One to two days per week. Multiple sets of 10 and 5 reps, 80 total contacts per session, double leg variations, boxes or hurdles no higher than 18 in.variations, boxes or hurdles no higher than 18 in. (about 46 cm).
Medicine ball	Same as in conditioning phase.

Competition Phase (6–8 weeks)	
Throwing	Volume—Complete 15–25 throws, 2–3 days per week, using regulation and light implements (1–2 lb. lighter than regulation). Focus—Quality is definitely more important than quantity at this point. Be sensitive to how the athletes feel. If they are too fatigued to perform the technique properly, then stop throwing and do some drills or just end the throwing session.
Lifting	Pulls—3 or 4 sets of 2–3 reps Presses—3 or 4 sets of 3–5 reps Supplementary—3 sets of 6–8 reps
Running	Run 2 days a week. Alternate between long and short sprints. Long sprint—8 × 80 m, walk 80 m for recovery. Short sprint—8 × 20–40 m, full recovery.
Plyometrics	One day per week. Multiple sets of 10 and 5 reps, 50 total contacts, double leg variations, boxes or hurdles no higher than 18 in. (about 46 cm).
Medicine ball	Same as in conditioning phase.

Unloading Peak Phase (7–10 days before main competition)	
Throwing	Volume—Complete 10–20 throws using regulation and mainly light implements (1–2 lb. lighter than regulation). A few throws the day before the competition can be a good idea to calm the nerves and get accustomed to the circle. Focus—Emphasize the rhythm of the throw and mental preparation for the competition.
Lifting	Pulls and presses—3 sets of 3 reps, light and quick (70-75% of max.)
Running	Run 2 days a week. Alternate between long and short sprints. Long sprint—6 × 60 m easy stride outs, walk 80 m for recovery. Short sprint—5 × 20 m, full recovery.
Plyometrics	No plyometrics
Medicine ball	One day this week cut volume to 1 set of 10 reps for the 4 selected exercises.

Competition

The competition phase needs more than technical and strength/power preparation. A large portion of the preparation is mental training. Use positive self-talk and mental imagery, projecting the ideal throw on the mind's movie screen. A rehearsal before each major meet reduces stress and increases confidence. The higher the caliber of competition, the greater the role of the mental dimension. An old quote from Henry Ford best sums this up, "Whether you believe you can or you believe you can't, you're right."

Two ways to implement mental imagery are to do it away from competition and also to implement it just before you throw. Go to a relaxed setting, perhaps your bedroom or some private area that allows for mental concentration. Listen to music that stimulates you, but allow for no other outside distractions. Close your eyes and see yourself competing. Let the music get you into the rhythm of the throw. See yourself completing the technique successfully, with quickness and explosiveness. Envision yourself competing the throw on balance and in control. Mentally rehearse the throw from the throwing position inside yourself as well as watching yourself from outside your body. See yourself on the victory stand.

Repeating the above technique will help the body learn correct form and also allow the athlete to feel the action. The second method involves the athletes at the competition site. While the athletes are waiting their turn, they should close their eyes, block out everything around them, and mentally rehearse the action.

Summary

Each athlete should strive to fully understand all aspects of the event. The better the athletes' understanding of proper training and technique, the quicker and more thoroughly they will develop good training methods and proper throwing technique. In essence, they need to become students of the sport, always striving to improve their knowledge and technique. This will also result in intrinsic motivation, which we all know is vital in individual sports like track.

15 Discus

Don Babbitt

In the discus event, distance is determined by the factors of size, technique, and strength combined with the elements of balance and speed to generate maximal power and rotational torque. The ideal athlete for discus throwing is tall, with long arms and legs, and has quick feet and good balance. The advantage of good leverage is illustrated by the fact that many of the world's top male throwers have measured almost 2 meters, or about 6 feet, 6 inches, in height, while many of the top female throwers are 5 feet, 10 inches (about 178 cm) or taller. Gabriele Reinsch, who holds the women's world record of 252 feet (76.81 m), stands 6 feet, 2 inches (188 cm), while Connie Price-Smith, who has been one of America's top discus throwers, stands 6 feet, 3 inches (190.5 cm)! At 6 feet, 6 inches (198 cm), and 243 pounds (about 110 kg), Lars Reidel, the current men's world champion, exemplifies the perfect discus body type.

The primary mechanical factors in determining performance in the discus are the thrower's abilities to execute a 630-degree turn with precision and speed while keeping the throwing arm loose and relaxed through the point of release. Throwers such as Jay Silvester, John Powell, and Mac Wilkins have been pioneers in developing the throwing technique that is used by many of today's successful throwers. The technical innovations of these great throwers still serve as models for how to turn and drive out the back of the ring, pivot in the middle of the ring, and set up the release at the end of the throw.

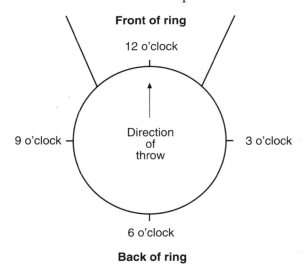

Front of ring

12 o'clock

9 o'clock

Direction
of
throw

3 o'clock

6 o'clock

Back of ring

Figure 15.1 Directional focus of circle, with 12 o'clock being the direction of the throw.

Technique

This section will cover the mechanics used to throw the discus as well as a teaching progression to introduce the event to throwers of varying levels. This will be followed by a section focusing on some of the most common technical errors, and will include some drills that can help correct these problems. All technical descriptions in the present and following sections will be for the right-handed thrower. For descriptive purposes, the different areas of the discus circle will be referred to by the hour positions on a clock. In this case, the back of the ring will be considered the 6 o'clock position, while the front of the ring will be considered the 12 o'clock position (see figure 15.1).

Beginning the Throw

The thrower will begin the throw by standing in the back of the ring, facing at 6 o'clock, with the feet apart at roughly shoulder width. The discus will wind behind the thrower's back with the arms extending out at a 90-degree angle from the trunk (see figure 15.2a). During the wind, the right foot will be flat against the

a   b   c   d

Figure 15.2 Discus technique: *(a)* the wind, *(b)* wide leg sweep of the right leg to unwind, *(c)* another right leg sweep, *(d)* pulling the right leg up to start the drive across the ring. *(continued)*

ground, while only the ball of the left foot will be in contact with the ground. The center of mass should be located halfway between the right and left legs, causing the thrower's weight to be equally distributed on both legs.

The thrower will then begin to unwind the discus by turning the torso to the left as the weight shifts onto the ball of the left foot. At this time also the right foot is picked up off the ground in preparation for a wide leg sweep while the thrower is turning on the ball of the left foot (see fig 15.2b). As the thrower continues to turn out the back of the ring by pivoting on the ball of the left foot, he or she sweeps the right leg in a wide arc until the left toe and chest are facing 1 o'clock (see fig. 15.2c). At this point, it is critical that the thrower's center of mass be directly over the ball of the left foot and that the shoulders be kept level with the ground to ensure good balance. The left arm should also be kept extended during the turn out the back of the ring to slow the upper body's rotation so that the discus can be kept back as far as possible.

Driving Across the Ring

Once the thrower has turned out the back of the ring and the left toe and chest are lined up with the right sector line (i.e., facing 1 o'clock), he or she will be in position to drive across the ring. This drive, or "sprint," across the ring will be caused by driving off the left leg while simultaneously pulling the right leg across the body as the right knee is pulled up to make a 90-degree angle between the right thigh and torso (see fig. 15.2d). The combined action of the right and left legs will cause the thrower to drive across the ring while gaining rotational momentum to complete the turn in the middle of the ring.

Turning in the Middle of the Ring

When the thrower has completed the push-off with the left leg, he or she will be in a short "flight phase" while turning in the middle of the ring. While turning in the air, the thrower tries to maintain the right thigh at a 90-degree angle with the torso until the right foot comes back in contact with the ground. While this is happening, the left leg is pulled in close to the right leg, in an effort to conserve rotational momentum (see fig. 15.2e).

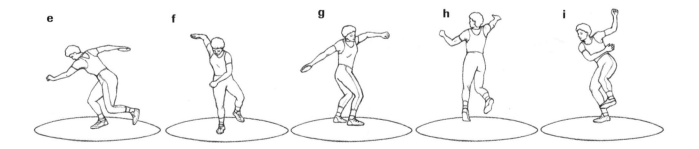

Figure 15.2 *(continued) (e)* turning in the center of the ring, *(f)* completion of the flight phase with the right toe facing between 7 and 9 o'clock, *(g)* start of the delivery phase, *(h)* block and release, and *(i)* the reverse.

The flight phase is completed when the thrower's right foot comes back in contact with the ground. At this point, only the ball of the right foot should be grounded and the toe should be facing anywhere between 7 and 9 o'clock. It is also important that the thrower's center of mass be located over the ball of the right foot upon recontact with the ground (see fig. 15.2f, page 237). The arms should be relaxed and stretched out, with the throwing arm at a 90-degree angle to the torso.

Once the ball of the right foot hits the ground, it begins to pivot in a counter-clockwise direction. As this pivoting motion is going on, the left foot is brought around to the front of the ring, as soon as possible after the touchdown of the right foot, and placed on the ground so that both feet are roughly a little more than shoulder-width apart. The thrower must keep the chest facing as close to 6 o'clock as possible until the left foot comes in contact with the ground. This ensures that the discus is extended as far behind the right hip as possible for maximum leverage (fig. 15.2f, page 237). It is also important that the heel of the right foot be lined up with the toe of the left foot so that the hips are able to rotate all the way through during the delivery phase.

The Delivery and Release

Once both feet are back on the ground (double-support phase), the delivery phase can begin. The delivery phase is initiated by the continued pivot of the right foot, which in turn leads the right hip ahead of the throwing shoulder and throwing arm (fig. 15.2g, page 237). The discus is pulled around in a wide orbit while the throwing arm continues to maintain a 90-degree angle with the trunk. As the discus is being pulled around from the 6 o'clock position to the release point at approximately 2 o'clock, the left side of the thrower's body firms up, or "blocks," as the right side of the body continues its rotational acceleration of the discus into the release (see 15.2h, page 237). At the point of release, the head is thrown back, which allows the chest and hips to rise to give lift to the discus.

The Reverse

The reverse is sometimes used by throwers to stop from fouling as they follow through after their release. Once the discus has been released, the thrower will kick the left leg out to the side and replace it with the right leg, causing a "reversal" of their body position (see fig. 15.2i, page 237). The reversal may be accompanied by a lowering of the center of mass in an effort to better control the body so that no foul occurs.

Teaching Progression

To begin, the thrower should hold the discus in the palm of the hand of the outstretched nonthrowing arm. He or she then places the right hand on top of the discus, with the fingertips extending over the edge of the lip of the discus. Each finger should be spread apart. This gives the thrower an idea of how the discus should feel in the hand. Once the thrower is comfortable with holding the discus, proceed through the following drills.

Pendulum Drill

Next, the thrower should hold the discus in the hand while the arm is dangling straight down from the shoulder. The thrower can then start swinging the arm back and forth like a pendulum. This shows the thrower how the discus should feel in the hand while it is moving. The "centrifugal force" generated by this swinging motion will help keep the discus in the thrower's hand and should reduce the thrower's need to want to grasp on to the discus.

Release Drill

An easy way to teach the proper direction in which to let go of the discus is to have the thrower hold the discus by the waist as described in the above section. From this position, the thrower tilts the hand backward and lets the discus roll out of the hand and fall to the ground. When this happens, the discus should roll forward off each finger, starting with the pinkie and ending with the index finger.

Discus Bowling Drill

The next step in teaching the proper release is to have the thrower *bowl* the discus. This exercise can be done with a partner who should start by standing roughly 10 yards away from the thrower who is about to bowl the discus. The throwers will roll the discus back and forth to each other on its edge, just as they would roll a bowling ball down a bowling alley. As the throwers get more proficient at this, they can increase the distance between themselves and work on releasing the discus with a little more pace.

Pendulum Drill Variation

Another release drill is an advanced variation of the pendulum drill (also called the height-release drill). The thrower begins by swinging the discus from a dangling arm; as the arm is swinging forward, the thrower releases the discus out the *front* of the hand, causing the discus to go straight up in the air. The coach should make sure that the discus has a good amount of rotation on it, and that the discus lands on its edge when it comes back to the ground.

Wind Up Drill

The next step in the teaching progression has the thrower swing the discus back and forth in a plane that is parallel to the ground. To begin this exercise, the thrower holds the discus in the outstretched palm of the nonthrowing hand, while the throwing hand is placed on top of the discus. The thrower swings the discus backward with an outstretched arm and then swings the discus back into the palm of the nonthrowing hand. As this exercise is being performed, the thrower should make an effort to keep the throwing hand on top of the discus while swinging the arm and not turn the discus over so the hand is underneath the discus. This should be repeated many times in succession, with no pause between the direction changes in the throwing arm.

Once the thrower is comfortable with swinging the discus back and forth and is able to do this without "cupping" or grabbing the discus, he or she should be ready to work on an actual throw.

Kneeling Throw Drill

Throwing from a kneeling position may seem strange, but it reduces the power that can be achieved by the thrower by eliminating the legs from the throw, which in turn will reduce the possibility of an errant throw. It also serves to focus the thrower on the upper body's role in the throwing action.

To begin this drill, the thrower assumes a kneeling position on one (the right) knee, with the left foot forward and the right knee supporting the body weight. The thrower then takes the discus and swings it back as he or she relaxes and lets the "centrifugal force" acting on the discus stretch out the throwing arm. The coach makes sure that the thrower rotates the trunk backward, along with the throwing arm, so that the whole upper body stays in "contact" with the discus. Once the arm has been pulled back as far as possible, the thrower "pulls" the discus through by turning the trunk and pulling the arm forward. The release should be flat, and the discus should land flat against the ground anywhere from 15 to 45 feet directly in front of the thrower.

Standing Throw Drill

To introduce the proper position for the stand throw, the coach should have the thrower stand in the front of the discus ring, facing the whole body out toward the center of the sector. From this position, the thrower steps back in toward the center of the discus ring so that the feet are a little more than shoulder-width apart and the right heel is lined up with the left toe. The thrower should bend the right knee and shift the weight back on to the ball of the right foot. At the same time, the thrower should swing the discus as far back behind the body as it will go, which will usually be a position back over the left heel. From this position, the thrower will immediately initiate the throw by pivoting the right foot, which will cause the right hip and shoulder to rotate through. This action will cause the throwing arm to be whipped around, and the discus will be released as in the previously described release drills.

The coach will also want to look for the following things when the thrower is performing the standing throw:

• The thrower pivots on the ball of the right foot during the throw, and finishes the pivot with the right foot pointing in the direction of the throw.

• The left leg (i.e., block leg) straightens out to form a solid block as the discus is being swung around to be released. The "block" is caused by a sudden deceleration of the left side of the body, which in turn causes an acceleration of the right side, thus accelerating the discus as it is released.

• The *orbit* is the path that the discus follows as it is being thrown. The orbit of the discus should follow a *high-low-high* pattern. This means that the discus will be at its highest point as it is fully drawn back (i.e., when it is over the left heel). The discus will hit the lowest point in its orbit when it is passing by the right foot. From this point the discus will start to rise back up to its high point as the throwing arm is brought around to release.

• The head should always be facing straight away from the chest during the throw. Make sure that the thrower does not turn the head away during the release. The head should be thrown back during the release to allow the chest to get up into the throw.

Half-Turn Drill

The half-turn drill teaches the fundamentals of pivoting on the right foot in the middle of the ring. The thrower can actually begin this drill without the discus, to focus his or her concentration on the pivoting action of the right foot and the turning of the body. The thrower should start this drill with the right foot placed in the center of the ring, with the weight bearing down on the ball of the right foot. The right leg should be bent, as it is at the beginning of a stand throw. The whole body should be lined up in a position similar to that at the beginning of a stand throw, except that the thrower is lined up to throw out the back of the ring.

Once the thrower is comfortable with the starting position for this drill, he or she begins by rotating the right hip, knee, and foot in unison to cause the body to start rotating around. The body of the thrower pivots as the body turns 180 degrees to the stand-throw position. At no time should the heel of the right foot touch the ground. While the right foot is pivoting, the left knee should be pulled close to the right leg, causing the knees to almost touch together in an effort to increase the speed of the body's rotation. As the thrower is finishing the 180-degree turn, he or she shoots out the left leg into a straightened position similar to that at the beginning of the stand throw. At the end of the 180-degree turn, the coach should take note to see that the thrower has maintained the following positions:

- The feet are in heel-toe alignment.
- The thrower's back is facing the throwing sector and the chest is facing toward the back of the ring.
- The thrower's weight is balanced over the ball of the right foot (i.e., pivot foot).
- The right leg is bent and the left leg is slightly flexed. The thrower should be in a position to deliver a solid stand throw.

The next step is for the thrower to perform this drill with the discus. The thrower starts by swinging the discus backward, at hip level, and then pushing it forward as the half-turn is initiated. As the thrower starts the half-turn, he or she will direct the discus in an upward path so the discus reaches its "high point" when it is closest to the front of the ring. By doing this, the thrower ensures that the discus has established its proper orbit, with a high point when the discus is near the front of the ring and a low point when the discus is positioned close to the back of the ring. The proper orbit enables the thrower to release the discus as it is ascending toward the high point of its orbit, which in turn results in a nice parabolic flight.

Step-In Drill

Once the thrower has mastered the half-turn, he or she can move on to the step-in drill. This drill begins with the thrower standing in the back of the ring with the ball of the left foot placed inside the back edge of the ring and is facing the front of the ring, or 12 0'clock. To begin, the thrower steps, with the right foot, into the center of the discus ring and settles the weight onto the ball of the right foot. At this point, the thrower should be in a position similar to the starting position for the half-turn. The thrower then proceeds to perform the half-turn and release. As the different parts of the step-in drill become more comfortable, they can be molded into one complete movement with no pauses in between positions. The coach makes sure that the heel of the right foot never touches the ground after the foot is placed in the middle of the ring. The emphasis of this drill should be the continued pivot of the right foot, and the coach should make sure that the thrower initiates the 180-degree turn by pivoting the right foot. The general rule of thumb is that you pivot to get into position to throw, not pivot as a reaction to the throw.

South African Drill

The South African drill begins just like the step-in except that the thrower drives the right leg into the middle of the ring as he or she pushes off the left leg to generate power out the back of the ring. This is an excellent drill for teaching the thrower to drive across the ring using the leg drive from both the right and left legs. As throwers perform this drill, the coach will want to check for the following things:

- The thrower keeps the upper body relaxed as he or she leads with the right leg into the center of the ring.
- The thrower should land in a balanced position on the ball of the right foot near the center of the ring.
- The thrower should always be on the balls of the feet during the throw.
- Make sure the discus follows the proper orbit.
- The thrower pushes off with the left leg out the back of the ring as the chest is facing the right sector line. At the same time, he or she sweeps the right leg outward and then across the body as the leg is driven toward the center of the discus ring.

360-Degree Turn Drill

This drill prepares the thrower to turn out the back of the ring. It begins with the thrower standing with the legs slightly flexed while the weight is balanced over the ball of the left foot. The feet will be slightly wider than shoulder-width apart, with the left leg flexed and the right leg only slightly bent. From this position the thrower will pivot in a complete circle on the ball of the left foot and come to a stop in the original starting position. The coach should make sure that the right leg stays wide as the turn is being performed. Many beginners will pull their ankles together in an attempt to gain more rotational speed. This should be discouraged, for this is not how the thrower will turn out the back of the ring during a full throw.

Full Throw Drill

When the thrower is able to perform all these drills, it should be an easy transition to a full throw. If the thrower is having trouble with a certain part of the full throw, he or she should go back and work on the drill that emphasizes the movement that is causing trouble. The coach should also make sure that the following technical elements occur during a full throw:

- Once the thrower reaches the stand throw position, the throwing arm makes a 90-degree angle with the torso. This 90-degree angle between the arm and the torso should be sustained through the release.
- The rhythm of the throw is from slow to fast (i.e., there will be a buildup of rotational speed throughout the throw).

Correcting Common Faults

Fault: Overrotating.

Cause: Overrotating occurs when the thrower rotates too long on the ball of the left foot when turning out the back of the ring. This will cause the thrower to drive

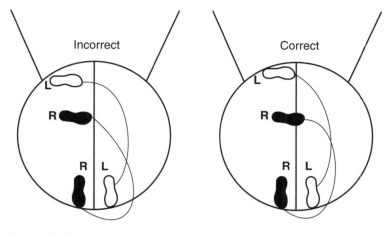

Figure 15.3   Overrotating.

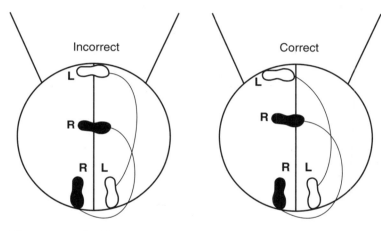

Figure 15.4   Locking-out.

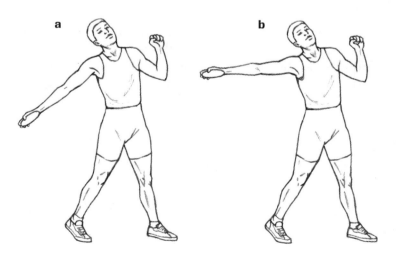

Figure 15.5   *(a)* Scooping occurs when the thrower releases the discus at a point when the throwing arm is at less than a 90-degree angle to the torso. *(b)* The correct throwing position with the arm at 90 degrees.

over to the left side of the ring instead of down the middle (see figure 15.3).

Correction: This can be corrected by having the thrower push off the left foot a little earlier as he or she turns into the entry.

Fault: Locking-out.

Cause: The thrower can "lock out" the hips by not having the heel-toe alignment necessary for rotating the hips to be square with the throwing sector (see figure 15.4). This problem usually occurs when the thrower does not pivot correctly in the center of the ring.

Correction: The 180-degree turn drill will help correct any pivoting problems.

Fault: Scooping.

Cause: Scooping occurs when the thrower releases the discus from a position where the throwing arm is at less than a 90-degree angle to the torso (see figure 15.5). This can be caused by the discus not being in the proper orbit, which in turn can be caused by overrotating out the back of the ring or by not carrying the discus in the correct position.

Correction: Throwing traffic cones can help solve scooping problems by slowing down the throwing arm and making the thrower more aware of the orbital path of the throwing hand.

Training

Training for the discus involves refining and improving both physiological and technical elements throughout the season. This section concentrates more on the physiological aspects of discus training, which will be separated into the preparation, precompetition, and competition phases. Physiologically, the discus thrower will work on developing speed, flexibility, and explosiveness through a combination of weight training, running, stretching, and plyometrics. Each of the three training phases is characterized by a specific emphasis on the volume and intensity of both the physical and technical training. These phases also follow a certain order and are designed to allow the athlete to "peak" for maximum performance at a specific point in the competitive season.

Table 15.1 provides general throwing ranges and records for high school, collegiate, and elite discus throwers. You can measure or compare the progression of your own athletes against these average and record throws at each level of competition.

TABLE 15.1   GENERAL THROWING RANGES FOR DISCUS

Women	Average Distance (ft./m)	Record (ft.-in./m)
High school	120–170/36.6–51.8	188–4/57.40
Collegiate	140–195/42.7–59.4	221–5/67.49
Elite: national class world class	165–205/50.3–62.5 200+/61+	216–0/65.84 252–0/76.81
Men		
High school (1.5 kg)	140–200/42.7–61	225–2 /68.63
Collegiate	160–200/48.8–61	220–0/67.06
Elite: national class world class	185–210/56.4–64 205+/62.5 +	237–4/72.34 243–0/74.07

Preparation Phase

The first phase of training is the preparation phase, which may begin in the early fall (September, October) for the collegiate or open athlete, or in the winter (January, February) for the high school athlete. This phase may also vary in length, from four to six weeks for some high school athletes to many months for higher-level athletes. Weight training in this phase is of low intensity and high volume, with emphasis on building an overall conditioning "base" for the athlete. This is also true for running workouts and low-intensity plyometrics. High-intensity plyometrics (e.g., depth jumps) should not be introduced into the workouts until the athletes have a fair amount of conditioning under their belts (four to six weeks).

Throwing workouts during the preparation phase will concentrate on establishing good fundamental technique, as well as addressing any technical weaknesses an individual may have. Specific drills used to help correct technical weaknesses are usually performed at high volume at 70–80% intensity to ensure the focus is on establishing proper neuromuscular patterns. Throwing drills can also be performed with knockenballs, powerballs, and implements of various weights to allow for an increase in the volume of throws and specific strength conditioning.

Precompetition Phase

This phase serves as a transitional period for training as the thrower gets ready for the competitive season. The precompetition phase can last anywhere from four weeks to two or three months. It is characterized by an increase in the intensity and a decrease in volume of both conditioning and throwing. Weight training, during this phase, switches from an emphasis on overall body conditioning to an emphasis on Olympic and power lifts for explosive development. Plyometrics are also increased in intensity and will be performed at the most intense level of any of the three training phases. Running workouts shift from an emphasis on cardiovascular conditioning to quicker, more explosive running that conditions the fast-twitch fibers.

In terms of throwing, there is an increase in the number of full throws taken with the discus, as the technical emphasis shifts from correcting individual weaknesses to developing throwing rhythm. Note that there should still be specific drill work at this time, isolating various aspects of the throw; but as the competition season begins, work should begin on developing a feel for the whole throw. Throwing intensity ranges from 70 to 90% during this training phase.

Competition Phase

The competition phase sees intensity in both throwing and conditioning reach its highest levels. This is accompanied by a decrease in the volume of throws taken and the amount of conditioning performed. Weight-lifting sessions are shorter and more intense, with fewer repetitions performed per set. Other aspects of conditioning, such as running and specific conditioning drills, emphasize development of maximal speed and explosiveness. The number of plyometric contacts begins to taper at this point in the season, so the thrower can peak for the major competitions that occur during this phase.

Throwing workouts during the competition phase are geared toward getting the thrower ready to perform at the highest level. Much of the throwing consists of full throws to develop a good throwing rhythm and to fine-tune the thrower's timing. Competitions can also be simulated in practice so that the thrower gets used to throwing at 100% intensity. Light implements may also be thrown during this phase to develop the thrower's speed, which is specific to the event.

For the best results, coaches must put together a general training plan for the preparation, precompetitive, and competitive phases. From there, weekly workouts can be planned. Tables 15.2 and 15.3 (see pages 246–247) are sample ways to plan your practices.

Competition

Preparing for competition is something that starts long before meet day. In fact, the more time that's devoted to physical and mental preparation prior to the competitive season, the easier the body will adapt to the stressors of competition. The following are things to consider when priming athletes for competition.

Physical Preparation for Competition

In preparation for competition, throwers taper training to rest their bodies so they can reach "peak" performance. As a general rule of thumb, the thrower will want

TABLE 15.2 GENERAL TRAINING PLAN FOR DISCUS

Type of training	Preparation phase	Precompetitive phase	Competitive phase
Weight training: Olympic lifts Power lifts Assistance lifts	4-5 sets; 6-8 reps 4-5 sets; 7-10 reps 3 sets; 10 reps	4-5 sets; 4-6 reps 4-5 sets; 4-6 reps 3 sets; 10 reps	3-4 sets; 2-4 reps 3-4 sets; 3-5 reps 3 sets; 8-10 reps mixed w/light/speed lifts
Plyometrics	Agility drills, bounding/ jumping on grass	Box bounding, stair jumps, bounding/ jumping on grass	Box bounding, depth jumps, hurdle hops
Running	Run straights/jog turns Stair runs 6 × 200 m at 70% 8 × 100 m strides Hill runs	Stair runs 50-100 m sprints Hill sprints	20-50 m sprints Hill sprints Stair sprints
Throwing	**Stand throws:** w/weighted balls, powerballs, or heavy discus **Technique drills:** half-turns, step-ins, cone drills, line drills, etc.	**Full throws:** 70-90% effort w/regulation or heavy discus **Technique drills:** half-turns, step-ins, cone drills, line drills, etc.	**Full throws:** 80-100% effort w/regulation or light discus **Practice competitions** **Selected technique drills:** half-turns, step- ins, cone drills, line drills, etc.

TABLE 15.3 SAMPLE WORKOUTS FOR DISCUS

	Preparation	Precompetition	Competition
Monday	Technical drills Cleans Run hills Military press Abdominal work Light/front squat	Full throws Technical drills Back squat Hill runs Weighted-ball throws Military press Abdominal work	Full throws Back squat Incline bench Hill sprints Military press Medicine ball Abdominal work
Tuesday	Bench press Bounding Medicine ball Leg curls Leg extension Abdominal work	Cleans Bounding Medicine ball Leg curls Leg extension Abdominal work Push press	Cleans 20-40 m sprints Bar twists Weighted-ball throw Abdominal work
Wednesday	Technical drills Snatch 8 × 100 m strides	Full throws Technical drills Bench press	Full throws Bench press Push press

	Arm curls Lunges Abdominal work	Light/stairs Bar twists Arm curls Lunges Abdominal work	Box jumps Lunges Flys Abdominal work
Thursday	Incline bench Bounding Stairs Push press Flys Abdominal work	Snatch Box jumps Flys Front arm-raises Medicine ball Abdominal work	Snatch 6 × 100 m sprints Leg curls Leg extension Medicine ball Abdominal work
Friday	Technical drills Back squat 8 × 100 m strides Medicine ball Lat pulls Abdominal work	Technical drills Incline bench Lat pulls 8 × 50 m sprints Abdominal work	Rest
Saturday	Rest	Rest or competition	Competition
Sunday	Rest	Rest	Rest

to rest the day before a meet to recover from the week's training. In regard to "peaking" for major competitions, the thrower's training plan may revolve around preparing for a single major meet such as the state meet, or the national championships. In this case, one may see throwers taper their amount of weight lifting and conditioning while increasing the intensity of their throwing so they can get used to performing at maximal effort. Peaking in this fashion can occur only one or two times during a season, so throwers should have a good idea of what meets they want to emphasize. This allows them to develop their training plan for the whole year.

Psychological Preparation

Psychological preparation leading up to a competition can take many forms. One method of mental preparation is to simulate competition conditions during practice so the thrower can get used to the stress that will be experienced during competition. Another method of psychological preparation is called mental rehearsal. This can be done by visualizing key aspects of the throw or by mentally rehearsing a successful throw over and over. Throwers should also determine their optimum mental arousal state to achieve maximum performance. This arousal state will be different for each person, and may be achieved by many different means (e.g., listening to music, quiet concentration, etc.). A final consideration for both the thrower and the coach is to have reasonable expectations based on the level of talent and on the level of training. Both the thrower and coach should recognize the performance limitations of a thrower based on experience, talent, phase of training, and conditions on meet day.

Suzy Powell's mental and physical preparation enabled her to reach peak performance at the 1996 Track and Field Championships and Olympic trials.

Warm-Up

When the warm-up for competition begins, throwers must make sure that their warm-up sequence fits into the time allowed them for warm-up. Although individual warm-up routines vary from thrower to thrower, everyone must take into account the wind conditions, ring surface, and number of competitors. Finally, it is also important that throwers develop a good throwing rhythm during warm-ups and that they carry this into actual competition. Many throwers will warm up hard and then lose their throwing rhythm by trying to "get a safe throw" on their first attempt. If the warm-up is done correctly, there should be no need for a thrower to back off and get a safe one in.

Summary

It takes many years for a thrower to reach his or her maximal level of performance. Throwers will find that their peak years may be in their late 20s and early 30s, due to that fact that one can maintain or improve strength levels into one's 30s. It also takes discus throwers many years to fine-tune their technique and figure out what exactly works for them. Consistency in training with regard to technique, weight lifting, flexibility, plyometrics, and running will lead to success in this event. Identifying the best combination of these training methods along with selecting the technique that works best for each individual will allow coaches to develop their discus throwers to their full potential.

16 Javelin

C. Harmon Brown
Bill Webb
Bob Sing

The javelin, like all other throwing events, is a dynamic, total body activity. While an explosive shoulder and arm is an asset for potential throwers, the javelin requires the use of the legs, hips, and abdominal muscles to throw well. Many young throwers have shortened their careers with elbow and shoulder damage by overusing the arms without learning to effectively use the whole body. Rather than being a "throw" which implies a predominantly arm activity, the javelin throw is an overarm, whip-and-flail motion that uses the entire body.

Another factor that distinguishes the javelin from other forms of throwing is the aerodynamic feature of the javelin itself. If the application of the forces made to the implement are not made so that the flight of the javelin follows the correct flight path, distances will be cut short.

In selecting candidates for the javelin, the coach has more latitude in body build than in the other throwing events, which require greater size and strength. Successful javelin athletes can come in all shapes and sizes. For example, champion male throwers have ranged in size from the small, dynamic Jorma Kinnunen at 5 feet, 9 inches (about 175 cm) and 170 pounds (about 77 kg) to the muscular bodybuilder Mark Murro. Women athletes have been tall and lithe like Petra Felke, or compact and muscular like Fatima Whitbread. However, successful javelin athletes should possess speed, explosive strength, good coordination and kinesthetics, overall flexibility, and a feel for overarm throwing that can be transferred to the javelin. In screening athletes for the javelin, tests such as the BAAB quadrathlon (30-meter sprint from standing start, two-handed overhead backward shot throw, standing long jump, and standing triple jump), as well as the softball throw for distance, are useful predictors.

General Principles

The javelin throw is essentially a linear, speed-oriented event, whose objective is to impart maximal release velocity to the implement in order to achieve maximal distance. To attain this objective, the athlete and coach must focus on several fundamental principles:

• Achieve the highest possible *controllable* runway speed, and maintain this speed into the final "block" stage of the throw and release.

• Withdraw the javelin so as to align it and the shoulder axis along the line of the throw, while keeping the hips forward as comfortably as possible so as to maintain running velocity.

• Execute the transition or "crossover" steps properly, so as to allow force to be generated from the legs and trunk, and allow the center of gravity to continue forward.

• Develop the proper tempo and rhythm from the above in order to summate all the forces and achieve a forceful "block" of the left side of the body (assuming a right-handed thrower).

• Maintain a relaxed upper body and arm as long as possible to allow for a delayed "whip-and-flail" action of the throwing arm. The throwing shoulder should be "pretorqued," with the hand and arm above the plane of the shoulder, and the tip of the javelin at chin to eye level, so that the release is an automatic response.

Aerodynamics

The javelin is an airfoil, whose flight is controlled by such factors as release velocity and release angle. In addition, wind direction and speed also play a major role in determining the flight distance. Thus, the release angle must be adjusted for the wind, with a lower angle being used when throwing into the wind. In practice, the optimal release angle is about 35 ± 3 degrees in relation to the horizontal.

Biomechanics

It is important for coaches and athletes to understand the terms that biomechanists and javelin coaches use to describe both javelin and athlete characteristics during the throw. These factors determine the flight characteristics of the implement and the distance attained. Many modern biomechanics studies are carried out using three-dimensional methods, which may give different values and information than older, two-dimensional reports (figure 16.1).

Release velocity—this is usually reported in meters per second (m/s). For elite males these values are 28–30 meters/second, and for females 25–26 meters/second.

Attitude angle—the angle of the javelin in relation to the horizontal.

Angle of release—the angle at which force is applied to the grip of the javelin at release, and which follows closely the path of the hand.

Angle of attack—the difference between the attitude angle and the release angle. This should be as close to 0 as possible, indicating that the athlete is "throwing through the point."

Tumbling angular velocity—a measure of the rotational forces applied to the shaft of the javelin, which cause it to oscillate (vibrate) and rotate forward (tumble).

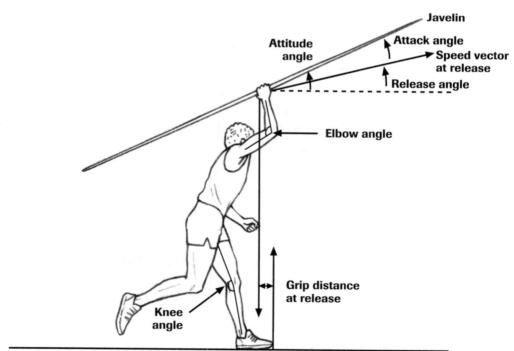

Figure 16.1 Biomechanics of javelin release.

Technique

The javelin event is usually divided into several phases:

1. Approach
2. Transition
3. Block and release
4. Follow-through

Approach

The approach run is the run-up phase prior to the withdrawal of the javelin. The run-up develops total body velocity, which is the energy that must be transferred to the throw itself. It should add 30–40% to the distance the javelin can be thrown from a standing position. Most throwers use a 12–15-step run-up, but some larger athletes find that 8–10 steps are adequate. The run-up should be a gradual acceleration, reaching the maximal *controllable* speed that can be maintained throughout the transition and release. The athlete should be as relaxed as possible during the run, especially in the upper body and shoulders. The javelin should be carried comfortably over the shoulder. Keeping it level or tip down aids in alignment during the withdrawal, as there is better eye-hand coordination.

Transition

This phase is used to withdraw the javelin in preparation for an optimal upper-body flail-and-whip action, and to prepare the lower body and trunk for a rapid, explosive drive into the block and release. This is usually accomplished with a five-step pattern (L,R,L,R,L for the right-handed thrower as in figure 16.2), although some athletes find it necessary to use a seven-step pattern to feel comfortably positioned for the body to strike the javelin. Those who use the seven-step rhythm must make a special effort to maintain velocity into and through the block-and-release phase.

Javelin withdrawal usually begins when the left foot lands (L1). The shoulders turn and the throwing arm is laid back with the palm up, so that the arm is above the plane of the shoulders, with the arm externally rotated at the shoulder (figure

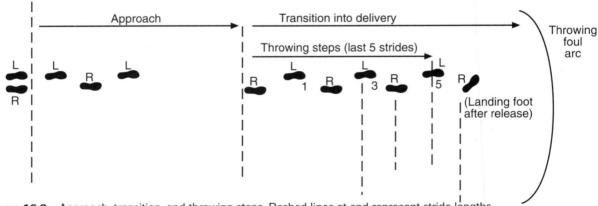

Figure 16.2 Approach, transition, and throwing steps. Dashed lines at end represent stride lengths.

16.3a-b). This "pretorque" position prepares the shoulder and arm for an automatic, high whip-and-flail release. The javelin tip is aligned at the level of the chin or eye, and the shoulders are kept level. The shoulders are aligned in the direction of the throw, with the left arm swung long and low across the chest to aid balance during the running strides.

The legs and hips are very active during this phase, with the left leg pulling and pushing the hips and trunk forward. The shoulder turn should dictate the amount of hip rotation and foot placement. Additional sideward turning of the hips and feet will cause deceleration, and defeat the main objective of the run-up—that is, speed into the block. The next-to-last (penultimate) step should be a vigorous forward drive off the left leg. This pull-push impulse of the active left leg (the "impulse step") aids in its rapid recovery and places the left leg in a fully extended position to be able to block at foot contact. The left foot should be beyond the right foot at right-foot touchdown. This stride drives the hips and trunk forward, and also lowers the center of gravity. The trunk is kept erect in order to maintain forward speed and allow rapid grounding of the left foot. The left arm is extended in the throwing direction, and the left shoulder raised slightly to open the chest and prepare for the hip and trunk strike. The eyes should be focused on a point about 50 meters into the field. The right leg is swung forward with the knee flexed and the toe turned up. This aids in pulling the hips forward during the forward drive from the left leg. The bent right leg is then thrust backward vigorously during grounding. The throw begins as soon as the right foot lands, with the thrower driving forward off the right foot against the blocked left side. This is the so-called soft-step action (figure 16.3c).

"Laying back" with the trunk to increase the "pull distance" is to be avoided, as this slows forward speed, and delays grounding of the blocking leg.

Block and Release

The block and release should be considered an explosive continuation of the preceding phases. Energy built up from the approach run and a properly executed transition can be converted into maximal release velocity only by a vigorously and correctly executed block and release. The hips and trunk are thrust forward against a straight, or nearly straight, left leg (figure 16.3d-f). The throw should be executed "from the ground up," with the right hip rotating about the hip axis, finishing with the hips facing in the direction of the throw. The left-leg block and the right-leg drive force the right hip to accelerate rapidly, stretching the trunk. The left foot should be planted in the throwing direction.

The left arm initially is extended in the throwing direction, to stabilize the shoulders and prevent premature rotation ("opening"). It is then brought down rapidly against the left side, as part of the left-sided block. The left shoulder should remain forward ("closed") as much as possible. This opens the chest and the torso, while the throwing arm remains relaxed and trailing.

These actions cause a prestretch of the chest and trunk muscles, resulting in reflex contraction of the trunk, and finally a flail-like action of the throwing arm. The athlete should finish with the hips, shoulders, head, and eyes focusing forward in the throwing direction (figure 16.3g-h).

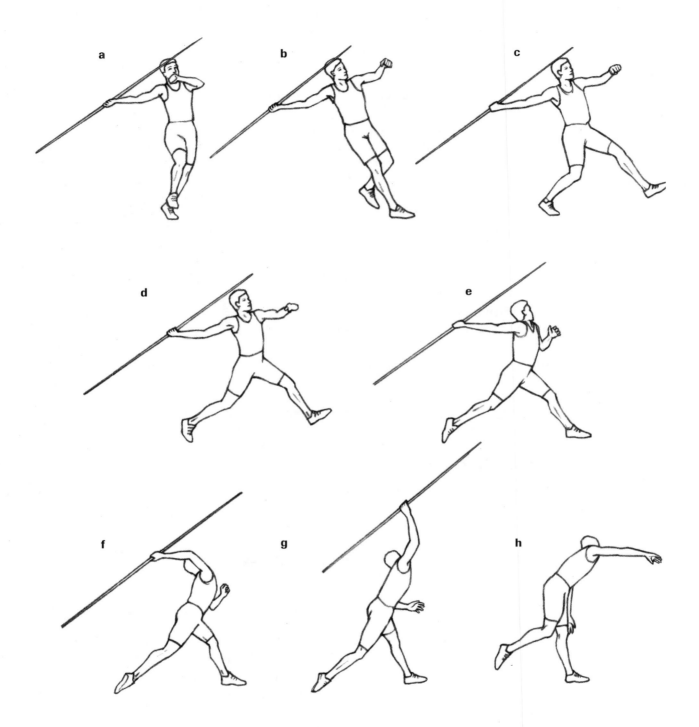

Figure 16.3 Transition, block, and release.

Follow-Through

The athlete must think of driving *through* the block, and not just *to* it. This will force the body high up onto the left toe after the release. A single final step should be used to check further forward momentum.

The approach run and steps should be established so as to allow seven to eight feet for this follow-through. Crowding the foul line in order to obtain added distance will cause premature deceleration and a poor effort.

Training

by Bill Webb and Bob Sing

The javelin event brings into play many ballistic and explosive forces that place great stress on all the body segments, especially the knees, low back, and shoulder and elbow. Training must be considered as a holistic program that prepares the body and mind to be able to withstand these stresses. The training program must encompass the elements of speed, strength, flexibility, technique development, ballistic explosiveness, and mental toughness and aggressiveness. All of these factors must be included in the training program, with the emphasis on any element or combination of elements varying during the training cycle. Ideally, for the mature athlete, the training process should occur through the entire year. However, for the younger athlete, especially in high school, each phase of the training cycle may need to be shortened to accommodate participation in other sports, weather conditions and available facilities, and the length of the permissible training and competition season.

Initially, the thrower should concentrate on building a sound strength base to prevent injuries when hard throwing sessions begin. During the beginning phases, bulk training in the form of weight lifting, running, bounding, and volume throwing (medicine balls and weighted balls) is the norm. A smooth transition should follow, moving toward less weight training and more technique work. Then the athlete should move gradually into the competitive season, with the emphasis shifting to power, technique, and psychological preparation.

Training Seasons

The training year is divided into four phases lasting three months each. The time frame of these phases can be altered according to the athlete's school year or work schedule. For students, an alternative eight-month training cycle consisting of four two-month phases can be planned.

Foundation Phase

The foundation phase lasts from September through November. It is concerned with building the strength and stamina base needed for the development of throwing power. Proper physical conditioning is also important to reduce injuries. A base of strength, flexibility, and overall conditioning is stressed. This is accomplished through weight training, running, and basic skill training. Bulk training, involving high-repetition, low-resistance exercises, occurs during the foundation phase.

During the competitive season, athletes should focus on perfecting their throwing technique.

Power-Development Phase

The power-development phase lasts from December through February. Overall power development is acquired through alternate-day weight training, primarily using the pyramid method of lifting (i.e., training with progressively increasing poundage with a corresponding decrease in repetitions). Power development for the specific throwing motion is improved by quantity-throwing sessions with overweight balls, medicine balls, and stubbies (short javelins with soft rubber ends used for indoor training). Distance runs and sprints (with and without the javelin), along with bounding and jumping exercises, round out the majority of the training during this phase. This power-development phase is the most intensive and time-consuming period of the year.

Early Competition Phase

The early competition phase takes place from March through May. Power training continues during this phase, but the loads are gradually reduced. Concentration on refining technique begins. Throwing underweight implements helps in the development of the explosive effort, as does concentration on mental imagery and rehearsal exercises. Flexibility exercises, especially when associated with mental (psychological) drills, are very beneficial to the physical and mental well-being, as well as performance, of the athlete. Sprint training and bounding exercises compose the majority of the running training. Early, small track meets are used to rehearse for upcoming major competitions.

Late Competition Phase

The late competition phase lasts from June through August. During the competitive months, the emphasis is on throwing, flexibility, and speed training. All other training modalities are used to a lesser extent, depending upon the athlete's competition schedule. Mental imagery and rehearsal exercises, with the mental emphasis on the "relaxed but explosive" final effort, are practiced regularly during this phase.

Sample training schedules are provided in tables 16.1 and 16.2. Of course, the amount of time spent on each activity should vary according to the training cycle.

Weight Training

The foundation for javelin throwing is the development of strength and power, which is best maximized by weight training. You and your athlete must always remember that although weight training is important, most important is the correct application of these power gains into the biomechanics of the throw.

The major weight-training exercises are squats, snatches, power cleans, lat pull-downs, pullovers (bent- and straight-arm), trunk twists (barbell on shoulders), jerks from the rack, and speed jerks (jumping jacks).

Other useful weight exercises include the bench press, inclined press, dead lift, triceps extension (French curls), rowing (standing and bent), shoulder press (military press), and "cheat" curls.

TABLE 16.1 JAVELIN TRAINING SCHEDULE FOR NONLIFTING DAYS

Daily practice	Time (min.)*
1. Warm-up jog	5
2. General flexibility exercises	30
3. Specific flexibility exercises	10

4. Technique work:
    a. Javelin drills
    b. Weighted balls
    c. Medicine balls
	60-120

5. Jumps and sprints	10-20
6. Cool-down jog and stretch	5
7. Mental training	No limit

Every week has 2 or 3 nonlifting days.
*Varies according to training phase.

TABLE 16.2 JAVELIN TRAINING SCHEDULE FOR LIFTING DAYS

Daily practice	Time (min.)*
1. Warm-up jog	5
2. General flexibility exercises	30
3. Specific flexibility exercises	10
4. Brief throwing session (optional)	30
5. Hopping, bounding, hurdle jumps, depth jumps in autumn	10-20
6. Weight training	60-120
7. Cool-down jog and stretch	5
8. Mental training	No limit

Every week has 3 lifting days.
*Varies according to training phase.

Drills

The following drills can assist in the development of the athlete's technical abilities. Each of them contributes to some aspect of the throw.

Standing Throws

Standing throws with the javelin

Standing throws with medicine balls (two-handed)

Standing throws with weighted implements (one-handed, using weighted balls and stubbies)

Overhead shot-put throws (8- and 12-pound/3.6 kg and 5.4 kg)

Short-Approach Throws

Three-step, five-step, and seven-step javelin throws

Approach Drills

Cariocas

Sprints with the javelin

Cross-step running with the javelin

Cross-step dragging a 5- to 10-pound (2.25 kg to 4.5 kg) weight

Other Drills

Vertical jumping

Depth jumping

Bounding exercises

Hopping over hurdles or boxes

Simulation exercises using cable or rubber tubing

Pulley-related exercises

Lunges

Axe swings (one- and two-handed)

Isometric-isotonic exercises (Exer-Genie)

Key Coaching Points

1. In the acceleration (driving and jumping) phase of the throw, look for these technical aspects:
   - Full extension of the left leg when driving into the throw
   - Aggressive forward and upward right-knee drive during the cross-step (keeping the right toe up in an attempt to land on the right mid-foot or heel)

- Forward, rather than upward, trajectory of the hips (center of gravity) into the throw
- Maximum controlled horizontal distance covered in the last two steps

2. To keep the trunk and head erect and in balance through the release, look for the following:

- Chin up, eyes straight ahead
- Trunk position similar to that of a triple jumper, with very little lateral or front-to-back deviation

3. When completing the delivery one javelin-length from the foul line, look for an aggressive follow-through step that uses up six to eight feet after the throw.

4. At the instant of touchdown with the right foot in the throwing stride, the thrower assumes a position of readiness. Look for these aspects:

- Left heel 8 to 12 inches in front of the right foot, so it can be regrounded quickly with a wide base
- Weight (center of gravity) over or behind a flexed right leg
- Throwing arm fully extended behind, with the javelin held close to the head (in the cheek-to-forehead area)
- Throwing hand about even with the middle of the back (as viewed from behind) and not sliding out as the left foot is regrounded; maintaining "maximum controlled torque/wrap"

5. With the left arm and right leg initiating throw, look for the following:

- Left arm and shoulder active, pulled forward and backward in a breaststroke fashion that stretches the upper chest, before the right-arm strike occurs
- Right hip and leg active in a turning manner before the right-arm strike

6. Left-side block and release completed in a full frontal position; look for these aspects:

- Shoulder and hip planes both facing straight forward at the instant of release

  (*Note:* For additional discussion of overrotation, see the following section on faults and corrections.)

- Complete extension of the left (blocking) leg occurring simultaneously with the javelin release
- After release, the hips and shoulders passing over the left leg and aggressively out toward the foul line

7. All things being equal, an improvement in general athletic ability (athletic quotient) improves the thrower's ability to create greater forces during the throw, thus increasing the throwing distance. You and your athlete should do the following:

- Periodically (two to four times/year) test various related one- and two-handed throws with different weight implements or medicine balls.
- Periodically (two to four times/year) test various related hopping and bounding tests off both one and two legs.
- Periodically (two to four times/year) test various strength and other fitness components to see whether continued progress is being made.

Correcting Common Faults

Fault: Excessive increase in the angle of attack during the throw, commonly referred to as *losing the point.*

Causes:

- Dropping the throwing arm and hand during the cross-step, allowing the javelin point to excessively elevate.
- Bending at the waist.
- Bending the plant leg during the throw.

Discussion: As the athlete performs the cross-step, you will note that the tip rises up because the rear, throwing hand drops. The athlete must maintain a high rear hand and not allow it to drop during the cross-step. Also, the hips must be high and solidly based if the throwing hand is to travel upward at the same positive angle as the attack angle of the javelin. If the thrower instead bends at the waist and keeps the hips low and behind the trunk, the forward motion of the trunk goes downward while the javelin tends to go up. The athlete consequently "pulls" down on the javelin, causing the javelin to bow and the point to go upward. The athlete's center of gravity also goes down if the athlete bends the plant leg excessively; so he or she again pulls down on the javelin.

Corrections: The thrower must prevent the throwing hand from dropping during the cross-step and must maintain the point at eye level, not letting it get away. Also, the thrower must keep the center of gravity up and forward to avoid pulling down on the javelin.

Fault: Inefficient transfer of the center of gravity.

Causes:

- Poor cross-step action.
- Initiating the throw before the plant foot hits the ground.

Discussion: Before the initiation of the throw, the right hip must start as far behind the right (drive) foot as possible. How far back the hips start is directly related to the cross-step. If a brisk cross-step is completed, the athlete's center of gravity (the hips) will be behind the drive foot during the landing after the crossover, often referred to as the *seat position.* The thrower then must wait until the plant foot strikes to complete the shift of the center of gravity from the drive leg onto the plant leg. In his 310 feet, 4 inches (94.59 m) world-record throw, in the 1976 Olympic Games in Montreal, Miklos Nemeth utilized an aggressive, brisk cross-step that allowed for the deep seat position that resulted in an extremely powerful hip drive and a stupendous hand speed.

A common mistake during the cross-step is the thrower's reaching for the ground with the drive leg and landing with a straight drive leg. In this case, the center of gravity is high over the drive leg, instead of behind it; therefore, there is no appreciable seat position. As a result, the athlete is unable to drive the right hip onto the plant leg, because the drive leg is already straight. Soft-step cannot occur, and the athlete literally falls onto the plant leg instead of driving into it.

The outside observer notes that (a) the thrower has no seat position, (b) the thrower gets off the drive leg too fast, and (c) the drive foot is lifted off the ground in a running motion as the javelin is being thrown. The thrower reports missing the throw, throwing with the arm only, or the throw had nothing behind it.

Sometimes the thrower experiences a sharp, jarring pain in the lower back because of the shock of crashing down onto the plant leg.

Corrections: The successful javelin thrower must develop a profound appreciation of cross-step mechanics. The cross-step must be aggressive, be low to the ground, and cover a lot of ground. The athlete must wait for the ground to "come up" to him or her; the athlete must not reach for the ground with the drive foot during the cross-step. The upper body must be delayed so that the center of gravity can be positioned underneath and in front of the upper body, resulting in the seat position. Also, the athlete should endeavor to use the landing of the plant foot (not the drive foot) as the focus of the explosive initiation of the throw.

Fault: Deceleration of the run-up during the transition steps and into the throw proper.

Causes:

- Poorly developed coordination and rhythm of the thrower.
- Too much acceleration in the run-up speed before the transition steps.
- Lack of confidence.

Discussion: The ideal is to accelerate into the throw. Any hint of deceleration markedly reduces the distance thrown. The final two steps absolutely must be the quickest.

Corrections: The thrower must practice acceleration drills going into the throw. These drills develop the coordination, rhythm, and, ultimately, the confidence necessary for the successful thrower. The athlete may have to consciously slow the run-up speed to then be able to accelerate through the transition steps.

Fault: Bending at the waist during the throw.

Causes:

- Premature halting of the hips, resulting in inefficient acceleration of the upper trunk ("rushing" the upper body).
- Inadequate trunk strength.

Discussion: Rushing the upper body, with subsequent bending at the waist, is a common error usually resulting from the thrower's attempt to throw hard and fast. The problem is that if the hips are going backward as the upper body is rushing forward, there is a decreased net forward motion. Therefore, the athlete is throwing off an unstable hip base (like shooting a rocket off a rowboat), and the feeling of acceleration is actually an illusion!

Corrections: The thrower must learn to relax and allow the throw to happen. He or she can practice the correct hip motion by making sure that the hips are high over the plant leg during throwing drills and medicine ball throws. Once the upward hip motion has improved, the throwing arm follows the path of least resistance, and the athlete finds it easier to deliver the javelin at the correct attack angle by this formation of a solid trunk throwing base. Improvement of trunk strength with various lifts, twists, and sit-ups is a must.

Fault: Throwing with the arm bent at the elbow.

Causes:

- Arm strike before the lower body can complete its part in the throw.
- Poor throwing shoulder flexibility.

Discussion: Throwing with a bent elbow is generally considered evidence of an early arm strike. This fault is usual in novice American throwers because of their initial attempts to throw the spear like a football or a baseball. In this respect, the correct javelin throw must be considered a "pull" rather than a simple throw. The problem can be corrected if the thrower starts the throw from as far as possible to the rear, allowing the pulling muscles of the trunk and shoulder (primarily the latissimus dorsi) to participate in the throw. Occasionally, though, a thrower comes along and throws very successfully with a bent arm.

Corrections: The javelin thrower must train to pull the spear from as far as possible to the rear. Pulley work and simulation exercises using rubber tubing help develop the pulling motion. Flexibility exercises involving the throwing shoulder are vital to correct throwing motion; they easily correct a bent arm if hindered shoulder mechanics is the problem (shoulder flexibility exercises are, in any case, a must for all javelin throwers).

Fault: Throwing the javelin like a dart.

Cause: Literally pushing the javelin out like a dart rather than pulling the spear from behind.

Discussion: Throwing the spear like a dart is a developmental bad habit resulting from an overemphasis on throwing "through the point" (applying all of the accumulated throwing force directly into the shaft of the javelin) during early coaching. The athlete learns to disregard the pulling motion completely in an effort to ensure that the hand action runs straight down the shaft, giving the observer the impression of a dart-throwing motion. Although throwing through the point is an admirable quality, it should not be forced at the expense of the pulling motion.

Corrections: The corrections are the same as those for throwing with a bent arm (the previous fault). The idea and feeling of pulling the javelin can be developed with simulation training by using pulleys and rubber tubing exercises.

Fault: Inefficient blocking of the nonthrowing side.

Causes:

- Excessive flexion (bending) of the plant leg.
- Overrotating the shoulders during the throw.
- Overrotating the hips by putting the plant foot too far to the side opposite the throwing arm.

Discussion: The distance the javelin is thrown is directly proportional to the horizontal velocity of the throwing-side hip, which is in turn directly proportional to the rate of the horizontal deceleration of the other hip. The thrower must block (stop and stabilize) the opposite side as quickly as possible to maximize this throwing-side acceleration. If the opposite side is not stabilized, the athlete will experience the "pirouette effect," continuing to spin off to the opposite side, and overrotating. This overrotation can be caused by any one of a number of mechanisms, or by a combination of them.

Corrections: The athlete must develop a firm opposite-side block by consciously making the effort to stop the opposite-side leg, trunk, and shoulder, and accelerating the throwing side around it. The sensation of the stable, tight opposite side must be pursued every time the javelin is thrown. Also, the thrower must learn to square off to the direction of the throw with the hips first, then the shoulders.

The next two faults include specific corrections for the inefficient blocking of the nonthrowing side.

Fault: Bent plant leg (excessive flexion of the plant leg).

Causes:

- Too much of the hip force being driven down into the plant leg instead of over it.
- Not producing enough power in the hip and thigh region.

Discussion: A bent plant leg causes the left hip to continue to move forward, causing energy to be absorbed, which reduces hip torque. The acceleration of the throwing side is directly proportional to the deceleration of the other side; in the case of the bent plant leg, the other side's deceleration is sluggish and incomplete. The plant leg should bend slightly (30 degrees at the most) before it must quickly straighten out at the instant of release.

Corrections: The athlete should try to throw high over the plant leg rather than drive down into it. Sometimes concentrating on getting up onto the toes of the plant foot as soon as the throw is off can help the athlete get higher. Quadriceps strengthening exercises, including knee extensions, squats, and cleans, are helpful in preventing excessive flexion of the plant knee during the throw. Medicine ball drills, with concentration on high release, improve the trunk-hip strength and assist in the development of the opposite-side block.

Fault: Putting the foot in the bucket (plant foot).

Cause: Starting the throw too early, before the plant foot hits the ground.

Discussion: By pointing the foot outward, away from the centerline and the throwing side, the thrower cannot effectively block the nonthrowing-side hip. This action, coupled with putting the foot too far away from the midline, is a mistake commonly called "putting the foot in the bucket." This action results from prematurely starting the hip drive before the plant foot lands, thereby swinging the plant foot too far from the throwing side.

Corrections: The thrower should delay starting the throw until after the plant foot has hit the ground. The plant foot should therefore land in a direct line with the throw, with the toes pointing straight forward in the direction of the throw.

Fault: Wrong mental attitude in competitive situations.

Causes:

- A mental and physical tightening feeling, commonly referred to as *choking*.
- Lack of confidence.

Discussion: The number of throwers who throw well in practice sessions and poorly in competitions is countless. How many throwers throw well after the competition, throwing what is sometimes called the "elusive seventh throw"?

Mental preparation is extremely important if the athlete is to excel in the javelin event. The thrower must be confident in his or her technique. The thrower must think in a positive manner. Instead of worrying about making mistakes and someone else winning, the thrower should be focusing on the throw at hand.

If not the first-place winner, the athlete should be consoled by knowing that he or she has trained as hard as possible for the competition. The thrower must view competition as an opportunity for expression of power and the athletic art.

Corrections: Have the athlete practice relaxation techniques (deep-breathing exercises, listening to music, and so forth) before and during competition. Develop rituals that are followed before every competition. Open discussions between the athlete and you on such topics as achievement, motivation, and goal setting can help relieve the heavy burdens that the athlete places upon him- or herself. You should develop imagery and rehearsal techniques so the athlete has a mental picture of how he or she is supposed to look and feel during a good throw. If all else fails, referral to a recognized sports psychologist may help.

Summary

Javelin throwing is an action that demands speed, strength, flexibility, technical precision, and mental aggressiveness. These are obviously not traits that are developed overnight. A complete training program that encompasses the above elements is necessary for achieving success. When it comes time to compete, the athlete who has prepared both the body and mind and who constantly strives for perfection will come out ahead.

17 Hammer

Ken Bantum

Perhaps the most intriguing of all throwing events, the hammer throw stands out for its uniqueness. I know of no other event that creates such fanatics and lifelong devotees, who, once bitten by the hammer, engage in the never-ending search for the perfect throw and the absolute technique.

Success in hammer throwing is determined by knowledge of the basic techniques, strength, agility, quickness, tireless dedication, and mental toughness.

The hammer requires a kinesthetic awareness of balance while turning at a high angular velocity. The thrower must maintain a delicate balance to prevent being yanked out of the circle by the spinning 16-pound ball or falling backward, pulled by the body's lean that counters the force of the ball.

Successful hammer throwers have come in a variety of sizes. However, the taller athlete with long arms has the distinct advantage of a longer radius. The shorter athlete must overcome this disadvantage by being able to create a higher rate of angular velocity through strength, power, and balance.

Fundamentals

The following are a few essentials about hammer throwing.

Common Terms

Many of the terms and coaching points are traditional. They have been passed down over many generations and are still applicable today. The following are terms that you must be familiar with:

Accelerate—To move faster.

Active—Using force.

Axis of rotation—The axis around which the hammer system rotates.

Block—Obstructs movement. There are positive and negative blocks in throwing.

Centrifugal force—A force that *appears* to cause a body or object that is traveling around a center to fly outward from its circular path.

Countering—Resisting pull of the hammer as it turns around the axis.

Flat—Refers to the plane of the hammer, which is horizontal or parallel to the ground.

Hammer system—The athlete and the hammer as one unit.

Hang—Countering the ball when the plane becomes steep. This position enables a deep collapse of the left leg. You are actually hanging down from the ball.

Heel-toe turn—Turning on the heel and toe.

Post—Having the foot drive down, as in driving a post into the ground.

Push—Pushing with the right arm and hand to create a wide rotation around the left side.

Radius—The distance from center or turning axis.

Release—The actual throwing of the hammer by the lower body and back, more so than by the arms.

Sit—A position done by bending the knees and lowering the hips during the turns to counter the hammer pull.

Skim—Executing a hard heel turn, keeping the ball of the foot close to the ground.

Toe turn—Turning completely around (360 degrees) on the toe.

Triangle—The isosceles triangle formed by the shoulders and hands.

Equipment

You'll need the following equipment to perform the drills in this chapter.

- Shoes—flat shoes, preferably hammer shoes
- Glove for left hand. Fingertips must be exposed.
- Implements—heavy, official, light

- Broom (type used for sweeping)
- Heavy rubber bands or surgical tubing
- Long athletic sock
- Lightweight indoor shot
- Medicine ball

Philosophy

Confidence is the key to success.

Do not attempt to overpower the implement. Learn to appreciate the science of the event. Follow the learning sequences. They are the building blocks. Confidence comes from accomplishing these small feats. Confidence allows the body to relax and perform more efficiently. Tension causes the body to become rigid and ineffective.

Teaching Progression

The following steps will aid in the development of a successful hammer thrower. All references are for right-handed throwers.

Appreciation of Radius

Before doing any throwing at all, perform this experiment. Take two athletic socks, one crew and one knee length. Place the lightweight indoor shot or a similar light weight in one of the socks. Wind up and release it. Place the weight in the other sock and repeat the wind up and release. You will find that the weight goes farther in the longer sock. This illustrates how the length of the radius (effective radius) influences ball-head speed, which is directly responsible for distance.

Grip

First grip with the left hand. Allow the handle to rest on the last digits of the fingers. Overlap with the right hand (figure 17.1).

Positioning and Countering

The following drills teach the thrower about the sense of the grip and feeling the long radius of the hammer, as well as about flat plane and centrifugal force.

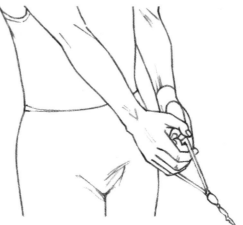

Figure 17.1   Right-handed grip.

Walk-Around Drill

The arms are held in front of the body in a relaxed manner with the feet fairly close together. Note the triangle made by the shoulders and hands. This must never break down. The head should be back, with the eyes focused on the ball. (Look under the bottom of eyeglasses or look continuously in the direction of the ball.) The thrower should turn counterclockwise in place using small steps to initiate movement and to stay centered. The faster the thrower turns, the more he or she has to resist the "centrifugal force" that appears to be created. As the thrower increases the turning speed, he is forced to sit more and more to counter the pull of the hammer (figure 17.2).

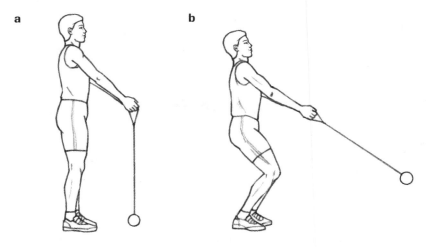

Figure 17.2 Walk-around drill: as the thrower's turning speed increases, he or she is forced to sit more and more to counter the pull of the hammer.

Tug of War Drill

If there is only one thrower, the coach holds the thrower's hands to teach correct posture. Hips underneath, head back, back straight. With two throwers, you can add a little fun by having them shuffle quickly clockwise and counterclockwise (figure 17.3).

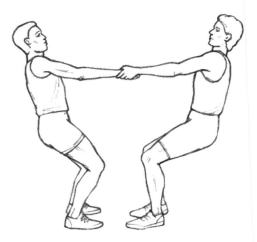

Figure 17.3 Tug of war drill.

Turning the Radius

The following drill is meant to teach throwers the proper arm and overall body position in relation to the hammer's wide arc.

Right Hand Drill

The thrower assumes the starting position at the back of the circle, facing 0 degrees, in an upright posture with feet slightly less than shoulder-width apart. Knees should be flexed. The thrower grasps the broom by the handle with the right hand and extends the arm out in front.

The thrower pivots on the heel of the left foot while keeping the ball of the foot close to the surface (skim). At the same time that the thrower drives and pivots the right foot counterclockwise, he pushes the broom in a wide arc. The broom should be parallel to the ground, with most of the weight transferred to the left foot (figure 17.4). The right knee should be close to the left knee and the right toe barely in contact with the ground. Have the thrower repeat this many times until done satisfactorily.

Next, increase the range of motion from 90 degrees to 180 degrees. The thrower initiates the same movement to 90 degrees; however, at 90 degrees he drives the right knee around and forward in a sprinting manner. The knee will go close to the left knee and be in a position similar to that of a sprinter (knee forward with toe down).

The weight should shift from the heel of the left foot to the ball to complete the 180-degree turn. When the turn is completed, the broom should be at 180 degrees. It should be slightly higher in plane than horizontal. Though the upper body remains upright, the plane of the movement forces the thrower to sit back slightly. The plane of the broom's movement also causes the left leg to collapse as well. The athlete should repeat this movement many times (figure 17.5).

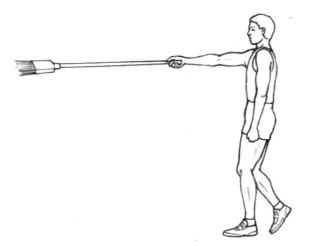

Figure 17.4 Right hand drill—finishing position after 90-degree range of motion.

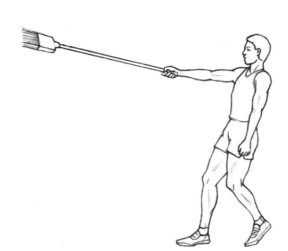

Figure 17.5 Right hand drill—finishing position after 180-degree range of motion.

In the preceding drill,

- the wide arc created by the broom represents the long radius we desire;
- the movement of the right foot is somewhat like that of a sprinter—the faster you turn, the higher your knee lifts;
- the faster the turn, the steeper the plane; and
- the faster you turn, the more you collapse.

What we should know about plane is that at 0 degrees the hammer is at its low point. At 180 degrees, the hammer is at its high point. At 90 degrees and 270 degrees, the hammer is horizontal. The arms should never be more than perpendicular to the body throughout the execution of the throw.

Winds

When practicing winds, throwers may want to use the long sock with a small weight inside instead of the hammer. After throwers have confidence that they will not injure themselves, they should execute the winds with the hammer.

One-Hand Winds

The thrower assumes the correct starting position at 0 degrees, then grasps the hammer with the right hand. The hammer rests behind and to the right of the right foot ("drag" or "pick up" position.) The thrower swings the hammer clockwise so that the handle is just overhead (figure 17.6a). As it moves overhead, the thrower twists the shoulders to the right and "catches" the hammer as it reaches approximately 270 degrees. Make sure the thrower raises the elbow as high as the top of the head, as this helps to make the winds flat. In the "catch" or "pick up" position, the arm should be extended. The thrower should do five sets of five repetitions, or until the drill is performed satisfactorily. Now the thrower grasps the hammer in the left hand and places it to the right of the right foot. As the thrower swings the hammer to the left, he must twist the shoulders again to the right. As the thrower twists to the right, he executes a high curling motion (figure 17.6b). After the hammer clears the top of the head, the arm is extended toward 270 degrees. Have the thrower do another five sets of five repetitions, or until you are satisfied with the execution.

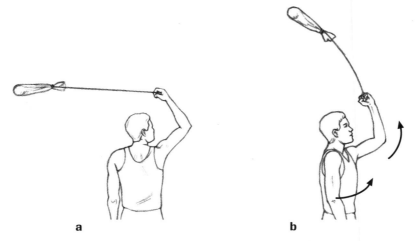

a   b

Figure 17.6 One hand winds: *(a)* clockwise swinging motion with the handle just overhead, *(b)* adding the curling motion.

Two-Hand Winds

The thrower places both hands on the handle and assumes the proper starting position. From the "drag" position, he executes five sets of five winds, or until they are done satisfactorily.

Walking Drill

A good drill to help the thrower gain confidence and control of the hammer is the "walking" drill. While winding the hammer about the head, the thrower walks about 10 steps with the legs in the deep flex position. After resting a few seconds, the thrower turns around and walks back, again executing the winds.

Make sure the winds are wide, flat, and fluid before proceeding to the next phase.

One-Hand, One-Turn Throw

The thrower assumes the correct starting position, with the hammer in the "drag" position. Taking one full wind, he sweeps the hammer as done with the broom. As the hammer moves in front, the thrower sweeps it wide and makes a full turn to 180 degrees. Because the weight of the hammer is greater than the broom, the hammer's pull will most likely cause the thrower's right foot to come down past 180 degrees, probably to 270 degrees, which is acceptable. When the right foot comes down, the thrower executes a drive pivot counterclockwise. The thrower sits back to shift his weight to the left and lifts to release the hammer. This is done 10–15 times. For most novice throwers this is enough for one day.

The thrower should review the preceding using the broom or sock device.

One-Turn Throws

The thrower assumes the starting position with both hands on the hammer. How the winds are initiated is an individual choice. Some take the hammer from a "drag" position. Some swing it from the left, up to the front and back to the right, before winding overhead.

At a controlled speed, the thrower takes two full winds around the head, making sure the winds are flat, wide, and fluid. After the second wind, the thrower executes a turn when the ball is out in front. The same footwork and upper-body work drilled on in previous passages on turning are executed here. The thrower should pay particular attention to the sweeping action of the right arm and hand, remembering that the right side of the body is the active side, while the left side lends itself more to control.

After several throws the athlete should have the sense that as the ball approaches 180 degrees, no more force can be exerted to it. This less active phase is where he catches up to the ball. Attempting to apply continuous force to the hammer will only cause the athlete to drag the ball around. This is the older, less effective method of throwing, outdated for over twenty years. We now have an active phase and a passive phase. The passive phase allows the athlete to collapse the left leg and create a hang from the hammer. It is at this time the thrower employs a quick right-foot plant. As the right foot hits, the athlete employs an explosive right-foot turn and back lift to the left side for an explosive release. Plate servings and/or medicine-ball throws are appropriate before the athlete attempts the one-turn throw and in-between throws. He should take as many as 30 one-turn throws—reviewing all aspects.

Two-Turn Throws

Before attempting the two-turn throw, athletes should do multiple turn drills and others to prepare for a successful transition from one-turn to two-turn throws.

180 Degrees to 180 Degrees Drill

The thrower holds a broom at the 180-degree position, then executes a full 360-degree turn back to the 180-degree position. This drill encourages the thrower to drive pivot more forcefully and sit back to complete the turn successfully (figure 17.7).

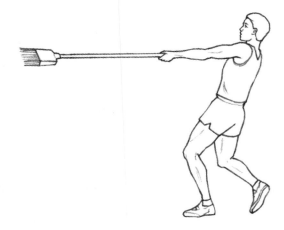

Figure 17.7   180 degrees to 180 degrees drill. The thrower must sit back to complete the turn successfully.

Wind/Turn Drill

If you have a long runway or discus circle, your athletes will receive more benefit from this drill because they will be able to do more turns. The thrower assumes the correct starting position. After two controlled winds, he executes one turn, then takes another two winds. Have the athlete repeat this as many times as the facility permits. On the last turn, the thrower executes the release.

Two-Hammer/Pipe Drill

The thrower takes two hammers, one in each hand. Holding them outstretched forward, the thrower does multiple turns. He then does the same thing with the hammers outstretched from the sides (figure 17.8). Or, taking a pipe seven to eight feet long, the thrower places it behind the neck and does multiple turns (figure 17.9).

Figure 17.8   Two hammer drill: hammers outstretched to the sides.

Figure 17.9   Pipe drill.

The athlete is now ready for two-turn throws with the hammer. The fundamentals are the same as for one-turn throws. The difficulty comes from the transition to another turn. You may also find that your throwers overturn. That is understandable—the hammer's pull causes it. However, we do not want to go past 270 degrees. The thrower must concentrate on grounding the right foot more quickly as he builds more speed into the turns.

Three-Turn Throws

Use same technique as two-turn throws. Increase drill work because transition is more difficult.

Four-Turn Throws

This is for the more advanced thrower, but not to be feared. The thrower who can master the four-turn technique may be able to gain a little more speed. Most four-turn throwers use a toe turn for their first turn. However, there are several top-notch four-turn throwers who are capable of executing four heel-toe turns. For the four-turn technique, the athlete slows down the winds and makes sure they are very flat. The athlete also may want to move the left foot to 0 degrees position to gain more room in the circle.

Bear in mind that the longtime record holder, the great Yuriy Syedikh, uses only three turns. He is tremendously fast and explosive.

Training

The following are important tips to remember when creating a training program.

- The focus of the day's workout should be based on a review of the previous day's practice. This is a good time to use the training devices to work on proper form and execution.

Key Coaching Points

- Because the hammer is moving rapidly around, it may be difficult to get the right foot down when and where the thrower wants it. Remind throwers to think, Early! Early! Early!
- The release should be thought of as another turn. The thrower should not gather for the "big one."
- To get the utmost from the legs and back at the moment of release, the thrower should think Turn! rather than, Explode! or, Stand! This thought will help the thrower maintain center and radius. Also, it will allow the thrower to achieve an effective block over and against the left leg.
- To keep the back against the ball and turn the right foot more explosively, the thrower should think, Turn! Turn! Turn! These commands could be barked out from the coach. The athlete should bark them out mentally as he executes the throw.
- To prevent dragging the hammer, the athlete keeps the eyes on the ball. To maintain correct posture, the athlete might imagine he or she is wearing eyeglasses and is looking under the lenses at the ball.
- The release angle should be between 42 and 45 degrees.

- Since we want to build and reinforce good motor patterns, select a drill that is specifically related to this end. For example, a medicine ball can be used to work on the proper release.

- Use reason instead of emotion in some decisions. Sometimes an athlete will get frustrated trying to execute a phase of the throw. It may be best to go to another phase. Once in a while the nervous system gets overly excited or agitated, and the best thing for the athlete to do is get completely away from the circle for a while.

- Generally the athlete should take about 30 throws in a practice session, depending on the weight of the implement. Obviously, taking 30 throws with the lightweight hammer is less stressing than 30 throws with the overweight hammer.

- Avoid rapid-fire throws. The athlete should take time between throws to critique the preceding throw and prepare for the next.

- I would suggest that your athletes work with the heavy implements early in the season and taper off as the championships near. At this time, increase the amount of work done with the light hammers. This is when maximum speed and explosiveness are important.

The entire conditioning program should be looked at as a triangle. We want our athletes to peak at the championship part of the season. The base of our conditioning program is composed of many cycles. The early part of the season consists of more conditioning and quantity. As we get near the championships, we want our athletes to be at maximum strength and explosiveness. The program should be designed to accomplish this. (See table 17.1.) Test before each cycle for new maximums. Structure programs based on the needs of the athlete. When all cycles are completed, start over with cycle three or four, depending on the length of your season. This should allow your athletes to peak in March and June.

TABLE 17.1 SAMPLE WORKOUTS FOR HAMMER

Where the lifts are heavy, the athlete should take two to three days of rest in between. Increase resistance 2-5% each week. Use discretion.

Cycle 1 : Four Weeks

Strength Training

Day	Exercise	Sets x Reps	Intensity
Monday	High pulls Back squats Front squats Hang cleans	3 × 12 3 × 12 3 × 12 3 × 12	40% of max. 30% of max. 20% of max. 25% of max.
Tuesday	Abdominal work		
Wednesday	Bench press Lat pull-downs Abdominal work	2 × 10 3 × 10	40% of max. 40% of max.
Thursday	Same as Monday		
Friday	Same as Wednesday		

The "General Conditioning" section that follows includes the box drill. In this drill, the athlete starts at one corner of the box, which is 20 yards by 20 yards, marked by cones. He performs a different skill at each side. The skills performed are carioca, backpedal, shuffle, and sprint. Executing the drill counterclockwise and clockwise is considered one repetition (figure 17.10).

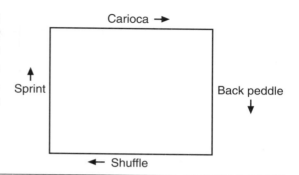

Figure 17.10 Box drill.

General Conditioning

Tuesday	Form sprint	10 × 100 m
Wednesday	Box drill	3 reps
Thursday	Run	1/2-mile to mile
Friday	Box drill	3 reps

Cycle 2 : Four Weeks

Strength Training

Day	Exercise	Sets x Reps	Intensity
Monday	High pulls	3 × 6	60% of max.
	Back squats	3 × 10	60% of max.
	Front squats	3 × 8	40% of max.
	Hang cleans	4 × 6	50% of max.
Tuesday	Abdominal work		
Wednesday	Bench press	3 × 8	60% of max.
	Lat pull-downs	3 × 8	60% of max.
	Abdominal work		
Thursday	Same as Mon.		
Friday	Same as Wed.		

General Conditioning

Repeat Cycle 1, with inclusion of stair hops on Wed. and Fri.

Cycle 3 : Four Weeks

Strength Training

Day	Exercise	Sets x Reps	Intensity
Monday	High pulls	3 × 6	70% of max.
	Back squats	3 × 8	70% of max.
	Hang cleans	4 × 4	60% of max.
Wednesday	Front squats	2 × 8	50% of max.
	Lat pull-downs	2 × 8	60% of max.
	Plate swings	3 × 15	Lightweight plate
	(Simulate hammer release)		
	Russian twists	3 × 15	Lightweight plate

(continued)

(continued)

Cycle 3 : Four Weeks			
Thursday	Same as Monday		
Friday	Front squats	2 × 8	50% of max.
	Lat pull-downs	2 × 8	60% of max.

General Conditioning

Stair bounding replaces box drill, which should become a large part of warm-up. Use a 10 × 10 yard box for warm-ups.

Tuesday	Form sprints	10 × 100 yd.
Wednesday	Stair/hurdle bounding	Bound up 10-20 stairs and down, 1-2 sets (5-10 times = 1 set) or 5 × 5 low hurdle hops*
Thursday	Run	1/2 mile to mile
Friday	Same as Wednesday	

* If you are not able to use high stairs, go immediately to hurdle hops.

Cycle 4 : Four Weeks

Strength Training

Day	Exercise	Sets × Reps	Intensity
Monday	Back squats*	4 × 6	70% of max.
	Hang cleans*	4 × 4	70% of max.
	Hang snatches*	5 × 3	40% of max.
Wednesday	Front squats	2 × 8	65% of max.
	Inclined press	2 × 8	60% of max.
	Lat pull-downs	2 × 8	60% of max.
	Plate swings	3 × 5	Increased weight
	Russian twists	3 × 10	Increased weight
Thursday	Same as Monday		
Friday	Front squats	2 × 8	65% of max.
	Inclined press	2 × 8	60% of max.
	Lat pull-downs	2 × 8	60% of max

* Form is most important here.

General Conditioning

Tuesday	80 × 60 m sprints
Wednesday	10 × 5 hurdles in low position
Thursday	1/2 to mile run
Friday	Same as Wednesday

Cycle 5 : Four Weeks

Strength Training

Day	Exercise	Sets × Reps	Intensity
Monday	Back squats	4 × 5	80% of max.
	Front squats	3 × 5	70% of max.
	Full snatches	2 × 8	70% of max.
Wednesday	Power cleans	5 × 3	70% of max.
	Bench press	2 × 8	60% of max.
	Lat pull-downs	1 × 12	60% of max.
	Plate swings	3 × 5	Increase weight
	Russian twists	3 × 10	Increase weight
Thursday	Same as Monday		
Friday	Bench press	2 × 8	60% of max.
	Lat Pull-downs	1 × 12	60% of max.

General Conditioning

Same as Cycle 4, but raise height of hurdles. For variety and for a challenge, do graduating hurdles or pyramid hurdles on Wednesday and Friday and 8-10 × 30 m sprints on Tuesday.

In addition to strength training through the more traditional resistance exercises, the athlete should work with heavier implements with short wires to build strength specific to the event. This is for off season, however. Throwing implements, such as medicine balls and the like, will also help. Newer resistance machines are available in most training facilities that offer turning resistance exercises. Hurdling and hurdling exercises and moderate plyometrics can also help.

Summary

The teaching progression in this chapter allows the athlete to first get a handle on the basic hammer throwing technique. From there, in addition to a comprehensive conditioning program, the athlete can continue to strive for technical perfection.

I have carefully omitted certain terms, like torque and lag, as they lend themselves to antiquated techniques and confusion. There are certain basic principles to successful throwing. We should not becloud the event by adding and alluding to terms that will only serve as road blocks.

Positive direction and reinforcement of the basics are the only true vehicles to success.

PART V

RACEWALKING AND MULTIPLE EVENTS

18 Racewalking

Jeff Salvage
Bohdan Bolwicaski
Gwen Robertson
Ian Whatley
Gary Westerfield

Because the training methods of racewalking are similar to those of running and because racewalking's technique is so important, this chapter focuses on the technique.

Racewalking is a contest to cover a set distance faster than the opposition, while abiding by two rules (USATF #39 and #150).

Racewalking is a unique sport of track and field. It combines endurance and technique as the two key ingredients for the athlete to focus on. Certainly strength and flexibility are also important biomotor abilities. The racewalker must have great mental concentration and tenacity to maintain proper form.

1. *Racewalking is a progression of steps so taken that the walker makes contact with the ground so that no visible (to the human eye) loss of contact occurs.* This means that before a racewalker lifts the rear foot off the ground, the leading foot must make contact with the ground. For a brief moment the heel of the leading foot and the toe of the rear foot appear to be in contact with the ground simultaneously.

2. *The advancing leg must be straightened (i.e., not bent at the knee) from the moment of first contact with the ground until in the vertical position.* On first hearing this rule, beginning walkers may think that they must walk with their legs straight all the time. This is not the case. The only stipulation is that when a racewalker's lead foot strikes the ground, his or her leg should be straight. It must stay straight until it passes under the body. Then it will have to bend to swing forward.

Proper racewalking technique is both efficient and legal. The primary objective is to maintain a constant velocity of the body's center of gravity without excessive vertical or side-to-side displacement. The visual impression of an elite racewalker is of a steady forward motion without excessive bouncing or side-to-side sway.

Technique

Our discussion of racewalking technique covers the actions of racewalking from most important action to least important. The most efficient motion for each action will be described, and *"Watch For"* sections will highlight common mistakes in technique.

Posture

The principle of good racewalking posture is simple. The body should be straight and relaxed throughout the entire stride. The lower back is flat throughout the stride without forward or backward tilt of the pelvis (figure 18.1).

Watch For:

- Bending forward at the waist (see figure 18.2.) This strains the lower back and limits hip movement. May be due to muscle weakness or an imbalance in the torso muscles.

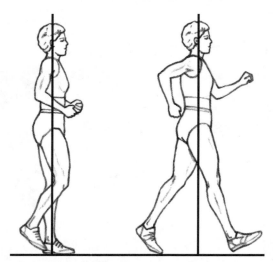

Figure 18.1 Proper racewalking posture.

Figure 18.2 Incorrect posture—bending forward at the waist.

Figure 18.3 Incorrect posture—swayback.

- Swayback (see figure 18.3). This limits the hip motion and moves the center of gravity backward. Additionally, it shortens the stride and may lead to an illegal stride. It may be due to a weakness or tightness of the lower back or abdominal muscles.

- Excessive forward or backward lean of the whole body. These are potentially injurious and reduce mechanical efficiency.

To maintain proper posture, a racewalker's head should be in a neutral position looking forward down the road.

Watch For:

Head pointed down. Usually caused by lack of concentration or weak neck muscles, this may lead to cramps in the neck and shoulders.

Hip Motion

The movement of the hips is the primary source of forward locomotion provided by the body. By rotating the hips forward (in a transverse plane parallel to the ground), the rear leg is pulled off the ground. The hips act like a motor, accelerating the knee and foot forward. In the later movements of the swing phase, the knee reaches a position forward of the hip. At ground contact, the heel is slightly forward of the knee.

Watch For:

- Excessive hip drop. Modern racewalking technique stresses hip rotation without much vertical movement of the hip joint.

- Excessive lateral hip motion. If the hips move from side to side, the body's center of gravity will move with them. This will slow forward movement and waste energy.

Stride Length

Correct hip action leads to increased stride length (see figure 18.4). This will also lead to correct foot placement along a straight line (see figure 18.5a). Insufficient hip rotation or limited flexibility in the pelvis may lead to foot placement on either side of a straight line (see figure 18.5, b-c).

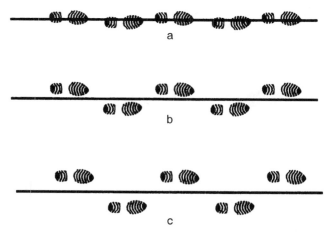

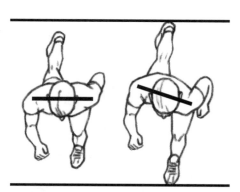

Figure 18.4 Correct hip action leads to increased stride length as seen in the figure on the right.

Figure 18.5 Foot placement: *(a)* Correct foot placement along a straight line. *(b, c)* Incorrect foot placement due to insufficient hip rotation or lack of flexibility.

A racewalker should not attempt to increase stride length by reaching out too far in front of the body using the foot, as this will cause overstriding. A racewalker should visualize the hips leading the legs and feet. Increasing the speed of the hips will directly increase the speed of the legs.

As an individual learns to racewalk, the increased use of the hips will cause the feet to land in almost an exact straight line. Be aware: if a non-racewalker attempts to mimic this foot placement without proper hip motion, he or she will place an unneeded stress across the knee.

Ideal foot placement has a racewalker's feet pointing straight ahead. Some people's foot placement will naturally point out or in because of the way they are built. These walkers should not try to change their foot placement. By using their hips properly, their footstrikes will occur in a straight line, but their feet will not be parallel. While this is less efficient, forcing the straightening of foot placement may cause stress on the legs, feet, and knees. Figure 18.6a shows the foot placement of a walker who is landing with the toes pointed in, and figure 18.6b shows that of a walker who is landing with the toes pointed out.

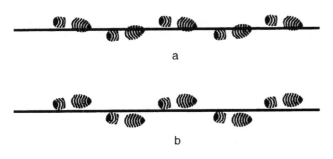

Figure 18.6 Foot placement of a walker landing with *(a)* toes pointed in, and *(b)* toes pointed out.

Knee Action

The knee must be straight from moment of heel contact until the support leg is in the vertical position (see figure 18.7.) The knee is flexed in the recovery swing, since short pendulums swing faster. The point at which the rear leg starts to bend varies from walker to walker. The optimum point for it to bend depends on the structure, flexibility, and strength of the athlete.

Watch For:

• The lead knee swinging through high. This is often due to a habit carried over from running (see figure 18.8). This wastes energy and may lead to illegal strides.

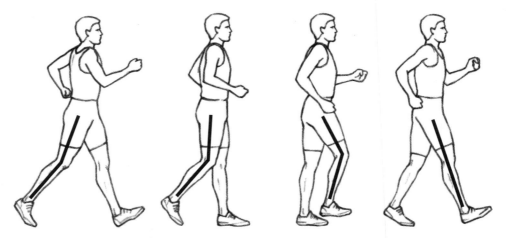

Figure 18.7 The athlete should maintain a straight knee from moment of heel contact until the support leg is in the vertical position.

- Bent knee on heel contact. This is illegal. Causes are overstriding in front of the body, inadequate quadriceps strength, and tight or weak hamstrings.
- The lead knee bending before the leg is vertically upright. This is illegal. It may be caused by the athlete trying to walk at speeds faster than his or her fitness level can sustain.

Foot Action

The heel strikes the ground first with the toes elevated, not flat-footed. Once the foot has made contact, it rolls forward, keeping the toes off the ground until the leg is supporting the body's weight. How long the toes are kept off the ground is directly related to the strength of the shin.

There is a push-off, with the calf causing the foot to roll to vertical, before leaving the ground. The foot of the swing leg is brought forward close to, but not brushing, the ground.

Watch For:

Landing flat-footed, or with the foot slapping too soon. This has a braking effect that wastes energy, shortens the stride, and may cause the knee to bend early. It may be caused by a lack of shin strength or lack of flexibility and/or lack of mobility in the hips.

Arm Action

The arm action in racewalking can vary from athlete to athlete. The elbows of a racewalker are bent at an angle between 90 degrees and 45 degrees. The elbow angle must be fixed, but with the muscles relaxed, throughout the arm swing. The arms each form a short pendulum and will swing more quickly than if they were held straight. The arms are driven predominantly backward and forward, not from side to side.

The hands trace an arc from just behind the hip at the level of the waistband to the sternum. The hands should not cross the centerline of the body. The arm movement is low and relaxed. There should not be tension between the shoulder blades nor hunching of the shoulders at the end of arm swing.

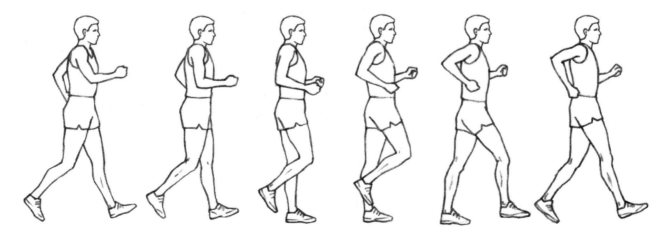

Figure 18.8 Swinging the lead knee through too high may lead to illegal strides.

Andrew Hermann strives for technical precision at the 1997 Outdoor Track and Field Championships.

A racewalker's hands should be relaxed. However, they should not dangle or flop with the arm swing. The wrist should be straight, while the hand should be held in a loose fist with the fingertips facing the hips as the arm swings past. If a racewalker is having trouble holding the hands in a relaxed manner, he or she should make a fist, holding it loosely, then place the thumb between the index finger and middle finger.

Watch For:

- Excessive side-to-side arm swing, which tends to cause side-to-side motion of the center of gravity and wastes energy. This is caused by incorrect motor skills learning.

- Elbow angle too tight (less than 45 degrees.) This may lead to a shortened stride and a bouncing motion that wastes energy. This tends to get worse as fatigue increases. It is caused by incorrect motor learning or loss of concentration.

- Elbow angle too large, which leads to a slower stride rate. This is caused by incorrect motor learning.

Summary

Racewalking improvement comes through the careful evaluation of technique. This not only helps the athlete avoid the tendency for illegal racewalking moves, it also improves the athlete's walking efficiency and, therefore, her or his chance for success.

For more information about racewalking, visit **www.racewalk.com**, or order "Walk Like an Athlete" by calling 1-888-WALK123.

19 Heptathlon

Cliff Rovelto

The heptathlon is the test for determining the most well-rounded female track and field athlete. The athlete competes in seven events over a two-day period. On day one, the athlete competes in the 100-meter hurdles, high jump, shot put, and 200-meter dash. Day two consists of the long jump, javelin, and 800-meter run. For the athlete to maximize her potential and achieve success, she must adopt a lifestyle that allows her to develop psychologically and physically. The heptathlete must be dedicated, determined, and possess great desire. Physically, she must concurrently develop all the biomotor abilities: speed, strength, stamina, skill (coordination), and suppleness.

Heptathlon Candidates

Potential candidates for the heptathlon can come from many disciplines. Historically speaking, in the United States most of our athletes have come into the heptathlon from the sprint-hurdle and/or jump disciplines. In other parts of the world, we have seen athletes who were very strong throwers achieve great success in the heptathlon. I feel it is a mistake to predetermine the pool of potential heptathletes. Jackie Joyner-Kersee, who is unquestionably the greatest heptathlete in history, was known as a great hurdler-long jumper, but her heptathlon personal records of 55 feet, 3 inches (about 16.8 m) in the shot put and 164 feet, 5 inches (about 50.1 m) in the javelin are great heptathlon throws marks in any frame of reference. Jane Frederick, the tenth-ranked heptathlete of all time and second-ranked American of all time, set her personal record of 6803 with throws of 50 feet, 10 inches (about 15.5 m) and 169 feet, 9 inches (about 51.7 m)—again, outstanding marks. At the 1997 World Championships in Athens, Sabine Braun, gold medalist, and Denise Lewis, silver medalist, both earned over 26% of their point totals in the two throwing events. The mean percentage for points earned from throws for the top 10 placers in this meet was under 25%. In short, outstanding heptathletes are very proficient in the throws.

Training Philosophy

In developing a training philosophy, the coach must consider the heptathlon scoring tables (see table 19.1), climate, facilities, and, more specifically, the age

TABLE 19.1 HEPTATHLON SCORING TABLES ANALYSIS

The first table gives a rough guide to the level of performance athletes are able to achieve by comparing their best performances to those in each table. Although not an exact score, this abbreviated table is more convenient than looking up the results on each event's complete scoring table.

The second table gives the coach the point value for adjusting scores relative to the amount of time or distance indicated.

Points	100 m hurdles	High jump	Shot put	200 m	Long jump	Javelin	800 m
500	17.89	4 ft. 6-3/4 in.	31 ft. 4 in.	29.75	15 ft. 8-1/4 in.	102 ft. 5 in.	2:46.60
600	16.97	4 ft. 10-1/4 in.	36 ft. 4 in.	28.40	16 ft. 10-3/4 in.	119 ft. 7 in.	2:37.70
700	16.12	5 ft. 1-3/4 in.	41 ft. 3-1/4 in.	27.14	18 ft. 1/2 in.	136 ft. 9 in.	2:29.47
800	15.32	5 ft. 5-1/4 in.	46 ft. 2-3/4 in.	25.97	19 ft. 2 in.	153 ft. 10 in.	2:21.77
900	14.56	5 ft. 8-1/2 in.	51 ft. 1-1/2 in.	24.86	20 ft. 3 in.	170 ft. 9 in.	2:14.52
1000	13.85	5 ft. 11-1/2 in.	56 ft.	23.80	21 ft. 3-1/4 in.	187 ft. 7 in.	2:00.00

Point value adjustments resulting from changes in performance			
100 m hurdles	.10 = 14 pts.	**Long jump**	5 cm = 15 pts.
High jump	3 cm = 39 pts.	**Javelin**	30 cm = 6 pts.
Shot put	30 cm = 20 pts.	**800 m**	1 sec. = 12-14 pts.
200 m	.10 = 9 pts.		

(chronological and training) and individual strengths and weaknesses of the athletes. These factors help determine an athlete's potential as a multi-event competitor. I feel it is in the athlete's best interest to emphasize her or his strengths and to work on eliminating weaknesses over time through her training program. The science of coaching empowers us with the knowledge of how to develop the biomotor ability areas of speed, strength, stamina, skill (coordination), and suppleness (flexibility and mobility). The art of coaching is identifying the athlete's current status of biomotor development through testing and evaluation and developing a prescription for addressing the athlete's needs. The coach must also consider the current stage of motor learning development. The coach must look at each athlete individually and prescribe an appropriate training program.

Given all of the physical areas to be developed and the technical components to be mastered, it should come as no surprise that the coach and athlete must accept that the pursuit of heptathlon excellence is a long-term project. The development of biomotor abilities and learning of motor skills should follow a progression of general to specific. To facilitate neuromuscular development, the training program must allow for the effective periodization of the biomotor abilities (see table 19.2).

TABLE 19.2 THE PERIODIZATION OF BIOMOTOR ABILITIES FOR THE HEPTATHLETE

	General preparation	Special preparation	Precompetitive	Competitive
Speed	Power/speed (30-40 m) Alactic speed (50-60 m) Glycolytic speed (40-60 m)	Power/speed (30-60 m) Alactic speed (60-80 m) Glycolytic speed (60-80 m)	Power/speed (30-60 m) Alactic speed (60-80 m) Glycolytic speed (60-80 m)	Power/speed (30-60 m) Alactic speed (60-80 m)
Strength	General strength Body weight circuits Strength circuits Hypertrophy Maximum strength Multiple jumps Multiple throws	General strength Maximum strength Power Multiple jumps Multiple throws Special strength Specific strength Eccentric strength	Maximum strength Power Multiple jumps Multiple throws Ballistic training Special strength Specific strength Eccentric strength	Maximum strength Power Multiple jumps Multiple throws Special strength Specific strength
Skill	General drills	General drills Special drills Specific drills	Special drills Specific drills Modeling	Special drills Specific drills Modeling
Stamina	Extensive tempo: *Aerobic capacity* *Aerobic power*	Extensive tempo: *Aerobic power*	Extensive tempo	Extensive tempo

(continued)

TABLE 19.2	THE PERIODIZATION OF BIOMOTOR ABILITIES FOR THE HEPTATHLETE *(continued)*			
	General preparation	**Special preparation**	**Precompetitive**	**Competitive**
	Intensive tempo: Aerobic power	Intensive tempo: Aerobic power Speed endurance Special endurance	Intensive tempo Speed endurance Special endurance Lactate tolerance	Intensive tempo Speed endurance Special endurance Lactate tolerance
Suppleness	Static flexibility Dynamic flexibility Mobility	Static flexibility Dynamic flexibility Mobility	Dynamic flexibility Mobility	Dynamic flexibility Mobility

Speed

Most heptathlon coaches will argue that speed is the most important biomotor ability, as it relates specifically to at least three of the seven events and indirectly to all seven events. Speed work is never absent from the effective training program.

Strength

Strength training is also very important. Types of strength work, volumes, and intensities vary significantly from one program to the next, but it is a biomotor ability that all coaches address. Age, body type, and event strengths and weaknesses will influence strength-training design.

Skill

Skill or technical training is greatly influenced by the athlete's learning curve with respect to motor skills. We know that learning is a continual process and moves back and forth through stages. (See Motor Learning sidebar.) Often, the athlete's inability to learn or master a skill is due to a physical limitation. That is, she may not be strong enough or flexible enough to get into or hold a desired position.

Motor Learning

Learning is a continual process. With respect to learning motor skills, we move through three stages: acquisition, refinement, and stabilization. However, we can and do move back and forth between these three stages.

1. Acquisition—neuromuscular patterns are developing the motor program.
   - It happens; the tape is being filled. As teachers we want it to happen correctly.
   - Communication is very critical; use general terms, particularly for athletes of a younger training age.
   - Use cues (trigger that fires gun) that are appropriate to each athlete; for example, in acquisition phase, use spatial cues—for example, where limbs are in space.

2. Refinement—perception begins to develop; this is what it feels like.
   - Structure is critical; there must be organization and feedback.
   - Self-confidence improves.
   - Anticipation increases; athlete can accept temporal cues—for example, rhythm and sequence.
   - Accuracy improves.
   - Automatic responses increase; you will see replication of desired action.
   - Be patient in moving through stages.
3. Stabilization—motor programs are developed.
   - Good, if learned correctly!
   - Self-evaluation.
   - Always review the basics.
   - Make sure the skill is always there and stored.
   - At the elite level, athletes are students of the technical aspects; they do not just go through the motions.

Stamina

Stamina training is not just for the 800 meters. The athlete must improve her work capacity to handle ever-increasing workloads. The "big picture," or total volume of training, must be taken into consideration in order to avoid overtraining.

Suppleness

Suppleness involves static flexibility; the goal should be to improve range of motion. Dynamic flexibility and general mobility are also important in the heptathlete's training program.

Based on the importance of the above five traits—speed, strength, skill, stamina, and suppleness—table 19.3 outlines a complete training inventory for the heptathlon.

Designing a Training Program

The planning of the training program for the heptathlete can be an intimidating process. If we as coaches follow the principles of periodization, we can with confidence greatly simplify the task. First, we must establish a theme for the year or macrocycle. With the young heptathlete, it is recommended that the coach alternate training emphasis from physical development to technical development from year to year. With the more experienced heptathlete, you could choose either biomotor abilities or events as the theme for each year. The process of developing the yearly plan begins with establishing goals for that year. The coach must determine the number of weeks or microcycles available for training and determine the importance of the planned competitions. The coach must work back from the most important competition for the athlete (e.g., conference, national, international). Obviously, the developmental level of the athlete will dictate this

TABLE 19.3 TRAINING INVENTORY FOR THE HEPTATHLON

Speed

Type of speed	Distance	Intensity	Rest (min.)	Total volume
Speed/power	30-60 m	90-100%	4-8	300-600 m
Alactic speed	50-80 m	90-100%	3-6	400-600 m
Glycolytic speed	40-80 m	90-100%	1-4	400-600 m

Strength

Anatomical adaptation (general): body weight circuits
Hypertrophy (strength endurance): high reps
Maximum strength: med. reps; concentric and eccentric
Power (speed-strength): low reps
Conversion (elastic-equivalent/static-dynamic): power, multiple jumps, multiple throws, ballistic training
Special: parachute, harness, hills, multiple throws, multiple jumps, medicine ball
Specific: for example, hurdle trail-leg drills with resistance

Skill/Coordination

For example: Drills; general to specific—for example, development of acceleration
1. sticks
2. resistance starts
3. crouch resistance starts
4. resistance let-gos
5. crouch starts with commands

Stamina

A. Metabolic (energy systems)
1. Extensive tempo: aerobic capacity, less than 70% of max. speed effort; aerobic power, 70-80%
   Examples:
   continuous tempo 3-5K runs
   3×1000 m (2 min. rest)
   $3 \times 3 \times 200$ m (1-3 min. rest)
2. Intensive tempo: anaerobic capacity; 80-90%
   Example: 5×300 m (5 min. rest)
3. Speed endurance: anaerobic power, 90-100%
   Example: $2 \times$ (80 m-100 m-120 m)(5-10 min. rest)
4. Special endurance: anaerobic power; 90-100%
   Example: 300 m-200 m-150 m (8 min. rest)
5. Lactate tolerance: 90-100% full recovery
   Example: 2×500 m (15 min. rest)

B. Neuromuscular
   Take into account the total volume of work—the "big picture"

Suppleness

Static flexibility
Dynamic/ballistic flexibility
Mobility

for the coach. The next step would be to distribute the preparation, competition, and transitional periods.

Recommended guidelines for macrocycle planning:

- Approximately 66–75% of available time should be spent in preparation period.
- Approximately 66–75% of time in preparation period should be in general preparation (training to train) phase.
- Approximately 25–33% of time in preparation period should be in special preparation (preparing to compete) phase.
- Approximately 25–33% of total time available will be spent in competition (training to compete) phase.
- A double or even triple periodized macrocycle is possible. The aforementioned percentage guidelines should be adhered to regardless of the type of macrocycle plan.
- Each competitive period should be followed by a transitional period to allow for psychological and physical rejuvenation.
- If the volume and intensity of the training load were quantified and graphed, these lines would cross in late special prep or early competition phases.
- Typically, athletes will experience greater improvements within double-periodized macrocycles; however, they will realize even greater long-term improvement if single- and double-periodized macrocycles are alternated.

The plan detailed in figure 19.1 is designed for the following athlete profile:

- This athlete has just finished her basketball season, which began in November. We are classifying this four-month period as General Preparation in nature.
- This athlete is a senior in high school who has three events that she will probably qualify to compete in at the individual state championships.
- This athlete will not compete past the state high school heptathlon championships.

Sample Macrocycle: High School Heptathlete

Month	March					April				May					June			
Week #	1	2	3	4	5	6	7	8	9	10	11	12	13	14	15	16	17	18
Period	Preparation									Competition								
Phase	General prep.					Special prep.				Early				Late		Champ.		
Mesocycle	I					I				I				II		III		
Events				Intrasquad		Spring break training camp / XY dual	AB dual	City invitational		Golden relays / CD dual		League champs.	District champs.	Regional champs. / State champs.		State HS hep. champs.		
Microcycle load — High			X				X				X		X			X		
Moderate	X	X			X	X			X	X			X			X		
Low				X				X				X		X				X

Figure 19.1   Sample macrocycle of a high school heptathlete.

The coach will then assign objectives to the various periods, phases, mesocycles, and microcycles. Once we have this blueprint, we begin! This plan should not be written in stone; it is only a guideline. The challenge for coaches is to make adjustments as needed because of injury, illness, comprehension plateaus, and the myriad of obstacles that will arise from time to time.

After developing the macrocycle, specific workouts should be put together that will allow the athletes to reach their goals and objectives set forth in the macrocycle. Table 19.4 presents sample weekly workouts for each part of the season.

Success Factors

There are nearly as many different philosophies about how to develop heptathletes as there are coaches. Every athlete and environment (geography, facility, climate, interpersonal dynamics of training group, etc.) is different. It stands to reason, therefore, that a superficial survey of programs will show their differences. However, a more in-depth analysis will reveal the similarities, particularly in programs that consistently produce successful heptathletes.

Recognizing Similarities Between Events

Due to the number of technical components of the heptathlon, most successful programs will identify the commonalities of the events involved and train their athletes accordingly. The events that make up the heptathlon are also similar with respect to metabolic and neurophysiological demands.

From a technical standpoint, there are numerous commonalities. The ability to overcome inertia through efficient application of force is a critical skill for the heptathlete, as it relates to virtually every event. This ability to accelerate can be universally trained using various general drills. Another example involves the high jump and javelin events. In these two events the rhythm of the approach, the mechanics of the penultimate step, and the posture at the point of percussion are all similar. From a metabolic standpoint, the improvement of work capacity is important for development of all the events. From a neurophysiological standpoint, multiple-jump and multiple-throw training is specific to both the throw and jump events in that we are developing a synchronization of firing and the ability to create impulse.

Using Compatible and Complementary Training

Another noticeable trait of successful programs is the use of compatible and complementary training. By "compatible," we mean that the different training components will work together harmoniously. By having the athletes perform certain training components together, we can actually enhance the training effect. An example of compatible training is performing multiple throws prior to acceleration development work. By "complementary," we mean that the different training components can act together to enhance a skill or to facilitate the sequencing of actions to complete a skill. An example of work sequence that would not be complementary is doing an extensive tempo workout prior to doing acceleration development work.

TABLE 19.4 SAMPLE WORKOUTS FOR HEPTATHLON

Always begin with a warm-up and end with a cool-down.

Day	General preparation phase	Special preparation phase
Monday	Hurdle drills Long jump drills Weight training	Multiple throws Hurdles High jump Multiple jumps Weight training
Tuesday	Shot put drills Extensive tempo Medicine ball circuit Abdominal circuit	Shot put Medicine ball Intensive tempo Pillar strength
Wednesday	High jump drills Javelin drills Weight training	Long jump Javelin Weight training
Thursday	Hurdle drills Long jump drills Pillar strength	Hurdle acceleration Shot put Speed endurance
Friday	Shot put Extensive tempo Medicine ball circuit	Multiple jumps Javelin Weight training
Saturday	Active rest 30 min. of basketball or volleyball	Extensive tempo/aerobic power Pillar strength
Sunday	Rest	Rest

Competition phase (10 days leading to and through event)

1	**Friday** Starts/acceleration Special endurance	4	**Monday** High jump approaches 4-6 jumps Shot put Weight training	8	**Friday** Heptathlon day 1
2	**Saturday** Shot put Weight training	5	**Tuesday** Long jump approaches 3-4 x half-approach jumps Javelin	9	**Saturday** Heptathlon day 2
3	**Sunday** Multiple throws Hurdle tune up Pillar strength	6	**Wednesday** Warm-up only	10	**Sunday** Pool workout
		7	**Thursday** Starts Approches		

DeDee Nathan's effective training program propelled her to success in the 1998 Goodwill Games. Here she is shown competing in the heptathlon high jump.

Establishing an Effective Training Environment

We also find that most successful heptathletes develop in environments that are remarkably similar. In most situations there is a single coach. The athlete is not shuffled among a number of coaches. This coach controls and monitors the training program. It is certainly appropriate to draw on other expertise, but the athlete can answer to only one master. The training plan includes some sort of two- to four-year plan that provides direction. Another constant is that successful heptathletes "grew up" in a system where they were permitted to develop generally before there was a great deal of specialization. They participated in other sports, experienced variety, and had fun. These athletes were taught motor skills properly and retained them through correct repetition.

Analyzing Point Percentages

There is information that can assist us in the planning process. In the 1997 World Championships held in Athens, Greece, an analysis of the top 10 placers revealed that on average 31% of their total score was accumulated in the 100-meter hurdles and 200-meter dash. They earned 30.2% in the high and long jumps. And 24.8% was earned in the shot put and javelin and 14% in the 800-meter run. If the goal is to compete at a high level, it makes sense to strive for this type of balance. Tenth place in this meet was 6253 points. We also know that for experienced heptathletes, on average there will be a 200–350 point difference between the athlete's personal record score and the sum of their heptathlon individual event personal records. This information tells us that to rank among the top 10 in world-class competition, the athlete must own heptathlon personal records totaling approximately 6450 to 6600 points. The more skewed her percentage breakdowns are, the greater the risk of inconsistent scores.

Realizing the Link Between Strength and Success

Recent history tells us that there are significant strength differences between the top-ranked heptathletes and the next lower rung of athletes. This is reflected by poorer throw marks and inconsistent scores. The proper periodization of strength is critical for the heptathlete's success, in part because of the throw events and also because of hormonal concerns related to the female athlete. (The levels of estrogen and testosterone effect strength significantly.)

Competition

Meet management by all athletes is a critical factor in the success or lack of success in any athletic competition. In the heptathlon, the athlete's ability to make successful transitions from one event to the next is perhaps the most critical factor in "putting a meet together." The athlete must manage her current state of biomotor development and psychological state of readiness and make the most of the competitive opportunity. A heptathlete has limited opportunities to perform, and it is inexcusable to make errors of ill preparation.

Premeet preparation must take into account tapering, blow-out workouts, technical tune-ups, and modeling. There are many logistical issues—travel, diet, hydration, nutritional supplementation, equipment, support group, and so on. Meet-day concerns include wakeup, both literal and neuromuscular, and nutrition before, during, and after the meet.

Transitions, both between events and between the two days, need to be addressed. There are logistical, psychological, neurophysiological, and metabolic demands to be considered. The effective planning, preparation, and coping for these transitions is absolutely necessary and unfortunately often overlooked. Issues such as the extent of warm-up, "safe" throws and jumps, and starting height need to be dealt with throughout the competition.

Summary

The heptathlon is a wonderful event contested by some of the finest athletes in all of sport. The "sorority," if you will, of participants and coaches is a special group. The competition itself is both the reward and a part of the continual developmental process. The pursuit of heptathlon excellence never ends.

20 Decathlon

Harry Marra

The decathlon is probably the most complex and time-consuming contest in track and field, yet all of its throws have some basic similarities, as do its jumps. A thorough study of the decathlon as a whole shows that it is a series of events that, with the exception of the 1500 meters, require short, explosive bursts of energy. The success of a multi-event athlete requires that those similarities be the starting point of the athlete's training. The true multi-event athlete will find no event too challenging.

The Events

First Day:	Second Day:
100-Meter Dash	110-Meter High Hurdles
Long Jump	Discus
Shot Put	Pole Vault
High Jump	Javelin
400-Meter Dash	1500-Meter Run

Characteristics of the Decathlete

Today's world-class decathletes are superior jumpers, sprinters, and throwers. An athlete cannot risk having a weak event or two. In fact, the decathlon scoring tables penalize the competitor who has a weak event. The best decathletes always have been fast, agile athletes with tremendous explosive power. They have had the willpower, persistence, and competitiveness to overcome all obstacles. These characteristics are a must for success at the elite level.

Desire is just as important as talent. The American decathlon champions succeeded despite many obstacles. Bruce Jenner (1976 champion and world-record holder) believes that all other things being equal, the decathlete who most wants victory (and is willing to commit himself toward that goal) will be the best. Psychological toughness and training are critical in the successful decathlete's development. He needs as much psychological preparation off the track as he does physical training on the practice field. The event is all-encompassing. For an athlete to prepare correctly, his lifestyle must revolve around his training.

Decathlon performances have improved sharply over the last decade. Studies of elite decathlon performers show that they were never untalented youths who became decathletes because they had no single strong event. Not to discourage less-talented athletes, but those who reach the top are generally among the cream of the crop even as junior-level athletes.

At the same time, the chart shows performance improvement does not come in a series of big jumps. It comes as regular, small improvements, a gradual rise in performance over several years (usually four to five years from the national level to the elite level).

For the young athlete at the national level (7500 to 7800 points), very gradual improvements in performance are the norm for most events, and balance across the events is a clear criterion of later success. Again, elite decathletes have no weak events.

The performances of elite athletes show that the events that improve the least are the high jump and the flat runs (100 meters, 400 meters, and 1500 meters). This is not because little training time goes into those events. Rather, they are the simplest events in terms of technique. The other, technical events yield larger point increases as they are mastered. Still, a coach must require a certain minimal level of skill in even the simplest events because those (except, again, for the 1500 meters) are the earliest "big-score" events for juniors.

Technique

Recognizing and utilizing the similarities between events makes for efficient and effective workouts. The following are some of the fundamental relationships between event groups.

Throws

"Balance" is a key word. Without proper balance at the start, and throughout delivery, all other aspects of throwing are negatively affected. Once balance is achieved, the following aspects are germane to success in the throws:

- Positive Acceleration—Followed by the sequential deceleration of body segments (blocking).
- Posture—The center of gravity (CG) is functionally lowered through ankle, knee, and hip flexion, as opposed to trunk flexion.
- Acceleration of the Implement—Through a full range of motion over the shortest time possible.
- Patience—There is a difference between being quick and being in a hurry! Remain rhythmical and patient at the start of each effort.
- Relaxation—A relaxed effort produces greater force and velocity.
- Starting Positions—Fundamental in all throwing events. An efficient starting position incorporates all of the previously mentioned parameters (1–5) and is essential for the correct initiation of movement patterns.

Jumps

The following similarities deal specifically with the approach and preparation for takeoff

1. Approach—A successful jump is predicated on a consistent, uniformly accelerated approach.
   - Length—The length of the approach is determined by the acceleration pattern and where the athlete achieves maximum controllable speed.
   - Starting Position
        stand/walk/jog
        posture/CG displacement
        relaxation/concentration
   - Rhythm—Should be constant throughout the approach.
   - Rhythm/Posture/Tempo—Final six strides.
2. Preparation for Takeoff
   - Penultimate Stride—The CG is lowered as a result of flexion in the ankle, knee, and hip of the support leg.
   - Punt Step—A tempo change at takeoff, which enables the athlete to create lift without significantly sacrificing velocity.

Dan O'Brien competing in the decathlon long jump competition during the 1998 Goodwill Games.

- Center of Gravity (CG)—Following the penultimate stride, the CG begins an upward trajectory through takeoff.

Running Events

1. Sprinting
   - Posture—Erect and tall from head to toe. Must be maintained throughout the run.
   - Turnover—To minimize reduction in velocity, you should emphasize stride frequency over length during the final stages of sprint races (key word—"active").
   - Rhythm and Relaxation—"Don't be in a hurry!" Smoothly complete all movements to generate maximum force. Special emphasis should be placed on rhythm and relaxation during the latter stages of all sprints.
   - Acceleration Patterns—Acceleration; speed–maintenance; deceleration. Each sprint encompasses these phases to varying degrees. To optimize performance, a smooth transition through each phase is required. Conditioning, running, mechanics, and relaxation help minimize deceleration.

2. 1500 Meters: Posture, rhythm, relaxation, and tempo (turnover) are important factors for successful 1500-meter running. Differences such as lower knee lift, increased surface area contact with the foot, shorter stride length, and more limited arm movements are necessary for efficient management of the race. Rhythm, posture, and tempo are interdependent and critical to the success of the race. Final acceleration (finishing sprint) is addressed by first increasing tempo (stride frequency) and ultimately combining tempo with stride length.

In the process of changing motor patterns, one must accept the fact that there will be initial regression in performance level. Athletes must be willing to remain motivated, focused, and look at the "big picture." Each athlete has the ability to improve upon his performance. Keep an open mind.

Training Philosophy

Once an athlete makes a commitment to the decathlon, his goals should be long-term. He cannot realistically hope to master 10 events in a short time. He must plan his training for the future, looking four to six years down the road. The aspiring decathlete should focus his attention in the early years on his weakest events and should build his training program around them. For example, a 13-foot pole vaulter must master the event so that heights of 16 feet and above become possible. Of course, once performance in a weak event is improved to a respectable level, the athlete must continue to work on the event.

Progress

Basic training goals for the younger athlete (after reaching a sub-4:40 1500 meters) might be at least 700 points for every one of the other nine events, along with 800 points for two to four "specialty" or "high-point" events. For the more mature athlete (in terms of total score), the goals should rise gradually to 800 points per event, with some events ranging toward the 900-point level. This approach has been the most popular one for several decades.

The thing to stress with young athletes is that improvements come gradually; they will not reach elite status overnight. The elite athletes averaged 7600 points at age 20. In four more years of competitive growth, they reached a mean score of 8350 points between ages 24 and 25. Most athletes did not have explosive improvements in their scores, except where still attaining full growth was a factor. Indeed, a striking fact is that for many of the athletes, there were no improvements in some of their high-scoring events.

Organizing Practices

The most common training pattern is to practice the events individually, most often in the order they occur in competition. When the training situation simulates the competitive situation, the athlete learns how to achieve the best results within the framework of the decathlon. For example, throwing the discus after first running the 110-meter hurdles, as in competition, is very different from throwing the discus as a fresh event. The legs are fatigued from the hurdles, not to mention from the five events of the previous day.

Knudson, Freeman, and Masloyski and Dubrogajev have, however, suggested changes in this training pattern. Krzesinski cites Polish studies showing that greater gains are made by more general training, developing the traits and skills that are shared by several events, thus making more efficient use of training time. For example, aspects of speed training and technique are involved in 7 of the 10 events. The start from blocks occurs three times. Certain takeoff patterns are used in all three of the jumps.

Rudski and Aptekman recommend dividing decathlon training into three stages. The first stage (ages 14 to 17) is the beginning training stage, stressing the development of endurance (rather than speed), strength, and mobility. The second stage (ages 18 to 20) concentrates on developing the specialized motor skills to master the technique of the events. The third stage (after age 20) is the stage of specialized training, emphasizing dynamic training and making the technical skills automatic.

The composition of the scoring tables is a major factor in planning training. Decathletes perform in a highly subjective environment; the scoring tables give an edge to the sprinter-jumper. In working with a young athlete, you should study the point tables and the athlete's best marks in each event, then plan the training in relation to the tables, using training time most effectively for potential scoring improvements.

As Sykes pointed out, more points are lost than are gained in a major competition. For that reason, the most important goal of a young athlete should be to improve his performance in every low-scoring event. After a stable skill base is developed, the tables can be restudied to probe for events that are potentially "easy"—sometimes easy relative to the scoring table, sometimes easy relative to the athlete's talents.

During this focused training time, however, the events that do not have priority must not be neglected. The athlete must train as a decathlete, not as a specialist in one event.

Conditioning Program

The decathlete should *not* train according to the plans and methods of specialists in the individual event groups. Thus, the decathlete should design a program to improve his athletic conditioning by considering that all 10 events should benefit.

Running

The decathlon is a contest that uses short, explosive bursts of speed in nearly all of the events; so speed/form running training should be a major concern to you and your decathlete. However, do not overlook aerobic conditioning early in the decathlete's career and early in each training year; sound conditioning is needed for all skills.

Sprinting Mechanics

Proper sprint mechanics, along with the movements that can help develop a sprinter's speed and explosiveness, should be worked on often in training. For example, long-jump approach work is an excellent way to reinforce both sprint mechanics and speed work, while simultaneously working on another event besides sprints. As a matter of adaptation, decathletes should always do two or three of their warm-up accelerations on the long jump runway while they prepare for the 100-meter event. Not only are they loosening up for the run, but getting a feel for the approach in the jump. The pole vault approach can be used in the same manner.

It is imperative that the mechanical efficiency of the runner not be overlooked as he works on speed development. At the same time, he must understand that given the explosive nature of the decathlon and the two-day, 10-event program, injuries are sometimes a part of the game. However, good performance mechanics decrease the likelihood of serious injury. The decathlete who enters the competition 100% healthy is a step ahead of his competitors.

Speed Endurance

Speed endurance (400 meters) is another important quality. The 400-meter dash is a key event in many ways. First, being in good shape for this event is a major step toward being in good shape for the entire decathlon. Second, there is a tremendous mental lift at the end of the first day if a decathlete has run a strong 400-meter dash. High school and college decathletes should run a leg on the 1600-meter relay at the end of each meet to develop their conditioning and their feel for running the event correctly and aggressively. At least three workout sessions per week should emphasize the 400-meter event.

Distance Running

Do not try to develop an outstanding decathlon 1500-meter runner at the expense of his nine other events; this can be disastrous. Take a long-range look at the event. Do not expect a young 4:55/1500-meter decathlete to run 4:10 the next year; such a time may be a realistic goal in four or five years. Commitment and willpower are a major factor in 1500-meter performance, though desire alone will not yet produce a 4:10. Approach the event logically. A decathlete should not put in the mileage of a 1500-meter specialist. Develop a broad-based aerobic foundation, then train for the event specifically. At the end of the regular Monday, Wednesday, and Friday sessions, emphasize the 400-meter event. Reserve Thursday for specific 1500-meter work. A sample workout follows:

Run 800 meters in 2:20, then rest 1 minute

Run 400 meters in 72 seconds, then rest 1 minute

Run a hard 300 meters in 45 seconds or less

The acute fatigue from such a workout will be tremendous; the decathlete will be totally spent. However, within 15 minutes he will have recovered. This workout accomplishes two major goals. First, the decathlete's legs are not heavy and flat, as they would be from excessive long, slow distance work. Second, the decathlete experiences how a 1500-meter run will feel in competition. Remember that this is Thursday and the decathlete is generally tired by this time of the week.

During the competitive phase, you must make some adjustments in training for both the 400 meters and the 1500 meters. Basically these changes are made to increase the speed (tempo) of the run and expand the recovery time between the work intervals. Quality is the key. The stronger the decathlete is as he enters the competitive season, the easier it is for him to carry his 400-meter and 1500-meter conditioning throughout the remainder of the year.

Strength Conditioning

The bottom line in strength conditioning is to apply it to the events. Strength without application is useless to a decathlete. There should be two to four strength sessions per week. When the decathlete is peaking for a major competition, the amount of time he spends in the weight room should decrease. Total body strength should be the training focus for the younger, less-experienced decathlete. As he matures physically, the lifts should be those that involve specific groups of muscles (cleans, squats, and such).

Power is the prime concern in the weight room. Thus, as the competitive phase draws near, the decathlete should train at 90–95% of his maximum lifts, performing about four to six repetitions. Do not permit the decathlete to use the weight room as a training crutch. Too often he may lose sight of the technical end of the event and try to master the skill simply by gaining strength.

The decathlete should not overlook a complete and thorough program of flexibility. Stretching at practice time is not enough. The decathlete should be encouraged to stretch at least twice a day. An ideal time for the second session is in the evening, before going to bed.

TABLE 20.1 GENERAL DECATHLON TRAINING PLAN		
	Fitness parameter	**% Work load**
Phase I		
General conditioning Oct. 1 through mid-Nov. (6 weeks)	Muscular endurance (ME) and cardiovascular/respiratory endurance (CVE) Muscular strength (MS, anaerobic) Neuromuscular conditioning (NM, technique)	85% 0% 15%
Phase II (a)		
Late general conditioning Mid-Nov. through first week of Dec. (3 weeks)	ME and CVE MS NM	45% 30% 25%
Phase II (b)		
Late, late general conditioning End of first week of Dec. through Jan. 1 (3 weeks)	ME and CVE MS NM	30% 45% 25%
Phase III		
Precompetitive season Jan. 1 through mid-Mar. (10 weeks)	ME and CVE MS NM	10% 50% 40%
Phase IV (a)		
Competitive season (Pre-USATF Champ.) Mid-Mar. through mid-June (12 weeks)	ME and CVE MS NM	5% 35% 60%
Phase IV (b)		
Competitive season (Post-USATF Champ.) Mid-June through Sept. 1 (12 weeks)	The post-USATF phase of the competitive season should be a microcosm of the annual training cycle. The length of each phase should be determined by the length of time before the next decathlon, and a post-USATF evaluation of performance there.	
Phase V		
Postcompetitive season September (4 weeks)	This is a period of time to recover both mentally and physically from the entire season. (Rest and/or active rest)	

TABLE 20.2 SAMPLE DECATHLON TRAINING SCHEDULE

San Mateo, California
Decathletes: Brian Brophy, Ross Kennedy, Darrin Steele

Sample Week: Fall Season (September-December)

1. Weight-training schedule:
   Mon. P.M. and Fri. P.M.—full program
   Wed. P.M.—auxiliary exercises

2. Medicine-ball schedule:
   Each Tues. and Sat. A.M. after weights

3. A.M. runs (low intensity):
   Each A.M. after hard running workout

4. Running workouts:
   Tues.—sprint mode, grass, form emphasis
   Thurs.—speed-endurance mode
   Sat./Sun.—strength, hills, 150–200 m length, short recovery

5. Technical/event work:
   Mon.—prior to weight training (2 events max.)
   Tues.—prior to runs (one event only)
   Wed.—nothing technical
   Thurs.—one-event dry run, drills
   Fri.—rest day; weights only P.M.
   Sat./Sun.—depending upon energy levels

6. Bounding schedule:
   After runs on Thurs. and/or Sat.

7. Multi-throws:
   As needed; change from medicine ball

8. Flexibility:
   2-3 times daily, especially P.M. before bed

Weekly Outline: Fall Program

	9 A.M.–11 A.M.	2 P.M.–6 P.M.
Monday	Physical therapy (regenerative things such as whirlpool or massage treatments) 1–2 events (throws or jumps)	Basketball warm-up Weight training Multi throws Flexibility
Tuesday	Medicine ball throws (20–25 min. routine)	1 event Sprint work Flexibility/abdominals
Wednesday	10-12 min. run Physical therapy	Multi throws Circuit-style weight training Flexibiliy
Thursday	Hurdle flexibility drills	1 event Speed endurance fartlek Bounds Flexibility
Friday	10-12 min. run Physical therapy	Weight training Flexibility
Saturday	Medicine ball 1–2 events Hill running Flexibility/abdominals	
Sunday	Recovery day: Swimming pool Form running drills Non-impact work	

Designing a Training Program

For any workout to be successful, coaches must consider the strengths and weaknesses of each athlete and alter the training program accordingly. Tables 20.1 and 20.2 illustrate a general training plan for decathletes and a decathlon schedule, respectively.

Competition

A proper warm-up for the decathlon is an art form. The best athletes fully understand what their bodies are telling them. The warm-up should be programmed to get the decathlete ready to compete at a superior level every time. There is no room for the excuse, "I warmed up too much" (or too little). When a decathlete is warming up for the first day of competition, he should be specifically concerned with the 100-meter event.

Staying warm between events is critical. Often a novice decathlete will walk around and talk with other decathletes. This is overtiring. The decathlete should consider the warm-up an integral part of his training program.

Preparation for the second day of competition actually begins at the end of the first day. A full, thorough cool-down is essential after sprinting an all-out 400 meters. A walk-jog of at least one mile should be the minimum cool-down. It should be done as soon as possible after the 400 meters. The decathlete should not lie around for a while before starting his cool-down.

The decathlete should wake up at least three or four hours before competition on the second day and, if possible, take a short four to six minute jog before eating and showering. This run can aid his performance in the 110-meter hurdles and get his body prepared for the rigors of further competition.

The thoroughly trained and prepared decathlete should be able to start three or four decathlons per year. The novice, no matter what his ability level, should do at least one per year. The experience gained in competition is extremely valuable. Normally an athlete should not begin another decathlon until at least three weeks after the previous one.

While preparing for a major competition, the athlete should make the last week one of rest and mental rehearsal. For example, the decathlete might warm up each day and check his final preparations for the events (such as long jump steps, high jump approach, and block setting). Of course, some specific runs are needed for sharpness even while he's generally resting for the competition.

A great way to prepare for multi-event competition is by having minimeets of three to four events, such as the 60-meter hurdles, the pole vault, and a 1000-meter run. The athlete can also go completely through the first or second day's events early in the season as a part of the preparation. These experiences are of tremendous value.

When a decathlete competes as part of a high school or college team, he should compete only in events that are not scheduled for the same time. He should do two or three events that he can concentrate on, rather than a number of events that have him running all over the place.

Summary

Decathletes must take part in a training program that develops their skills in every event. They cannot afford to have a weak event. A successful decathlete must contain the physical and mental perseverance to tackle such a grueling contest.

BIBLIOGRAPHY

Chapter 1

Bush, J. , and D. Weiskopf. *Dynamic Track and Field*. Boston: Allyn & Bacon, 1978.

Carr, G. *Fundamentals of Track and Field*. Champaign, IL: Leisure Press, 1991.

Gambetta, V., editor. *The Athletics Congress's Track and Field Coaching Manual*. Champaign, IL: Leisure Press, 1989.

Stolley, S., and E. Derse. *AAF/CIF Track and Field Coaching Manual*. Los Angeles, CA: Amateur Athletics Foundation, 1991.

Thompson, P. *Introduction to Coaching Theory*. London: International Amateur Athletics Federation, 1991.

Chapter 8

Cavanaugh, P. R. *Biomechanics of Distance Running*. Champaign, IL: Human Kinetics, 1990.

Daniels, J. *Running Formula*. Champaign, IL: Human Kinetics, 1998.

Gambetta, V., editor. *The Athletics Congress's Track and Field Coaching Manual*. Champaign, IL: Leisure Press, 1981.

Martin, D., and P. Coe. *Better Training for Distance Runners*. Champaign, IL: Human Kinetics, 1997.

Stolley, S., and E. Derse. *AAF/CIF Cross Country Coaching Manual*. Los Angeles, CA: Amateur Athletic Foundation, 1994.

Vigil, J. "Methodical Approach to Training by the Energy Systems." 1984.

Chapter 13

Attig, R. "Pole Vault Technique and Training Sequence." *Track & Field Quarterly Review* 90, no. 4 (winter 1990): 29.

Falk, B. "Taking the Mystery Out of Fiberglass Pole Vaulting: Book 4." M-F Athletic Company, 1993.

Houvion, M. "Perfecting Pole Vaulting Technique." *Track & Field Quarterly Review* 8, no. 4 (winter 1985): 34.

Kochel, G. *Tactical Coaching for the Pole Vault*. Ames, IA: Championship Books, 1981.

Fraley, B., and E. Jacoby. *The Complete Book of Jumps*. Champaign, IL: Human Kinetics, 1995.

Krzesinski, A. "My Views on Pole Vaulting." *Track & Field Quarterly Review* 81, no. 4 (winter 1981): 42.

Petrov, V. "Pole Vaulting Technique." Lecture presented at European Athletics Congress, Birmingham, England, 1995.

Ward, J. "Plant Food for Thought." Paper presented at USA Pole Vault Elite Athlete Clinic, Lawrence, Kansas, 1985.

Chapter 14

Dunn, G. Jr. "Develping the Young Shot Putter." *New Studies in Athletics,* March 1990.

Dunn, G. D., Jr., and K. McGill. *The Throws Manual*. Mountain View, CA: Tafnews Press, 1991.

Judge, L. W. "Coaching Young Shot Putters—Detecting, Correcting Technical Flaws." *American Athletics,* Winter 1992.

Lasosrsa, R. "Glide Shot Put Teaching Progression." USATF Men & Women's Development Super Clinic Notes, 1996.

Jarver, J., editor, *The Throws,* 3d ed. Los Altos, CA: Tafnews Press, 1985.

Stolley, S., and E. Derse. *AAF/CIF Track and Field Coaching Manual.* Los Angeles, CA: Amateur Athletics Foundation, 1991.

Venegas, A. "UCLA Shot Put—Discus Conditioning Program."XI International Track & Field Coaches Association Congress, Barcelona, Spain, December 1988.

Chapter 15

Arbeit, E., K. Bartoneitz, and L. Hillebrand. "Differences in Throwing Technique in the Discus for Men and Women." In *The Throws: Official Report, Federation of European Track Coaches,* edited by J. Boète and J.L. Gastaldello, 75–81. Paris: L'Amicale des Entraineurs Francais D'Athletisme, 1987.

Jarver, J. "Discus Fundamentals for the Novice." In *The Throws,* 3d ed., edited by J. Jarver, 82–88. Los Altos, CA: Tafnews Press, 1985.

Tidow, G. "Model Technique Analysis Sheets Part IX: The Discus Throw." *New Studies in Athletics* 9, no. 3 (1994): 47–68.

Venegas, A. "UCLA Shot Put-Discus Conditioning Program." *Track & Field Quarterly Review* 89, no. 3 (fall 1989): 6–8.

Vrabel, J. "Problems of Technique of Advanced Discus Throwers." In *The Throws: Official Report, Federation of European Track Coaches,* edited by J. Boète and J.L. Gastaldello, 91–103. Paris: L'Amicale des Entraineurs Francais D'Athletisme, 1987.

Ward, P. "The Discus." In *The Athletics Congress's Track and Field Coaching Manual,* edited by V. Gambetta, 117–31. Champaign, IL: Leisure Press, 1981.

Wilkins, M. "Technique Conditioning Drills for the Discus." In *The Throws: Official Report, Federation of European Track Coaches,* edited by J. Boète and J.L. Gastaldello, 83–89. Paris: L'Amicale des Entraineurs Francais D'Athletisme, 1987.

Woicik, M. "The Discus." In *The Throws,* 3d ed., edited by J. Jarver, 93–97. Los Altos, CA: Tafnews Press, 1985.

Yingbo, Z. "Pre-Competition Preparation for Throwers." *New Studies in Athletics* 9, no. 1 (1994): 43–45.

Chapter 16

Brown, C.H. "Javelin Throwing, British Style." *Track Technique* 120 (1992): 3824–26.

———. Letter to the editor. *Track Technique* 123 (1993): 3939.

Brown, C.H., and J. Stevenson. "The Biodynamics of Javelin Release." *Track Technique* 128 (1994): 4087–88, 4101.

Komi, P., A. Mero, and T. Korjus. "3-D Kinematics of Olympic Javelin Throwers." Report to the IOC Medical Commission, Subcommission for Biomechanics and Sport Physiology, 1993.

Lawler, P. "The Javelin Throw—The Past, Present and Future." *New Studies in Athletics* 8 no. 3: 15–23.

Naclerio, T. *The Teaching Progressions of the Shot Put, Discus, and Javelin.* Rockaway, NJ: T. Naclerio, 1988.

Ogiolda, P. "The Javelin Throw and the Role of Speed in Throwing Events." *New Studies in Athletics* 8, no. 3: 7–13.

Paish, W. "The Training of Power." *Track Technique* 120: 3827–29.

Shannon, K., C.H. Brown, and J. Donins. "The Javelin Throw." *The Athletics Congress's Track and Field Coaching Manual,* 1st ed., edited by V. Gambetta, 133–41. Champaign, IL: Leisure Press, 1981.

Webb, B., and B.F. Sing. "The Javelin." In *The Athletics Congress's Track and Field Coaching Manual,* 2d ed., edited by V. Gambetta, 189–99. Champaign, IL: Leisure Press, 1989

Chapter 17

Connolly, H. "What Makes Syedikh's Technique So Effective." *Track and Field Technique* 102 (Winter 1988): 260.

Dunn, G. D., Jr., and K. McGill. *The Throws Manual*. Mountain View, CA: Tafnews Press, 1991.

Gambetta, V., editor. *The Athletics Congress's Track and Field Coaching Manual*. Champaign, IL: Leisure Press, 1981.

Kohlhepp, T., editor. *USA Thrower* (Multiple articles on top national and international throwers and coaches).

McGill, K. "Hammer." *Track & Field Quarterly Review* 89, no. 3 (fall 1989).

Payne, H. "The Mechanics of Hammer Throwing." Conference proceedings from Techniques in Athletics first international conference, Vol.1. Cologne, Germany: Deutsche-Sporthochschule, 1990. 146-197.

Chapter 19

Bompa, T.O. *Theory and Methodology of Training*. Dubuque, IA: Kendall/Hunt, 1983.

———. *Periodization of Strength: The New Wave in Strength Training*. Toronto, Ont.: Veritas, 1993.

Myers, B. "The Heptathlon." In *The Athletics Congress's Track and Field Coaching Manual*, edited by V. Gambetta, 209–18. Champaign, IL: Leisure Press, 1989.

Schmolinsky, G., editor. *Track and Field*. 2d ed. Berlin: Sportverlag, 1983.

Chapter 20

Dick, F.W. "Jumps and the Combined Events." *Track & Field Quarterly Review* 86 (summer 1986): 50–54.

Freeman, W.H. "An Analysis of Elite Decathlon Performances." *Track & Field Quarterly Review* 79 (summer 1979): 49–52.

———. "Decathlon Performance Success: Progress and Age Factors." *Track Technique* 96 (1986): 3050–52.

Henson, P.L. "Coaching Athletes for Multiple Events." *Track & Field Quarterly Review* 86 (summer 1986): 48–49.

Jenner, B. "Bruce Jenner on the Decathlon." *Track & Field Quarterly Review* 86 (summer 1986): 26–29.

Knudson, L. "International Combined Events Congress (Summary of Presentations)." *Track & Field Quarterly Review* 79 (summer 1979): 63.

Krzesinski, A. "The Specific Features of the Decathlon." *Track Technique* 89 (1984): 2828–30.

Masloyski, E., and I. Dubrogajev. "The Order of Events in Training (Decathlon)." *Track & Field Quarterly Review* 79 (summer 1979): 19.

Rudski, A., and B. Aptekman. "Stages in the Training of Decathloners." *Track & Field Quarterly Review* 86 (summer 1986): 16–17.

Sykes, R.C. "Balance: The Decathlon Keyword." *Track Technique* 45 (1971): 1442–43.

Tolsma, B. "A Scientific View of Decathlon Training." In *Proceedings of the International Track and Field Coaches Association IX Congress*, edited by G.W. Dales, 121–24. Kalamazoo, MI: NCAA Division I Track Coaches Association, 1984.

Yang, C.K. "Decathlon Training in Preparation for Competition." *Track & Field Quarterly Review* 87 (spring 1987): 57–58.

Zarnowski, C.F. *The Decathlon*. Champaign, IL: Leisure Press, 1989.

———. *A Basic Guide to the Decathlon*. Glendale, CA: Griffin Publishers (USOC Series), 1996.

ABOUT USA TRACK & FIELD

USA Track & Field (USATF) is the national governing body for track and field, long-distance running, racewalking and cross country. It is the United States' member of the International Amateur Athletic Federation, the world governing body for Athletics, as well as a Group A member of the U.S. Olympic Committee.

Through their nationwide membership of more than 2500 clubs, schools, colleges, universities, and other organizations interested in track and field, long-distance running, and racewalking, USATF promotes programs of training and competition for men and women and boys and girls of all ages; protects the interests and eligibility of its some 125,000 member-athletes; and establishes and maintains the sports' rules of competition. The USATF is comprised of 56 member Associations.

USA Track & Field's mission is to continue its leadership role as the world's preeminent national governing body in Athletics—from the grassroots to the elite level. It will provide opportunities for athletes of all ages to pursue excellence in long-distance running, racewalking, and track and field in the USA. USA Track & Field is located in Indianapolis, Indiana.